BATTLE CRIES

For Shirley, Ken and Amirah, Rose and Eve

This 2008 edition published by Metro Books,
by arrangement with Murdoch Books Pty Limited.

Chief Executive: Juliet Rogers
Publisher: Kay Scarlett
Commissioning Editor: Diana Hill
Editor: Sarah Baker
Concept and Design: Hugh Ford
Picture Research: Amanda McKittrick
Production: Kita George

Metro Books
122 Fifth Avenue
New York, NY 10011

ISBN-13: 978-1-4351-1090-8

Printed and bound in China

1 3 5 7 9 10 8 6 4 2

BATTLE CRIES

The most stirring speeches from history's greatest warriors, activists, and revolutionaries

JAMES INGLIS

METRO BOOKS

NEW YORK

WAR OF WORDS

Battle Cries shows us at our best and worst. Featuring a wide variety of speeches, writings, songs, poems, cartoons, propaganda, famous last words, short quotes, and aphorisms, it examines the motives of the speakers, writers, and composers, both stated and concealed. Set out chronologically, it focuses on important speeches and documents from each era — from Pericles to Patton, from Joan of Arc to Margaret Thatcher — and examines the way language is used as well as the verbal and emotional tricks employed by the speakers and writers to further their ambition.

This book is not restricted to military matters; some of the speakers are fighting different battles — against apartheid, racism, and sexism. Others speak (often successfully) in favor of such prejudices, and we wonder how anyone could have taken them seriously in the first place. Some of the words are remarkable for their honesty, others for their duplicity. The great majority are inspirational. Many are honest, many are composed of outrageous lies. Some are hilarious, often unintentionally: the reader may find a kind of grisly humor in the bigoted philistinism revealed by Adolf Hitler in his comment about modern art: "Anyone who sees and paints a sky green and fields blue

Winston Churchill, British prime minister for most of World War II, inspired his people to victory with some of the greatest speeches in the English language.

should be sterilized." Sarcasm and irony are well represented, unsurprisingly. All the speakers show passion and a love of either war or peace (or, in some cases, both). There are bigoted rants designed to dehumanize, inspiring calls-to-arms, impassioned railings, and motivational gee-ups.

As we look back into history, and around the modern world, we can see there is no apparent respite from war in the foreseeable future. Perhaps the territorial disease that blights the world is only held by extremists, nationalists, and those who hold power; most people everywhere have the same simple ambitions: to safely and peacefully earn a living while supporting their family and enjoying their friends. As a species, this is our greatest challenge.

War has always been a method of claiming a particular disputed territory, but where is the territory in the so-called "war on terror"? Everywhere, of course. Can it be won? By definition, it cannot. The very term, which tries to give life to a non-existent nonsense, is fighting talk at its weasel worst.

Perhaps one day we will learn to sublimate the counterproductive aspects of our inherent competitiveness, and agree to settle our differences with, say, a sporting contest. Or a debate — that would indeed be the pinnacle of fighting talk!

Part 1

GOD-KINGS & HEROES

The Ancient World

The death of Pisander in the Trojan War
From Homer, *The Iliad*, c. 750 BCE

Little is known about Homer and, in fact, many scholars believe there was no such person, and that the works attributed to him are actually collections of traditional oral poetry composed by others.

Believed to be the oldest surviving work of Greek, and hence European, literature, *The Iliad* is an epic poem about events during the tenth and final year in the Greek siege of the city of Ilion during the Trojan War; the word *iliad* means "pertaining to Ilion," the capital city of Troy, in modern-day Turkey.

Some scholars believe there is a historical basis to *The Iliad*, others that Homer's stories are a fusion of different tales of wars and expeditions by Greeks during the Bronze Age (about the twelfth or eleventh centuries BCE).

The roots of the Trojan War were planted when two powerful gods, Zeus and Poseidon, tried to seduce the sea-goddess Thetis. But Zeus's wife Themis warned them that any son of Thetis would inevitably usurp them and eventually rule Olympus, the Greek pantheon of the twelve major gods, so Zeus decided to marry off Thetis to Peleus, a mortal.

All the gods and goddesses were invited to the wedding except Eris, the goddess of discord and strife. Furious at this slight, Eris lobbed a golden apple, inscribed "For the fairest," into the wedding assembly. Three powerful goddesses — Hera, Athena, and Aphrodite — each claimed the prize, and asked Zeus to arbitrate on who was "the fairest." But Zeus referred the decision to Paris, a Trojan prince. Each goddess offered Paris a reward: Athena would make him a great war leader and hero, Hera promised to install him as ruler of the most powerful kingdom on earth, while Aphrodite promised him the hand in marriage of the most beautiful woman in the world — Helen, the wife of Menelaus of Sparta, who would later become known as Helen of Troy.

Paris chose Helen, thereby enraging the two most powerful goddesses in the pantheon. Helen duly fell in love with Paris, who abducted her and took her to Troy. Infuriated, for ten years the Greeks besieged Troy under the leadership of Agamemnon, the King of Mycenae, eventually achieving victory after the Trojans were duped by the Trojan Horse ruse.

In the ensuing bloody war, the Greeks slaughtered the Trojans and desecrated their temples, thus incurring the wrath of the gods. On their way home, the surviving Greeks, under the leadership of Odysseus (Ulysses), encountered shipwrecks, storms, and other god-given disasters. In this excerpt Menelaus of Sparta kills the Trojan Pisander and gloats over his body. Homer makes the point that unless we apply reason and self-control to our emotions, virtuous anger can deteriorate into trivial resentment or unmanageable rage.

Pisander then made straight at Menelaus — his evil destiny luring him on to his doom, for he was to fall in fight with you, O Menelaus. When the two were hard by one another the spear of the son of Atreus turned aside and he missed his aim; Pisander then struck the shield of brave Menelaus but could not pierce it, for the shield stayed the spear and broke the shaft; nevertheless he was glad and made sure of victory; forthwith, however, the son of Atreus drew his sword and sprang upon him. Pisander then seized the bronze battle-axe, with its long and polished handle of olive wood that hung by his side under his shield, and the two made at one another. Pisander struck the peak of Menelaus's crested helmet just under the crest itself, and Menelaus hit Pisander as he was coming towards him, on the forehead, just at the rise of his nose; the bones cracked and his two gore-bedrabbled eyes fell by his feet in the dust. He fell backwards to the ground, and Menelaus set his heel upon him, stripped him of his armor, and vaunted over him saying, "Even thus shall you Trojans leave the ships of the Achaeans, proud and insatiate of battle though you be: nor shall you lack any of the disgrace and shame which you have heaped upon myself. Cowardly she-wolves that you are, you feared not the anger of dread Jove, avenger of violated hospitality, who will one day destroy your city; you stole my wedded wife and wickedly carried off much treasure when you were her guest, and now you would fling fire upon our ships, and kill our heroes. A day will come when, rage as you may, you shall be stayed. O father Jove, you, who they say art above all both gods and men in wisdom, and from whom all things that befall us do proceed, how can you thus favor the Trojans — men so proud and overweening, that they are never tired of fighting? All things pall after a while — sleep, love, sweet song, and stately dance — still these are things of which a man would surely have his fill rather than of battle, whereas it is of battle that the Trojans are insatiate."

So saying Menelaus stripped the blood-stained armor from the body of Pisander, and handed it over to his men; then he again ranged himself among those who were in the front of the fight.

Homer as imagined by a Greek sculptor. Some historians believe that Homer is actually a fictitious name.

The fall of Miletus, 494 BCE
From Herodotus, *The Histories*, c. 440 BCE

Not a great deal is known about the "Father of History," the Greek historian Herodotus (c. 484–c. 425 BCE). His aim in writing *The Histories*, a nine-volume record of his observations on his travels, is to "prevent the great and wonderful actions of the Greeks and the Barbarians [Persians] from losing their due mead of glory; and to put on record what causes first brought them into conflict." He reports on recent wars, particularly the Greek victory in the Greco-Persian Wars of 490 and 480 BCE following a Greek revolt against occupation by the powerful Persians, who forbade the Greeks to trade while exacting exorbitant taxes.

These excerpts describe Persian attacks on the Greek stronghold of Miletus, in modern-day Turkey. The first sets out the horrendous implications of a refusal to surrender, also promising: "…if they submit, no harm shall happen to them…" This time-honored tactic is still used today. The second notes Herodotus's admiration of Persian leader Alyattes's policy of not destroying buildings, thus allowing the people to resume farming "…so each time that he invaded the country he might find something to plunder."

BOOK I

On the side of the barbarians the number of vessels was six hundred. These assembled off the coast of Milesia, while the land army collected upon the shore; but the leaders, learning the strength of the Ionian fleet, began to fear lest they might fail to defeat them, in which case, not having the mastery at sea, they would be unable to reduce Miletus, and might in consequence receive rough treatment at the hands of Darius. So when they thought of all these things, they resolved on the following course: calling together the Ionian tyrants, who had fled to the Medes for refuge when Aristagoras deposed them from their governments, and who were now in camp, having joined in the expedition against Miletus, the Persians addressed them thus: "Men of Ionia, now is the fit time to show your zeal for the house of the king. Use your best efforts, every one of you, to detach your fellow-countrymen from the general body. Hold forth to them the promise that, if they submit, no harm shall happen to them on account of their rebellion; their temples shall not be burnt, nor any of their private buildings; neither shall they be treated with greater harshness than before the outbreak. But if they refuse to yield, and determine to try the chance of

Herodotus is depicted reading his works to the Greek people.

a battle, threaten them with the fate which shall assuredly overtake them in that case. Tell them, when they are vanquished in fight, they shall be enslaved; their boys shall be made eunuchs, and their maidens transported to Bactra; while their country shall be delivered into the hands of foreigners."

Thus spake the Persians. The Ionian tyrants sent accordingly by night to their respective citizens, and reported the words of the Persians; but the people were all staunch, and refused to betray their countrymen, those of each state thinking that they alone had had overtures made to them...these events happened on the first appearance of the Persians before Miletus.

Afterwards, while the Ionian fleet was still assembled at Lade, councils were held, and speeches made by divers persons — among the rest by Dionysius, the Phocaean captain, who thus expressed himself: "Our affairs hang on the razor's edge, men of Ionia, either to be free or to be slaves; and slaves, too, who have shown themselves runaways. Now, then, you have to choose whether you will endure hardships, and so for the present lead a life of toil, but thereby gain ability to overcome your enemies and establish your own freedom; or whether you will persist in this slothfulness and disorder, in which case I see no hope of your escaping the king's vengeance for your rebellion. I beseech you, be persuaded by me, and trust yourselves to my guidance. Then, if the gods only hold the balance fairly between us, I undertake to say that our foes will either decline a battle, or, if they fight, suffer complete discomfiture."

BOOK VI
This prince [Alyattes] waged war with the Medes under Cyaxares, the grandson of Deioces, drove the Cimmerians out of Asia, conquered Smyrna, the Colophonian colony, and invaded Clazomenae. From this last contest he did not come off as he could have wished, but met with a sore defeat; still, however, in the course of his reign, he performed other actions very worthy of note, of which I will now proceed to give an account.

Inheriting from his father a war with the Milesians, he pressed the siege against the city by attacking it in the following manner. When the harvest was ripe on the ground he marched his army into Milesia to the sound of pipes and harps, and flutes masculine and feminine. The buildings that were scattered over the country he neither pulled down nor burnt, nor did he even tear away the doors, but left them standing as they were. He cut down, however, and utterly destroyed all the trees and all the corn throughout the land, and then returned to his own dominions. It was idle for his army to sit down before the place, as the Milesians were masters of the sea. The reason that he did not demolish their buildings was that the inhabitants might be tempted to use them as homesteads from which to go forth to sow and till their lands; and so each time that he invaded the country he might find something to plunder.

Pericles's funeral oration, 430 BCE
From Thucydides, *History of the Peloponnesian War*

Another pioneering Greek historian was Thucydides (c. 460–c. 395 BCE), the author of *History of the Peloponnesian War* (431 BCE), a war conducted between Sparta and Athens in the fifth century BCE. Thucydides is regarded as the father of logical, empirical history because he examines events in terms of cause and effect rather than attributing their causes to divine intervention by moralistic gods. He analyses human nature to explain behavior and consequences, whereas traditionally the gods were seen as rewarding or punishing people and societies. His writing is full of colorful literary and rhetorical flourishes, particularly in the speeches he quotes.

In contemporary Athens it was customary to hold an annual public funeral to honor the war dead, culminating in a speech delivered by an eminent citizen. This speech was delivered in 430 BCE by Pericles, a prominent Athenian politician and orator, at the end of the first year of the Peloponnesian War. Pericles was an enthusiastic patron of the arts, ordering the construction of most of the buildings on the Acropolis, including the Parthenon (see also page 24).

Thucydides does not claim that his speech transcripts are verbatim; rather they are meant to be a summary, an accurate interpretation of the speaker's intentions and words. This oration is significant because it is much wider ranging than the usual Athenian funeral speech. It can be seen as a eulogy to Greek society itself (much as Michelangelo's *David* sculpture was seen as a metaphor and exemplar of the nascent, flourishing Italian Republic). The speech lauds Athens's achievements, and is also intended to raise the morale of a people at war.

...Our constitution does not copy the laws of neighboring states; we are rather a pattern to others than imitators ourselves. Its administration favors the many instead of the few; this is why it is called a democracy. If we look to the laws, they afford equal justice to all in their private differences; if no social standing, advancement in public life falls to reputation for capacity, class considerations not being allowed to interfere with merit; nor again does poverty bar the way, if a man is able to serve the state, he is not hindered by the obscurity of his condition. The freedom which we enjoy in our government extends also to our ordinary life. There, far from exercising a jealous surveillance over each other, we do not feel called upon to be

ΠΕΡΙΚΛΗΣ

Jn.º Condé Del.   M.rs Bovi Sculp.t late Pupil to F. Bartolozzi R.A.

angry with our neighbor for doing what he likes, or even to indulge in those injurious looks which cannot fail to be offensive, although they inflict no positive penalty. But all this ease in our private relations does not make us lawless as citizens. Against this fear is our chief safeguard, teaching us to obey the magistrates and the laws, particularly such as regard the protection of the injured, whether they are actually on the statute book, or belong to that code which, although unwritten, yet cannot be broken without acknowledged disgrace.

Further, we provide plenty of means for the mind to refresh itself from business. We celebrate games and sacrifices all the year round, and the elegance of our private establishments forms a daily source of pleasure and helps to banish the spleen; while the magnitude of our city draws the produce of the world into our harbor, so that to the Athenian the fruits of other countries are as familiar a luxury as those of his own.

If we turn to our military policy, there also we differ from our antagonists. We throw open our city to the world, and never by alien acts exclude foreigners from any opportunity of learning or observing, although the eyes of an enemy may occasionally profit by our liberality; trusting less in system and policy than to the native spirit of our citizens; while in education, where our rivals from their very cradles by a painful discipline seek after manliness, at Athens we live exactly as we please, and yet are just as ready to encounter every legitimate danger. In proof of this it may be noticed that the Lacedaemonians do not invade our country alone, but bring with them all their confederates; while we Athenians advance unsupported into the territory of a neighbor, and fighting upon a foreign soil usually vanquish with ease men who are defending their homes. Our united force was never yet encountered by any enemy, because we have at once to attend to our marine and to despatch our citizens by land upon a hundred different services; so that, wherever they engage with some such fraction of our strength, a success against a detachment is magnified into a victory over the nation, and a defeat into a reverse suffered at the hands of our entire people. And yet if with habits not of labor but of ease, and courage not of art but of nature, we are still willing to encounter danger, we have the double advantage of escaping the experience of hardships in anticipation and of facing them in the hour of need as fearlessly as those who are never free from them.

Nor are these the only points in which our city is worthy of admiration. We cultivate refinement without extravagance and knowledge without

The historian Thucydides honored Pericles with the designation "the first citizen of Athens."

effeminacy; wealth we employ more for use than for show, and place the real disgrace of poverty not in owning to the fact but in declining the struggle against it. Our public men have, besides politics, their private affairs to attend to, and our ordinary citizens, though occupied with the pursuits of industry, are still fair judges of public matters; for, unlike any other nation, regarding him who takes no part in these duties not as unambitious but as useless, we Athenians are able to judge at all events if we cannot originate, and, instead of looking on discussion as a stumbling block in the way of action, we think it an indispensable preliminary to any wise action at all. Again, in our enterprises we present the singular spectacle of daring and deliberation, each carried to its highest point, and both united in the same persons; although usually decision is the fruit of ignorance, hesitation of reflection. But the palm of courage will surely be adjudged most justly to those who best know the difference between hardship and pleasure and yet are never tempted to shrink from danger. In generosity we are equally singular, acquiring our friends by conferring, not by receiving, favors. Yet, of course, the doer of the favor is the firmer friend of the two, in order by continued kindness to keep the recipient in his debt; while the debtor feels less keenly from the very consciousness that the return he makes will be a payment, not a free gift. And it is only the Athenians, who, fearless of consequences, confer their benefits not from calculations of expediency, but in the confidence of liberality.

In short, I say that as a city we are the school of Hellas, while I doubt if the world can produce a man who, where he has only himself to depend upon, is equal to so many emergencies, and graced by so happy a versatility, as the Athenian. And that this is no mere boast thrown out for the occasion, but plain matter of fact, the power of the state acquired by these habits proves. For Athens alone of her contemporaries is found when tested to be greater than her reputation, and alone gives no occasion to her assailants to blush at the antagonist by whom they have been worsted, or to her subjects to question her title by merit to rule. Rather, the admiration of the present and succeeding ages will be ours, since we have not left our power without witness, but have shown it by mighty proofs; and far from needing a Homer for our panegyrist, or other of his craft whose verses might charm for the moment only for the impression which they gave to melt at the touch of fact, we have forced every sea and land to be the highway of our daring, and everywhere, whether for evil or for good, have left imperishable monuments behind us. Such is the

Athens for which these men, in the assertion of their resolve not to lose her, nobly fought and died; and well may every one of their survivors be ready to suffer in her cause...

For heroes have the whole earth for their tomb; and in lands far from their own, where the column with its epitaph declares it, there is enshrined in every breast a record unwritten with no tablet to preserve it, except that of the heart. These take as your model and, judging happiness to be the fruit of freedom and freedom of valor, never decline the dangers of war. For it is not the miserable that would most justly be unsparing of their lives; these have nothing to hope for: it is rather they to whom continued life may bring reverses as yet unknown, and to whom a fall, if it came, would be most tremendous in its consequences. And surely, to a man of spirit, the degradation of cowardice must be immeasurably more grievous than the unfelt death which strikes him in the midst of his strength and patriotism!

Comfort, therefore, not condolence, is what I have to offer to the parents of the dead who may be here. Numberless are the chances to which, as they know, the life of man is subject; but fortunate indeed are they who draw for their lot a death so glorious as that which has caused your mourning, and to whom life has been so exactly measured as to terminate in the happiness in which it has been passed. Still I know that this is a hard saying, especially when those are in question of whom you will constantly be reminded by seeing in the homes of others blessings of which once you also boasted: for grief is felt not so much for the want of what we have never known, as for the loss of that to which we have been long accustomed. Yet you who are still of an age to beget children must bear up in the hope of having others in their stead; not only will they help you to forget those whom you have lost, but will be to the state at once a reinforcement and a security; for never can a fair or just policy be expected of the citizen who does not, like his fellows, bring to the decision the interests and apprehensions of a father. While those of you who have passed your prime must congratulate yourselves with the thought that the best part of your life was fortunate, and that the brief span that remains will be cheered by the fame of the departed. For it is only the love of honor that never grows old; and honor it is, not gain, as some would have it, that rejoices the heart of age and helplessness...

FIGHTING WORDS

"It is entirely seemly for a young man killed in battle to lie mangled by the bronze spear. In his death all things appear fair. But when dogs shame the gray head and gray chin and nakedness of an old man killed, it is the most piteous thing that happens among wretched mortals."
Homer, *The Iliad*, c. eighth century BCE
This quote was inspired by the success of the Trojan Horse ruse, which led to the Greek defeat of the Trojans following the siege of Troy.

"All warfare is based on deception...Be extremely subtle, even to the point of formlessness. Be extremely mysterious, even to the point of soundlessness. Thereby you can be the director of the opponent's fate."
"The supreme warrior attacks his enemy's strategy, the next best attacks his alliances. The third best attacks his armed forces, while the most inept attacks his walled cities...The best result of all is to subdue others' armies without fighting."
Chinese writer Sun Tzu (c. 544–496 BCE) was one of the earliest pragmatists in the theory of international relations. These quotes are from his highly influential book on military strategy, *The Art of War* (sixth century BCE).

"In war, truth is the first casualty."
Ancient Greek playwright Aeschylus (525–456 BCE) is usually recognized as the founder of the tragedy genre. Only seven of his estimated seventy plays survive to this day. Numerous other speakers have since used adaptations of this famous quote.

"Eat well, for tomorrow we dine in Hades."
In 480 BCE Sparta was warring with Persia when the Spartan king Leonidas and about 300 troops, vastly outnumbered, fought a successful rearguard battle at Thermopylae that allowed his main army of about 7000 to escape overnight. Sure enough, he and all his troops were killed the next day.

"Ten soldiers wisely led will beat a hundred without a head."
Playwright and philosopher Euripides (c. 480–406 BCE) was possibly the greatest of the Greek tragedians. Sophocles is quoted as saying: "I portray people as they ought to be, whereas Euripides portrays them as they are."

"No one is so foolish as to prefer war to peace, in which, instead of sons burying their fathers, fathers bury their sons. But the gods willed it so."
Herodotus, *The Histories*, c. 440 BCE
The "father of history" offers his observation on why humans seem to be compelled to kill each other.

"We make war that we may live in peace."
Greek philosopher Aristotle (384–322 BCE) was a student of Plato and teacher of Alexander the Great. A brilliant polymath, he made groundbreaking contributions to physics, logic, poetry, biology, theater and ethics, among many other fields.

"*Veni, vidi, vici.* I came, I saw, I conquered."
This was Roman emperor Julius Caesar's concise report back to Rome after defeating Pharnaces II at Zela in Asia Minor in just five days, in 47 BCE. It is roughly pronounced, but should not be translated as: "Weeny, weedy, weaky."

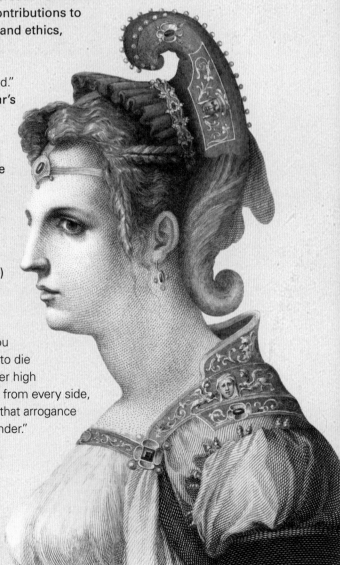

"The body of a dead enemy always smells sweet."
Emperor Vespasian (9–79 CE) took part in the Roman invasion of Britain (43 CE) and later ordered the construction of Rome's coliseum.

"You demand my surrender as though you were not aware that Cleopatra preferred to die a Queen rather than remain alive, however high her rank…If [the forces] we are expecting from every side, shall arrive, you will, of a surety, lay aside that arrogance with which you now command my surrender."
Queen Zenobia (pictured) of Palmyra (240–after 274 CE), then ruler of Egypt, to Aurelian, the Roman emperor

Conclusion of Socrates's final speech, 399 BCE
From Plato, "The Apology (The Defence of Socrates)" in *Great Dialogues of Plato*, fifth century BCE

The classical Greek philosopher Socrates of Athens (c. 470–399 BCE) is renowned for developing the "Socratic method," whereby the teacher asks the student a series of questions aimed at inspiring a basic moral insight into the subject at hand. He made fundamental, ground-breaking contributions to the fields of epistemology, ethics, and logic, and is generally regarded as the most influential philosopher of his era, exerting a powerful influence upon such thinkers as Plato and Aristotle.

Socrates was born into the dawning of the "Golden Age of Greece." Pericles had just risen to power, introducing people's courts and other proto-democratic measures, using the public treasury to promote the arts and embarking on an ambitious building program that included the construction of the Acropolis and the Parthenon. These measures were designed to not only glorify Greece but also provide employment and wealth-creation opportunities for the lower classes.

In this hotbed of democracy and liberalism, Socrates somehow managed to acquire a set of values and beliefs that were at odds with many of his fellow citizens. He was neither a democrat nor an egalitarian, believing that people were like a herd of sheep, in need of wise guidance by an educated elite. These ideas flew in the face of the principles of Athenian democracy, and Socrates attracted many enemies who would often physically attack him as he went about expressing his dialectic and moral viewpoints in public places, often in a confrontational manner. He was said to react to these attacks with patience, logic, and a remarkable lack of anger or fear.

In 399 BCE a jury of prominent citizens charged and convicted Socrates with impiety and corrupting youth. The following speech was made after all the evidence had been heard. It is his address to the jury, his last chance to apologize, or plead innocence or mitigation, before they decide his fate. But his tone is decidedly unapologetic. As he leads the court into a philosophical meditation on the nature of death and the function of compassion, Socrates displays equanimity and good humor.

The jury sentenced him to death. They probably had little choice, since Socrates makes it clear that he renounces none of his beliefs or actions; on the contrary, if he were freed, he would follow the same path that led to his arrest and trial.

Throughout the trial, Socrates sought not to persuade jurors, but rather to harangue and goad them. If so, Socrates's suicide — he chose to take hemlock, the customary alternative to execution — was made on the altar of free speech; he correctly predicts that history would judge his persecution and martyrdom as a blight on Greek society.

Most scholars see Socrates's conviction and execution as a fulfilment of his conscious choice.

…Men of Athens, do not interrupt, but hear me; there was an agreement between us that you should hear me out. And I think that what I am going to say will do you good: for I have something more to say, at which you may be inclined to cry out; but I beg that you will not do this. I would have you know that, if you kill such a one as I am, you will injure yourselves more than you will injure me. Meletus and Anytus will not injure me: they cannot; for it is not in the nature of things that a bad man should injure a better than himself. I do not deny that he may, perhaps, kill him, or drive him into exile, or deprive him of civil rights; and he may imagine, and others may imagine, that he is doing him a great injury: but in that I do not agree with him; for the evil of doing as Anytus is doing — of unjustly taking away another man's life — is greater far.

And now, Athenians, I am not going to argue for my own sake, as you may think, but for yours, that you may not sin against the God, or lightly reject his boon by condemning me. For if you kill me you will not easily find another like me, who, if I may use such a ludicrous figure of speech, am a sort of gadfly, given to the state by the God; and the state is like a great and noble steed who is tardy in his motions owing to his very size, and requires to be stirred into life. I am that gadfly which God has given the state and all day long and in all places am always fastening upon you, arousing and persuading and reproaching you. And as you will not easily find another like me, I would advise you to spare me. I dare say that you may feel irritated at being suddenly awakened when you are caught napping; and you may think that if you were to strike me dead, as Anytus advises, which you easily might, then you would sleep on for the remainder of your lives, unless God in his care of you gives you another gadfly. And that I am given to you by God is proved by this: that if I had been like other men, I should not have neglected all my own concerns, or patiently seen the neglect of them during all these years, and have been doing yours, coming to you individually, like a father or elder brother, exhorting you to regard virtue; this I say, would not be like human nature. And had I gained anything, or if my exhortations had been paid, there would have been some sense in that: but now, as you will perceive, not even the impudence of my accusers dares to say that I have ever exacted or sought pay of anyone; they have no witness of that. And I have a witness of the truth of what I say; my poverty is a sufficient witness...

Well, Athenians, this and the like of this is nearly all the defence which I have to offer. Yet a word more. Perhaps there may be someone who is offended at me, when he calls to mind how he himself, on a similar or even a less serious occasion, had recourse to prayers and supplications with many tears, and how he produced his children in court, which was a moving spectacle, together with a posse of his relations and friends; whereas I, who am probably in danger of my life, will do none of these things. Perhaps this may come into his mind, and he may be set against me, and vote in anger because he is displeased at this. Now if there be such a person among you, which I am far from affirming, I may fairly reply to him: My friend, I am a man, and like other men, a creature of flesh and blood, and not of wood or stone, as Homer says; and I have a family, yes, and sons. O Athenians, three in number, one of whom is growing up, and the two others are still young; and yet I will not bring any of them hither in order to petition you for an acquittal. And why not? Not from any self-will or disregard of you. Whether I am or am not afraid of death is another question, of which I will not now speak. But my reason simply is that I feel such conduct to be discreditable to myself, and you, and the whole state. One who has reached my years, and who has a name for wisdom, whether deserved or not, ought not to debase himself. At any rate, the world has decided that Socrates is in some way superior to other men. And if those among you who are said to be superior in wisdom and courage, and any other virtue, demean themselves in this way, how shameful is their conduct! I have seen men of reputation, when they have been condemned, behaving in the strangest manner: they seemed to fancy that they were going to suffer something dreadful if they died, and that they could be immortal if you only allowed them to live; and I think that they were a dishonor to the state, and that any stranger coming in would say of them that the most eminent men of Athens, to whom the Athenians themselves give honor and command, are no better than women. And I say that these things ought not to be done by those of us who are of reputation; and if they are done, you ought not to permit them; you ought rather to show that you are more inclined to condemn, not the man who is quiet, but the man who gets up a doleful scene, and makes the city ridiculous.

But, setting aside the question of dishonor, there seems to be something wrong in petitioning a judge, and thus procuring an acquittal instead of informing and convincing him. For his duty is, not to make a present of justice, but to give judgment; and he has sworn that he will judge according to the laws, and not according to his own good pleasure; and neither he nor we should get into the habit of perjuring ourselves — there can be no piety in that. Do not then require me to do what I consider dishonorable and impious and wrong, especially now, when I am being tried for impiety on the indictment of Meletus. For if, O men of Athens, by force of persuasion and entreaty, I could overpower your oaths, then I should be teaching you to believe that there are no gods, and convict myself, in my own defence, of not believing in them. But that is not the case; for I do believe that there are gods, and in a far higher sense than that in which any of my accusers believe in them. And to you and to God I commit my cause, to be determined by you as is best for you and me…

The Thirteenth Rock Edict
King Asoka, c. 264 BCE

Asoka (304–232 BCE) was the third monarch of the Indian Mauryan dynasty whose vast empire included present-day Afghanistan, Pakistan, and Iran, and most of India. Of him British author and historian H. G. Wells wrote: "Amidst the tens of thousands of names of monarchs that crowd the columns of history...the name of Asoka shines, and shines almost alone, a star." In the nineteenth century a large number of his edicts were discovered inscribed on rocks and pillars in India, Nepal, Afghanistan, and Pakistan, stating his policies and providing insights into his attempt to establish an empire based on justice and virtue.

The edicts provide little information about his life. He assumed the title Devanampiya Piyadasi ("Beloved-of-the-Gods"). In 262 BCE, eight years after his ascension, Asoka's armies attacked and conquered Kalinga, now the north-eastern Indian state of Orissa. The horrors of the war seemed to bring about a change in his outlook: Asoka spent the rest of his life applying pacifist principles to his government as he helped Buddhism to spread throughout India and nearby states. In this edict, "Dharma" (Law) refers to the inherent order and harmony in nature, and a life lived in accord with that order.

Beloved-of-the-Gods, King Piyadasi, conquered the Kalingas eight years after his coronation. One hundred and fifty thousand were deported and one hundred thousand killed. After the Kalingas had been conquered, Beloved-of-the-Gods came to feel a strong inclination towards the Dharma, a love for the Dharma and for instruction in Dharma. Now Beloved-of-the-Gods feels deep remorse for having conquered the Kalingas.

Indeed, Beloved-of-the-Gods is deeply pained by the killing, dying, and deportation that take place when an unconquered country is conquered. But Beloved-of-the-Gods is pained even more by this — that Brahmans, ascetics, and householders of different religions who live in those countries, and who are respectful to superiors, to mother and father, to elders, and who behave properly and have strong loyalty towards friends, acquaintances, companions, relatives, servants, and employees — that they are injured, killed, or separated from their loved ones. Even those who are not affected (by all this) suffer when they see friends, acquaintances, companions, and relatives affected. These misfortunes befall all (as a result of war), and this pains Beloved-of-the-Gods.

Asoka established several monuments celebrating various stages in the life of Buddha.

There is no country, except among the Greeks, where these two groups, Brahmans and ascetics, are not found, and there is no country where people are not devoted to one or another religion. Therefore the killing, death, or deportation of a hundredth, or even a thousandth part of those who died during the conquest of Kalinga now pains Beloved-of-the-Gods. Now Beloved-of-the-Gods thinks that even those who do wrong should be forgiven where forgiveness is possible.

Even the forest people...are entreated and reasoned with to act properly. They are told that despite his remorse Beloved-of-the-Gods has the power to punish them if necessary, so that they should be ashamed of their wrong and not be killed. Truly, Beloved-of-the-Gods desires non-injury, restraint, and impartiality to all beings, even where wrong has been done.

MESSENGERS OF WAR

The ability of an army's various divisions to communicate quickly and accurately with each other is crucial, perhaps second only to military strength. Efficient communication enables a leader to take maximum advantage of his forces as well as of secret intelligence gathered by spies or reconnaissance agents. But if messages are intercepted by the enemy, the result may well be more disastrous than if they had not been sent at all. Over the centuries many techniques have been used to ensure the reliability and secrecy of such exchanges, including the use of secret codes.

Talking knots

For about 5000 years, the ancient Inca empire of South America and its predecessors employed the *quipu*, or "talking knot," usually a series of looped or woven lama or alpaca threads with up to 2000 knotted cords attached. This base 10 positional system was used for accounting purposes as well as for recording the census, the calendar, accounts of battles, and possibly historical events and literature.

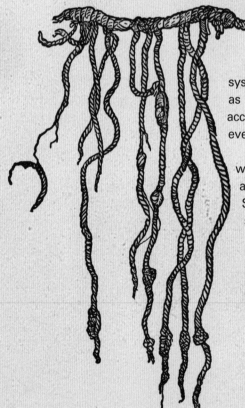

The ability to create and translate these was confined to just a few experts, known as Quipucamayocs. The fourteenth century Spanish conquistadors, or conquerors, soon banned the talking knots, realising they could not interpret them, and that captured Quipucamayocs frequently provided false translations; indeed, modern scholars have not yet been able to translate most of their details.

Similar systems were used in Samoa, India, China, Tibet, and Africa, although not always for military purposes.

Smoke signals

Useful for communicating simple pieces of information over large distances, smoke signals were developed in ancient China, Australia, and the Americas. A covering, such as a blanket, was used to cover and uncover a fire, resulting in puffs of various sizes over different intervals, which were used in prearranged sequences between the sender and the receiver.

Ciphers and runners

To communicate in times of war, the ancient Greeks used transposition ciphers (a staple of modern cryptography), where one letter or number is substituted for another; Julius Caesar used such a cipher, called the Caesar Cipher, to communicate with his generals. The historian Herodotus recorded that the Greeks also used steganography, the art and science of writing hidden messages — they concealed secret messages under wax on wooden tablets, or tattooed them on a slave's head, where they were eventually hidden by regrown hair; the latter method was obviously of limited use for urgent messages.

It's interesting to note that the modern-day marathon race is based on the story of the runner Phidippides, who was despatched from Marathon to Athens, 26 miles south, to inform the city of the Greeks' victory over a numerically superior Persian force. Once he reached his destination, Phidippides collapsed and died, but not before he delivered his message.

Optical telegraph

The optical telegraph, a relayed system of visual signals, was used by the ancient Chinese, and in the eighteenth century this invention made great advances all over the world. Messages were relayed from point to point by flags, lights, fires, and other methods such as patterns of open or closed windows in tall structures.

In 1792, at the height of the French Revolution, French engineers Claude and Ignatius Chappe invented a system of telescopes and rods of varying angles that eventually consisted of 556 stations stretching across France; it was used for both civilian and military communications until the 1850s. Similar systems were subsequently set up in Spain, Sweden, and England.

Carrier pigeons

Carrier pigeons have been used in war since ancient Roman times. Although they are not very reliable, and can only travel "home" in one direction, they were particularly useful in sieges and other situations where troop movement was restricted. In the twelfth century, Mongol warlord Genghis Khan set up a system of pigeon relay posts across Asia and eastern Europe.

During the siege of Paris (1870–71) in the Franco-Prussian war, hot-air balloons transported pigeons to distant locations, returning to the besieged city with photographs and other information. Nonetheless, Paris was starved into submission and eventual defeat, and the French territory of Alsace-Lorraine was added to the Prussian Empire as part of the peace settlement.

Carrier pigeons were widely used by both sides in World War I. One heroic American bird, known as The Mocker, flew fifty-two successful missions before he was wounded and retired from action.

In October 1918 another pigeon, the legendary Cher Ami, Dear Friend, was awarded the high military honor Croix de Guerre (War Cross) after conveying a message that saved the lives of some 200 US 77th Infantry Division troops who, encircled by German forces, were being bombed by their own forces in the Argonne forest in north-eastern France. About 300 soldiers had already been killed by this "friendly fire" when Cher Ami, despite being shot by German bullets that hit his breastbone and almost severed his leg, managed to return to headquarters with the following message:

"We are along the road parallel to 276.4. Our own artillery is dropping a barrage directly on us. For Heaven's sake, stop it."

The intrepid bird became a world-famous war hero, featuring in many newspapers and magazines. After the war a poem was composed in his honor by anthologist Harry Webb Farrington. The poem reads, in part:

> The bullets buzzed by like a bee,
> So close, it almost frightened me;
> One struck the feathers of this sail,
> Another went right through my tail...

Grateful soldiers made a wooden leg for Cher Ami, but he eventually died of his wounds on 13 June 1919. In 1931 he was inducted into the Carrier Pigeon Hall of Fame. His body is on display in the National Museum of American History, Smithsonian Institution, Washington, DC.

Enigma code

In World War II the German Enigma code, an ever-changing code created on a machine of several revolving wheels, was so complicated that it was considered impossible to break. But Allied cryptanalysts found a way to decode its messages, and, equally importantly, managed to conceal that fact until after the war ended (much the same thing happened in World War I). This was one of the most important strategic advantages possessed by the Allies in the war (see also page 227).

The twenty-first century

With the advent of satellites, the internet, and mobile telephones, military communications are easier than ever — and encryption more important than ever. Terrorist organisations, knowing that all telephone calls, faxes, and emails are permanently logged by the US-based "Echelon" eavesdropping system, have resorted to sending cryptic messages on untraceable phones, or on websites such as YouTube.

WAR CRIES

A war cry, or battle cry, is a shout or chant used in battle by members of the same military force. The nature and content vary, depending on whether the motive is to threaten, frighten the foe, inspire the reluctant soldier, invoke a family or tribal name, communicate to cohorts that they have assistance, promote a sense of camaraderie and strength or call on a superior being for help.

Massed voices in the distance give an advance impression of a formidable, united fighting force. We can assume that war cries have existed since our ancestors first yelled at wild animals and enemies to scare them away; humans must have roared as they attacked the Neanderthals and drove them to extinction.

Shouting stimulates the diaphragm, the muscle below the ribs that controls the lungs and the human center of gravity, and many martial arts advocate a yell at the moment of release.

Schools and sports teams all over the world use formalized and traditional war cries in their sport competitions, while some tennis players find that a shriek at the moment of service is advantageous (with the added benefit that the opponent cannot hear the ball hitting the racquet). The haka, the fierce war dance traditionally performed by Maori warriors, is still a feature of the All Blacks rugby team's international matches.

It's interesting to note that the word "slogan" derives from the Gaelic *sluagh-gairm*: *sluagh* is "people"; *gairm* "call or "declaration," meaning "gathering-cry" or, in times of war, "war cry." In English the word evolved through "slughorn" and "sluggorne" to "slogan."

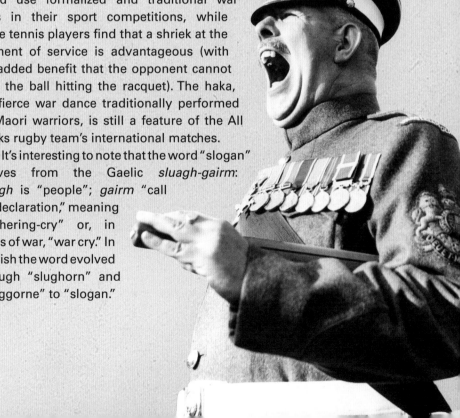

First oration against Catiline
Cicero, Roman Senate, 63 BCE

A Roman humanist lawyer, politician, and philosopher, Marcus Tullius Cicero (106–43 BCE) is considered one of Rome's greatest orators and wordsmiths. He was elected consul of Rome for the year 63 BCE at a time when the Republic, to whose ideals he was devoted, was disintegrating in the process of a fierce civil war between loyal forces and followers of the usurper Catiline (see page 39).

He survived numerous conspiracies, including several led by Catiline. In the Senate, Cicero delivered a series of orations against Catiline and his cohorts, whom he was trying to drive away from the city. The following year, after a series of battles, the exiled Catiline was defeated and killed in the battle of Pistoria.

This, the first of his anti-Catiline orations, is remarkably fluent and erudite in its bold, second person attack on Catiline (who was present).

When, oh Catiline, do you intend to cease abusing our patience? How long is that madness of yours still to mock us? When is there to be an end of that unbridled audacity of yours, swaggering about as it does now?...

Though there are some men in this body who either do not see what threatens, or dissemble what they do see; who have fed the hope of Catiline by mild sentiments, and have strengthened the rising conspiracy by not believing it; influenced by whose authority many, and they not wicked, but only ignorant, if I punished him would say that I had acted cruelly and tyrannically. But I know that if he arrives at the camp of Manlius to which he is going, there will be no one so stupid as not to see that there has been a conspiracy, no one so hardened as not to confess it...

But if this man alone were put to death, I know that this disease of the Republic would be only checked for a while, not eradicated forever. But if he banishes himself, and takes with him all his friends, and collects at one point all the ruined men from every quarter, then not only will this full-grown plague of the Republic be extinguished and eradicated, but also the root and seed of all future evils.

We have now for a long time, O conscript fathers, lived among these dangers and machinations of conspiracy; but somehow or other, the ripeness of all wickedness, and of this long-standing madness and audacity, has come to a head at the time of my consulship. But if this man

alone is removed from this piratical crew, we may appear, perhaps, for a short time relieved from fear and anxiety, but the danger will settle down and lie hid in the veins and bowels of the Republic. As it often happens that men afflicted with a severe disease, when they are tortured with heat and fever, if they drink cold water, seem at first to be relieved, but afterward suffer more and more severely; so this disease which is in the Republic, if relieved by the punishment of this man, will only get worse and worse, as the rest will be still alive.

Wherefore, O conscript fathers, let the worthless be gone, let them separate themselves from the good, let them collect in one place, let them, as I have often said before, be separated from us by a wall; let them cease to plot against the consul in his own house, to surround the tribunal of the city praetor, to besiege the senate-house with swords, to prepare brands and torches to burn the city; let it, in short, be written on the brow of every citizen, what his sentiments are about the Republic. I promise you, this, O conscript fathers, that there shall be so much diligence in us the consuls, so much authority in you, so much virtue in the Roman knights, so much unanimity in all good men that you shall see everything made plain and manifest by the departure of Catiline, everything checked and punished.

With these omens, O Catiline, be gone to your impious and nefarious war, to the great safety of the Republic, to your own misfortune and injury, and to the destruction of those who have joined themselves to you in every wickedness and atrocity. Then do you, O Jupiter, who were consecrated by Romulus with the same auspices as this city, whom we rightly call the stay of this city and empire, repel this man and his companions from your altars and from the other temples, from the houses and walls of the city, from the lives and fortunes of all the citizens; and overwhelm all the enemies of good men, the foes of the Republic, the robbers of Italy, men bound together by a treaty and infamous alliance of crimes, dead and alive, with eternal punishments.

Cicero delivers his speech against Catiline at the orator's stand in the Roman Senate.

JULIUS CAESAR

Roman political and military leader Julius Caesar (100–44 BCE) transformed the Roman Republic into the Roman Empire with a series of brilliant victories.

"The die is cast."
On crossing the Rubicon River, the boundary of Gaul, thus invading Italy and beginning a civil war with Pompey, 49 BCE

"Gaul is subdued."
Julius Caesar informs the Roman Senate of his victory in 5 BCE.

"Fortune, which has a great deal of power in other matters but especially in war, can bring about great changes in a situation through very slight forces."
From Caesar's *The Civil War*

The following quotes have been attributed to Julius Caesar.

"Cowards die many times before their actual deaths."

"I have lived long enough to satisfy both nature and glory."

"I love the name of honor, more than I fear death."

"In war, events of importance are the result of trivial causes."

Catiline prepares for battle at Pistoria, Italy, January 63 BCE
From Sallust, *The Conspiracy of Catiline*, date unknown

Lucius Catiline was a charismatic Roman senator and military general with a reputation for debauchery. According to the Roman historian Sallust, Catiline could "endure hunger, cold and want of sleep to an incredible extent...A man of flaming passions, he was as covetous of other men's possessions as he was prodigal of his own...His monstrous ambition hankered continually after things extravagant, impossible, beyond his reach."

Catiline spent much of his time plotting against fellow senator Cicero. After the Senate exiled him from Rome, Catiline cobbled together an army of supporters and attempted to escape through northern Italy to Gaul. But at Pistoria his militia was surrounded by a vast Roman army. Whether they fought or surrendered, death was certain. Catiline decided to fight; this is the speech he gave to his doomed troops before their final battle.

I am well aware, soldiers, that words cannot inspire courage; and that a spiritless army cannot be rendered active, or a timid army valiant, by the speech of its commander. Whatever courage is in the heart of a man, whether from nature or from habit, so much will be shown by him in the field; and on him whom neither glory nor danger can move, exhortation is bestowed in vain; for the terror in his breast stops his ears...

Whithersoever we would go, we must open a passage with our swords. I conjure you, therefore, to maintain a brave and resolute spirit; and to remember, when you advance to battle, that on your own right hands depend riches, honor and glory, with the enjoyment of your liberty and of your country. If we conquer, all will be safe; we shall have provisions in abundance, and the colonies and corporate towns will open their gates to us. But if we lose the victory through want of courage, those same places will turn against us; for neither place nor friend will protect him whom his arms have not protected. Besides, soldiers, the same exigency does not press upon our adversaries, as presses upon us; we fight for our country, for our liberty, for our life; they contend for what but little concerns them, the power of a small party. Attack them, therefore, with so much the greater confidence, and call to mind your achievements of old.

We might, with the utmost ignominy, have passed the rest of our days in exile. Some of you, after losing your property, might have waited

The Roman Senate survived the fall of the Roman Empire and is the model for most modern-day senates.

at Rome for assistance from others. But because such a life, to men of spirit, was disgusting and unendurable, you resolved upon your present course. If you wish to quit it, you must exert all your resolution, for none but conquerors have exchanged war for peace. To hope for safety in flight, when you have turned away from the enemy, the arms by which the body is defended, is indeed madness. In battle, those who are most afraid are always in most danger, but courage is equivalent to a rampart.

When I contemplate you, soldiers, and when I consider your past exploits, a strong hope of victory animates me. Your spirit, your age, your valor, give me confidence — to say nothing of necessity, which makes even cowards brave. To prevent the numbers of the enemy from surrounding us, our confined situation is sufficient. But should fortune be unjust to your valor, take care not to lose your lives unavenged; take care not to be taken and butchered like cattle, rather than fighting like men, to leave to your enemies a bloody and mournful victory.

FAMOUS LAST WORDS

"To the strongest"
Alexander III (Alexander the Great),
Greek empire-builder and emperor,
on his deathbed, when his generals
asked which one of them should
take control of the empire, 323 BCE

"*Et tu, Brute?* And you, Brutus?"
Gaius Julius Caesar, Roman
emperor, to one of his
assassins on the Ides of
March, 44 BCE

"*Vivo!* I live!"
Caligula (Gaius Julius Caesar
Augustus Germanicus), Roman
emperor, as his own soldiers
murdered him, 41 BCE

"Did I play my role well? If so, then
applause, because the comedy is finished!"
Caesar Augustus, 14 CE. After his death the
Roman Senate declared him a god.

"What an artist dies in me."
Nero, pictured, Roman emperor
and patron of the arts and
athletics, 68 CE

"I think I am becoming a God."
Titus Flavius Vespasian, successful
military leader and Roman emperor,
when fatally ill, 79 CE

Boudicca addresses her army, 60 or 61 CE
From Tacitus, *Annals*, 109 CE

Boudicca (also known as Boudica; formerly Boadicea) was a queen of the Iceni tribe of eastern Britain who led an uprising against the occupying Roman forces. This speech, reported by Roman historian Tacitus, was made in an unsuccessful attempt to inspire her troops to victory — her army was slaughtered and she died, although the time and place remain unknown. She invokes her lost liberty, war wounds, and raped daughters, and states that her cause is honorable and favored by the gods. She finishes with a dig at her male charges: "...the men, if they please, may survive with infamy, and live in bondage."

> Boudicca, in a [chariot], with her two daughters before her, drove through the ranks. She harangued the different nations in their turn: "This," she said, "is not the first time that the Britons have been led to battle by a woman." But now she did not come to boast the pride of a long line of ancestry, nor even to recover her kingdom and the plundered wealth of her family. She took the field, like the meanest among them, to assert the cause of public liberty, and to seek revenge for her body seamed with ignominious stripes, and her two daughters infamously ravished. "From the pride and arrogance of the Romans nothing is sacred; all are subject to violation; the old endure the scourge, and the virgins are deflowered. But the vindictive gods are now at hand. A Roman legion dared to face the war-like Britons: with their lives they paid for their rashness; those who survived the carnage of that day, lie poorly hid behind their entrenchments, meditating nothing but how to save themselves by an ignominious flight. From the din of preparation, and the shouts of the British army, the Romans, even now, shrink back with terror. What will be their case when the assault begins? Look round, and view your numbers. Behold the proud display of war-like spirits, and consider the motives for which we draw the avenging sword. On this spot we must either conquer, or die with glory. There is no alternative. Though a woman, my resolution is fixed: the men, if they please, may survive with infamy, and live in bondage."

Boudicca, Queen of the Iceni tribe, prepares for battle.

C.H.S. delt.   Aquatinted by R. Havell.

Boadicea, Queen  *of the Iceni.*

Published June 1.1815. by R. Havell, 3, Chapel Street, London.

FIGHTING POEMS
Beowulf

Beowulf spake, and a battle-vow made
his last of all: "I have lived through many
wars in my youth; now once again,
old folk-defender, feud will I seek,
do doughty deeds, if the dark destroyer
forth from his cavern come to fight me!"
Then hailed he the helmeted heroes all,
for the last time greeting his liegemen dear,
comrades of war: "I should carry no weapon,
no sword to the serpent, if sure I knew
how, with such enemy, else my vows
I could gain as I did in Grendel's day.
But fire in this fight I must fear me now,
and poisonous breath; so I bring with me
breastplate and board. From the barrow's keeper
no footbreadth flee I. One fight shall end
our war by the wall, as Wyrd allots,
all mankind's master. My mood is bold
but forbears to boast o'er this battling-flyer.
— Now abide by the barrow, ye breastplate-mailed,
ye heroes in harness, which of us twain
better from battle-rush bear his wounds.
Wait ye the finish. The fight is not yours,
nor meet for any but me alone
to measure might with this monster here
and play the hero. Hardily I
shall win that wealth, or war shall seize,
cruel killing, your king and lord!"

This anonymous Anglo-Saxon poem dates from between the eighth and
eleventh centuries and tells the story of the hero Beowulf, who battles
various adversaries in his quest to keep Geat (modern-day Sweden) free
from various invaders, including a dragon. This excerpt takes place just
before Beowulf slays the dragon, but he dies from the injuries he receives.

The Story of Burnt Njal (Njal's Saga)

Blood rains
From the cloudy web
On the broad loom of slaughter.
The web of man,
Gray as armor,
Is now being woven;
The Valkyries
Will cross it
With a crimson weft.

The warp is made
Of human entrails;
Human heads
Are used as weights
The heddle-rods
Are blood-wet spears;
The shafts are iron-bound,
And arrows are the shuttles.
With swords we will weave
This web of battle.

It is terrible now
To look around,
As a blood-red cloud
Darkens the sky.
The heavens are stained
With the blood of men,
As the Valkyries
Sing their song…

Written in Icelandic by an unknown Norse poet, this thirteenth century poem (reproduced here in part) describes a vision of the Valkyries after the Viking defeat at the Battle of Clontarf in Ireland in 1014. These minor goddesses of Norse mythology chose the most heroic men among the slain and carried them to Valhalla, "Hall of the Slain," so they could fight alongside Odin in the battle at the end of the world.

Part 2

NO MERCY IN THE AGE OF MIRACLES

The Medieval World

"Be Ye the Avengers of Noble Blood"
William the Conqueror, Battle of Hastings, 1066

In 1051 William, Duke of Normandy in northern France, visited his cousin, Edward the Confessor, King of England. He believed (or claimed) that the heirless Edward had offered him the English throne upon his death, but in 1066, Earl Harold of Wessex was crowned instead. Enraged at this betrayal, William invaded the south of England while the English army was occupied with defeating Norse invaders in the north.

On 14 October, after several weeks of undisturbed looting and pillaging, William's troops faced Harold's returning army at the Battle of Hastings. Within hours Harold had been killed, his army routed, and all effective resistance ended. William was crowned on Christmas Day, and by 1072 had conquered and united all of England.

William made this speech to inspire his troops on the morning of the Battle of Hastings. Consisting mostly of a series of rhetorical questions, it recalls past glories, and calls for vengeance against previous English atrocities and betrayals.

Normans! bravest of nations! I have no doubt of your courage, and none of your victory, which never by any chance or obstacle escaped your efforts. If indeed you had, once only, failed to conquer, there might be a need now to inflame your courage by exhortation; but your native spirit does not require to be roused. Bravest of men, what could the power of the Frankish King effect with all his people, from Lorraine to Spain, against Hastings my predecessor? What he wanted of France he took, and gave to the King only what he pleased. What he had, he held as long as it suited him, and relinquished it only for something better. Did not Rollo my ancestor, founder of our nation, with our fathers conquer at Paris the King of the Franks in the heart of his kingdom, nor had the King of the Franks any hope of safety until he humbly offered his daughter and possession of the country, which, after you, is called Normandy.

Did not your fathers capture the King of the Franks at Rouen, and keep him there until he restored Normandy to Duke Richard, then a boy; with this condition, that, in every conference between the King of France and the Duke of Normandy, the duke should wear his sword, while the King should not be permitted to carry a sword nor even a dagger. This

concession your fathers compelled the great King to submit to, as binding for ever. Did not the same duke lead your fathers to Mirmande, at the foot of the Alpes, and enforce submission from the lord of the town, his son-in-law, to his own wife, the duke's daughter? Nor was it enough for you to conquer men, he conquered the devil himself, with whom he wrestled, cast down and bound him with his hands behind his back, and left him a shameful spectacle to angels. But why do I talk of former times? Did not you, in our own time, engage the Franks at Mortemer? Did not the Franks prefer flight to battle, and use their spurs? While you — Ralph, the commander of the Franks having been slain — reaped the honor and the spoil as the natural result of your usual success. Ah! let any one of the English whom, a hundred times, our predecessors, both Danes and Normans, have defeated in battle, come forth and show that the race of Rollo ever suffered a defeat from his time until now, and I will withdraw conquered. Is it not, therefore, shameful that a people accustomed to be conquered, a people ignorant of war, a people even without arrows, should proceed in order of battle against you, my brave men? Is it not a shame that King Harold, perjured as he was in your presence, should dare to show his face to you? It is amazing to me that you have been allowed to see those who, by a horrible crime, beheaded your relations and Alfred my kinsman, and that their own heads are still on their shoulders. Raise your standards, my brave men, and set neither measure nor limit to your merited rage. May the lightning of your glory be seen and the thunders of your onset heard from east to west, and be ye the avengers of noble blood.

The Battle of Hastings. According to tradition, King Harold was shot through the eye with an arrow.

Address at the Council of Clermont
Pope Urban, Clermont, France, 1095

In 1095 Byzantine (Greek) emperor Alexius I Comnenus requested assistance from Christian Europeans against the Muslim Persians, who occupied the Holy Land and were heading westward with imperialist ambitions. Pope Urban (1042–1099) called an audience of French nobles and clergymen to Clermont with the aim of inspiring them to take up arms.

Lest his listeners fail to be seized by religious zeal, Urban puts a pragmatic spin on his call to arms: Europe is so small and overcrowded, while the Holy Land "floweth with milk and honey"; Muslims are vile and heathen, and participation in a Holy War will ensure a future "in the kingdom of heaven." His call was successful, leading to the first of many Crusades, and the defeat of the Persians in Jerusalem in 1099.

Oh, race of Franks, race from across the mountains, race beloved and chosen by God...set apart from all other nations...by your Catholic faith and the honor which you render to the holy Church: to you our discourse is addressed, and for you our exhortations are intended. We wish you to know what a grievous cause has led us to your country, for it is the imminent peril threatening you and all the faithful which has brought us hither.

From the confines of Jerusalem and from the city of Constantinople a grievous report has gone forth and has repeatedly been brought to our ears; namely, that a race from the kingdom of the Persians, an accursed race, a race wholly alienated from God, "a generation that set not their heart aright, and whose spirit was not steadfast with God," has violently invaded the lands of those Christians and has depopulated them by pillage and fire. They have led away a part of the captives into their own country, and a part they have killed by cruel tortures. They have either destroyed the churches of God or appropriated them for the rites of their own religion. They destroy the altars, after having defiled them with their uncleanness...The kingdom of the Greeks is now dismembered by them and has been deprived of territory so vast in extent that it could not be traversed in two months' time.

On whom, therefore, is the labor of avenging these wrongs and of recovering this territory incumbent, if not upon you — you, upon whom, above all other nations, God has conferred remarkable glory in arms, great courage, bodily activity, and strength to humble the heads of those who resist you? Let the deeds of your ancestors encourage you and incite

Pope Urban preaching the First Crusade in the Clermont marketplace.

your minds to manly achievements: the glory and greatness of King Charlemagne, and of his son Louis, and of your other monarchs, who have destroyed the kingdoms of the Turks and have extended the sway of the holy Church over lands previously pagan. Let the holy sepulchre of our Lord and Savior, which is possessed by the unclean nations, especially arouse you, and the holy places which are now treated with ignominy and irreverently polluted with the filth of the unclean...

But if you are hindered by love of children, parents, or wife, remember what the Lord says in the Gospel, "He that loveth father or mother more than me is not worthy of me." "Every one that hath forsaken houses, or brethren, or sisters, or father, or mother, or wife, or children, or lands, for my name's sake, shall receive an hundredfold, and shall inherit everlasting life." Let none of your possessions retain you, nor solicitude for your family affairs. For this land which you inhabit, shut in on all sides by the seas and surrounded by the mountain peaks, is too narrow for your large population; nor does it abound in wealth; and it furnishes scarcely food enough for its cultivators. Hence it is that you murder and devour one another, that you wage war, and that very many among you perish in intestine strife.

Let hatred therefore depart from among you, let your quarrels end, let wars cease, and let all dissensions and controversies slumber. Enter upon the road to the Holy Sepulchre; wrest that land from the wicked race, and subject it to yourselves. That land which, as the Scripture says, "floweth with milk and honey" was given by God into the power of the children of Israel. Jerusalem is the center of the earth; the land is fruitful above all others, like another paradise of delights. This spot the Redeemer of mankind has made illustrious by his advent, has beautified by his sojourn, has consecrated by his passion, has redeemed by his death, has glorified by his burial.

This royal city, however, situated at the center of the earth, is now held captive by the enemies of Christ and is subjected, by those who do not know God, to the worship of the heathen. She seeks, therefore, and desires to be liberated and ceases not to implore you to come to her aid. From you especially she asks succor, because, as we have already said, God has conferred upon you above all other nations' great glory in arms. Accordingly, undertake this journey eagerly for the remission of your sins, with the assurance of the reward of imperishable glory in the kingdom of heaven.

FIGHTING WORDS

"When battle is joined, no noble knight thinks of anything other than breaking heads and arms."
Bertran de Born, French baron and troubadour (c. 1140–1215)

"What is the function of knights? To guard the Church, to fight unbelievers, to venerate the priesthood, to protect the poor from injuries, to pour out their blood for their brothers…and if need be, to lay down their lives."
John of Salisbury (c. 1120–1180), English author and diplomat, who became Bishop of Chartres, France, in his *Policraticus* (1159)

"Nothing is of greater importance in time of war than in knowing how to make the best use of a fair opportunity when it is offered."
Niccoló Machiavelli (1469–1527), pictured, Florentine diplomat, philosopher and writer, in his *Art of War* (1520)

"…with all extremity destroy, burn and kill, man, woman and child, the terrible example of all others."
Henry VIII of England's (1491–1547) instruction to the Duke of Norfolk after the uprising in Lincolnshire, 1536

"Though I be a woman yet I have as good a courage answerable to my place as ever my father had. I am your anointed Queen…I thank God I am endued with such qualities that if I were turned out of the Realm in my petticoat I were able to live in any place in Christendom."
Elizabeth I of England, in response to Parliament, October 1566

Sermon at Blackheath
John Ball, Blackheath, England, June 1381

John Ball (c. 1330–1381) was an itinerant radical priest who railed against the injustices of serfdom and the riches of the Church. He made this speech during a rebellion that has come to be known as the Peasants' Revolt, regarded by many historians as perhaps the first (and certainly the most successful) popular uprising in English history. The Black Death (1338) had recently killed perhaps half the population, with the result that surviving commoners were forced into even greater servitude. This resulted in a series of minor, local uprisings for little result.

In June 1381, rebels led by Wat Tyler marched on London, killing the Archbishop of Canterbury, the Lord Chancellor, and the Lord Treasurer (who were discovered hiding in the Tower of London). They confronted King Richard II, who acceded to their demands, but later reneged, ordering the death of more than 1500 of the rebels.

But the rebellion marked the beginning of the end of feudalism in England, and a progressive increase in rights for the lowest classes.

What have we deserves, or why should we be kept thus in [servitude]? We be all come from one father and mother, Adam and Eve. Whereby can they say or show that [the noblemen] be greater lords than we be...? They are clothed in velvet...and we be [covered] with poor cloth. They have their wines, spices, and good bread, and we have the rye bran and drink water. They dwell in fair houses, and we have the...rain and wind in the fields. And by that cometh from our labors they keep and maintain their estates. We be called their bondsmen and [unless] we do readily them service, we be beaten. And we have no [representatives] to whom we may complain, nor that will hear us nor do us right. Let us go to the King, he is young, and show him [our harsh conditions]...And if we go together, all manner of people that be now in any bondage, will follow us...to be made free. And when the King seeth us, we shall have some remedy, either by fairness or otherwise.

The French chronicler Jean Froissart called John Ball "the mad priest of Kent."

Letter to King Henry VI of England
Joan of Arc, 22 March 1429

Joan of Arc (Jeanne d'Arc, c. 1412–1431) was born in Domrémy, in eastern France, during the Hundred Years' War between France and England. During her childhood, her village was raided and burned several times.

By the age of 17, Joan commanded the entire French army. Late in the Hundred Years' War, she declared that she had visions from God, telling her to recover her homeland from the English. King Charles VII of France, impressed by her piety, determination, and her claim that she was a prophet sent by God to save France, ordered her to the English siege at Orleans as part of a rescue mission. She lifted the siege in just nine days and went on to complete several more rapid victories.

Joan was captured by the Burgundians at La-Charité-sur-Loire, in central France, while defending against another siege. The Burgundians sold her to their English allies, and she was subsequently tried and convicted of heresy and witchcraft by an ecclesiastical court led by Bishop Cauchon, an English partisan. She was burnt at the stake by the English on 30 May 1431 when she was just 19 years old. In 1456 Pope Callixtus III reviewed the conviction, found her innocent and declared her a martyr. In 1909, a mere five centuries later, the Catholic Church beatified her; in 1920 it canonized her as a saint.

In this letter to the English king, Joan gives the English an opportunity to capitulate at Orleans, and warns of the consequences should they refuse. She speaks of government in holy terms, and switches back and forth between the first and third person, emphasising the idea that she is both human and divine.

King of England, render account to the King of Heaven of your royal blood. Return the keys of all the good cities which you have seized, to the Maid. She is sent by God to reclaim the royal blood, and is fully prepared to make peace, if you will give her satisfaction; that is, you must render justice, and pay back all that you have taken.

King of England, if you do not do these things, I am the commander of the military; and in whatever place I shall find your men in France, I will make them flee the country, whether they wish to or not; and if they will not obey, the Maid will have them all killed. She comes sent by the King of Heaven, body for body, to take you out of France, and the Maid promises and certifies to you that if you do not leave France she and her troops will

Henry VI (1421–1471), only child of Henry V of England and Catherine of Valois, became King of England in 1429 and King of France two years later.

HENRY THE SIXTH 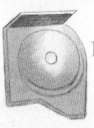 KING OF ENGLAND,

A.D.1422.

Joan is carried to her place of execution in 1431.

raise a mighty outcry as has not been heard in France in a thousand years. And believe that the King of Heaven has sent her so much power that you will not be able to harm her or her brave army.

To you, archers, noble companions in arms, and all people who are before Orleans, I say to you in God's name, go home to your own country; if you do not do so, beware of the Maid, and of the damages you will suffer. Do not attempt to remain, for you have no rights in France from God, the King of Heaven, and the Son of the Virgin Mary. It is Charles, the rightful heir, to whom God has given France, who will shortly enter Paris in a grand company. If you do not believe the news written of God and the Maid, then in whatever place we may find you, we will soon see who has the better right, God or you…

Duke of Bedford, who call yourself regent of France for the King of England, the Maid asks you not to make her destroy you. If you do not render her satisfaction, she and the French will perform the greatest feat ever done in the name of Christianity.

Done on the Tuesday of Holy Week. HEAR THE WORDS OF GOD AND THE MAID.

JOAN OF ARC

Joan of Arc was a fifteenth century Catholic visionary who led the French army to several major (and unlikely) victories (see page 58).

"The blood of our soldiers is flowing, why did they not tell me? My arms, my arms!"

"*Bon cœur, bonne espérance*, the hour is at hand."

"I shall only last a year: take the good of me as long as it is possible."

"Fall upon them! Go at them boldly. If they were in the clouds we should have them. The gentle King will now gain the greatest victory he has ever had."

"Dear friends and children, I have to tell you that I have been sold and betrayed, and will soon be given up to death. I beg of you to pray for me; for soon I shall no longer have any power to serve the King and the kingdom."

"Of the love or hatred God has for the English, I know nothing, but I do know that they will all be thrown out of France, except those who die there."

"You say you are my judge; I warn you to take care what you are doing, for I am sent from God, and you are putting yourself in much peril."

"I can say nothing else to you; and if I saw the fire before me, I should say only that which I say, and could do nothing else."

"When I have done that for which I was sent by God, I will then take back a woman's dress."

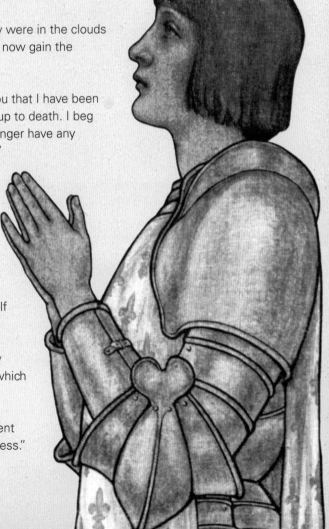

WAR CRIES

"*Santiago y cierra, España!* St. James and attack, Spain!
This war cry was used by Spanish soldiers during the Reconquista, a
700-year-long series of wars that started in 718 BCE and saw Spain and
other European countries gradually take over the Iberian Peninsula from
the resident Arabs. It was also used during the Spanish conquests in
America. The speakers, or criers, are requesting holy assistance from
St. James, the patron saint of Spain.

"*Dex Aie!* God help us!"
Used by the Norman invaders at the Battle of Hastings in 1066 in Sussex,
England, and also by the British Royal Guernsey Light Infantry in World
War I. During the later Roman Empire, soldiers used a passive variation
— "*Nobiscum Deus*, God be with us."

"*Olicrosse!* Holy Cross!" and "*Godamite!* God Almighty!"
Used by senior Saxon army officers at the Battle of Hastings, on
14 October 1066, against the Norman invaders. The foot soldiers
cried: "*Ut! Ut! Ut!* Out! Out! Out!"

"*Denique caelum!* Heaven at last!
Latin war cry used by European Christian soldiers during their Crusades,
from the eleventh to the thirteenth centuries.

"I have the heart of a king..."
Elizabeth I of England, Tilbury Fort, Essex, 1588

Elizabeth I (1533–1603), daughter of Henry VIII and Anne Boleyn, and often known as "the Virgin Queen," was one of Britain's most loved monarchs. Her reign saw a decrease in sectarian violence between Catholics and Protestants, and a blossoming of literature, particularly drama.

Elizabeth's refusal to marry allowed her to shrewdly avoid taking sides in the numerous intrigues that confronted her, and led her suitors (and potential usurpers) to treat her with deference in the hope of gaining future favors. She refused to accept that women could be inferior to men, and gained acceptance among her subjects for her habits of spitting, swearing, and enjoying a few beers.

In 1588 King Philip II of Spain, with the blessing and sponsorship of the Pope, intended to invade England and put an end to the Protestant reformation. His 130-strong fleet arrived in the English Channel on 20 July, but suffered a series of losses and defeats in skirmishes with the British navy. Faced with superior firepower and the brilliant tactics of Vice-Admiral Francis Drake, the defeated Spanish were soon forced to retreat northwards, but many of their ships were wrecked by storms on the west coast of Ireland and Scotland as they limped homewards. The Spanish had lost 65 ships and 10 000 men, the British fewer than 100 men and no ships.

This famous speech was addressed to the English army and navy at Tilbury Fort, at the mouth of the Thames River, at the height of the hostilities. There is an element of hyperbole, in that Elizabeth was not actually about to "take up arms," as she states, but the inspirational quality of her words is unmistakable.

My loving people, we have been persuaded by some, that are careful of our safety, to take heed how we commit ourselves to armed multitudes, for fear of treachery; but I assure you, I do not desire to live to distrust my faithful and loving people.

Let tyrants fear; I have always so behaved myself that, under God, I have placed my chiefest strength and safeguard in the loyal hearts and good will of my subjects. And therefore I am come amongst you at this time, not as for my recreation or sport, but being resolved, in the midst and heat of the battle, to live or die amongst you all; to lay down, for my God, and for my kingdom, and for my people, my honor and my blood, even the dust.

Known as the Armada Portrait (note the Armada scenes behind her), this portrait of Elizabeth I shows her resting her right hand on the globe, her fingers on the Americas.

I know I have but the body of a weak and feeble woman; but I have the heart of a king, and of a king of England, too; and think foul scorn that Parma or Spain, or any prince of Europe, should dare to invade the borders of my realms: to which, rather than any dishonor should grow by me, I myself will take up arms; I myself will be your general, judge, and rewarder of every one of your virtues in the field.

I know already, by your forwardness, that you have deserved rewards and crowns; and we do assure you, on the word of a prince, they shall be duly paid you. In the mean my lieutenant general shall be in my stead, than whom never prince commanded a more noble and worthy subject; not doubting by your obedience to my general, by your concord in the camp, and by your valor in the field, we shall shortly have a famous victory over the enemies of my God, of my kingdom and of my people.

FAMOUS LAST WORDS

"I have loved justice and hated iniquity; therefore I die in exile."
Pope Gregory VII, before dying in exile in Salerno, Italy, 1085

"For the name of Jesus and the protection of the Church
I am ready to embrace death."
Thomas à Becket, murdered by Henry II's followers
in Canterbury Cathedral, 1170

"My design is to make what haste I can to be gone."
Legend has it that Genghis Khan, pictured, was thrown
from his horse and contracted a fatal fever in 1227.

"Now, God be with you, my dear children. I have breakfasted
with you and shall sup with my Lord Jesus Christ."
Robert the Bruce died of an "unclean ailment" in 1329.

"I see Heaven open and Jesus on the right hand of God."
Thomas Cranmer, Archbishop of Canterbury, before
he was burnt at the stake as a traitor, in the reign of
Mary I, 1556

"Strike, man, strike!"
Sir Walter Raleigh, before being beheaded
at Whitehall in the reign of James I, 1618

"Go, announce to the Duke of Friedland that I am
mortally wounded; but I die content, having learned
that the bitter enemy of our holy religion is dead."
Gustavus Adolphus of Sweden, mortally
wounded at the Battle of Lutzen, 1632

"Let not my end disarm you...let the enemy
be my death."
Oliver Cromwell, Lord Protector of England,
Ireland, and Scotland, 1658

FIGHTING POEMS
The Song of Roland

The Prince Grandoyne was a good knight and gallant,
Strong of his hands and valorous in battle;
Athwart him now comes Roland the great captain;
He'd never met him, but he knew him instanter
By his proud aspect, and by his noble stature,
His haughty looks, and his bearing and manner.
He cannot help it, a mortal fear unmans him;
Fain would he fly, but what's the good? He cannot.
The Count assails him with such ferocious valor
That to the nasal the whole helmet is shattered,
Cloven the nose, and the teeth and the palate,
The jaz' rain hauberk and the breastbone and backbone,
Both silver bows from off the golden saddle;
Horseman and horse clean asunder he slashes,
Lifeless he leaves them and the pieces past patching.
The men of Spain fall a-wailing for sadness:
The French all cry: "What strokes! And what a champion!"

Regarded as the most outstanding example of the medieval literary
form *chanson de geste* (epic poem celebrating a hero's exploits),
The Song of Roland is the oldest surviving major work of French
literature. It commemorates the Battle of Roncevaux in which
Charlemagne's Frankish troops were massacred by Basques in
August 778; Roland, Charlemagne's nephew, led the rear guard.
In the poem, the Basques have become Moors, "men of Spain."

"Once more unto the breach…"

Once more unto the breach, dear friends, once more;
Or close the wall up with our English dead.
In peace there's nothing so becomes a man
As modest stillness and humility:
But when the blast of war blows in our ears,
Then imitate the action of the tiger;
Stiffen the sinews, summon up the blood,
Disguise fair nature with hard-favor'd rage;
Then lend the eye a terrible aspect;
Let pry through the portage of the head
Like the brass cannon; let the brow o'erwhelm it
As fearfully as doth a galled rock
O'erhang and jutty his confounded base,
Swill'd with the wild and wasteful ocean.
Now set the teeth and stretch the nostril wide,
Hold hard the breath and bend up every spirit
To his full height. On, on, you noblest English.
Whose blood is fet from fathers of war-proof!
Fathers that, like so many Alexanders,
Have in these parts from morn till even fought
And sheathed their swords for lack of argument:
Dishonor not your mothers; now attest
That those whom you call'd fathers did beget you.
Be copy now to men of grosser blood,
And teach them how to war. And you, good yeoman,
Whose limbs were made in England, show us here
The mettle of your pasture; let us swear
That you are worth your breeding; which I doubt not;
For there is none of you so mean and base,
That hath not noble luster in your eyes.
I see you stand like greyhounds in the slips,
Straining upon the start. The game's afoot:
Follow your spirit, and upon this charge
Cry "God for Harry, England, and Saint George!"

This famous speech — from Shakespeare's *Henry V* (1599), Act III, Scene I — takes place during the Battle of Agincourt during the Hundred Years' War between England and France, shortly after Henry's fleet arrives in France in search of conquest. His troops are holding the city of Harfleur under siege. The "breach" is a gap in the wall of the city. Henry encourages his troops to attack again, even if they have to "close the wall with English dead."

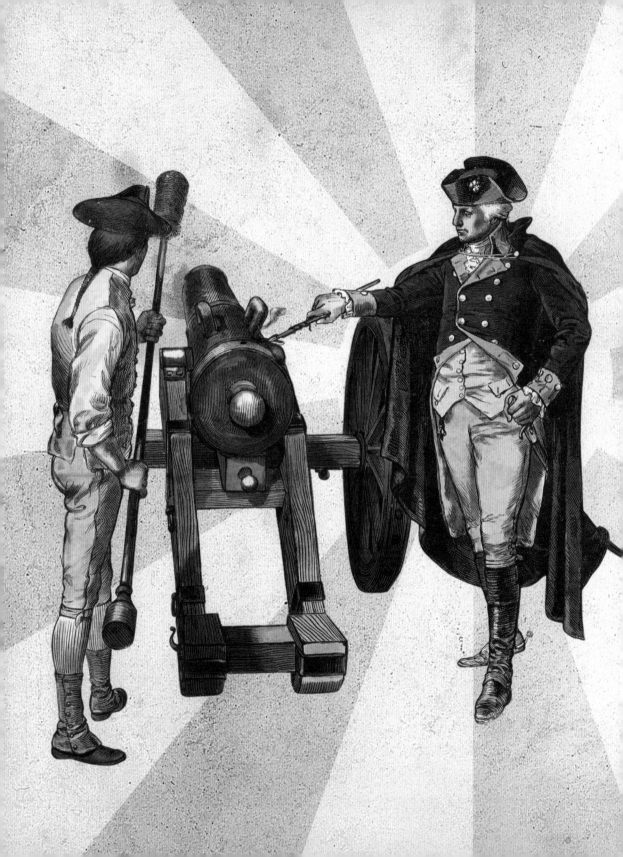

Part 3

AN ERA OF ENLIGHTENMENT, LIBERATION, & BLOODY REVOLUTION

"

The Early Modern Era

"The subject of war"
From Jonathan Swift, *Gulliver's Travels*, 1726

Jonathan Swift (1667–1745) was an Anglo-Irish satirist, essayist, poet, political pamphleteer, and priest, regarded by many as the preeminent English language satirist. *Gulliver's Travels* is a satirical novel, depicting the voyages of Lemuel Gulliver, a ship's surgeon who inadvertently travels to several unknown islands populated by various strange beings.

This excerpt, in which Gulliver describes England (or perhaps Europe), records a conversation with one of the Houyhnhnms — horse-like people who rule themselves democratically, care for their own and don't even have words for "lying" or "compulsion." Swift makes an ironic case that, whatever the problem is, the answer is war: "Sometimes a war is entered upon, because the enemy is too strong; and sometimes, because he is too weak."

The Yahoos, the other creatures inhabiting the island, represent human nature at its most primitive — violent, disgusting, treacherous, greedy, and spiteful — but not necessarily blameworthy, because they are uneducated. They are descended from two civilized Yahoos who were once shipwrecked on the Houyhnhnm's shore, and whose offspring revealed their primal nature as the cloak of culture fell away. Swift's point is that reason does not necessarily remove these vices; instead, it allows the small-minded to justify and amplify them.

In this passage, Swift's aim is to destroy some of the optimistic illusions about human progress that were prevalent among Enlightenment thinkers. The warmth, kindness, and simple decency of the Houyhnmnms are set in dramatic contrast to the Yahoos' behavior, and Gulliver's descriptions of war, legal b******ry, and politics.

He asked me, "what were the usual causes or motives that made one country go to war with another?" I answered "they were innumerable; but I should only mention a few of the chief. Sometimes the ambition of princes, who never think they have land or people enough to govern; sometimes the corruption of ministers, who engage their master in a war, in order to stifle or divert the clamor of the subjects against their evil administration. Difference in opinions has cost many millions of lives: for instance, whether flesh be bread, or bread be flesh; whether the juice of a certain berry be blood or wine; whether whistling be a vice or a virtue; whether it be better to kiss a post, or throw it into the fire; what is the best color for a coat, whether black, white, red, or gray; and whether it should be long or short, narrow or wide, dirty or clean; with many more. Neither are any wars so furious and bloody, or of so long a continuance, as those occasioned by difference in opinion, especially if it be in things indifferent.

"Sometimes the quarrel between two princes is to decide which of them shall dispossess a third of his dominions, where neither of them pretend to any right. Sometimes one prince quarrels with another for fear the other should quarrel with him. Sometimes a war is entered upon, because the enemy is too strong; and sometimes, because he is too weak. Sometimes our neighbors want the things which we have, or have the things which we want, and we both fight, till they take ours, or give us theirs. It is a very justifiable cause of a war, to invade a country after the people have been wasted by famine, destroyed by pestilence, or embroiled by factions among themselves. It is justifiable to enter into war against our nearest ally, when one of his towns lies convenient for us, or a territory of land, that would render our dominions round and complete. If a prince sends forces into a nation, where the people are poor and ignorant, he may lawfully put half of them to death, and make slaves of the rest, in order to civilize and reduce them from their barbarous way of living. It is a very kingly, honorable and frequent practice, when one prince desires the assistance of another, to secure him against an invasion, that the assistant, when he has driven out the invader, should seize on the dominions himself, and kill, imprison or banish the prince he came to relieve. Alliance by blood, or marriage, is a frequent cause of war between princes; and the nearer the kindred is, the greater their disposition to quarrel; poor nations are hungry, and rich nations are proud; and pride and hunger will ever be at variance. For these reasons, the trade of a soldier is held the most honorable of all others; because a soldier is a Yahoo hired to kill, in cold blood, as many of his own species, who have never offended him, as possibly he can.

"There is likewise a kind of beggarly princes in Europe, not able to make war by themselves, who hire out their troops to richer nations, for so much a day to each man; of which they keep three-fourths to themselves, and it is the best part of their maintenance: such are those in many northern parts of Europe."

"What you have told me," said my master, "upon the subject of war, does indeed discover most admirably the effects of that reason you pretend to: however, it is happy that the shame is greater than the danger; and that nature has left you utterly incapable of doing much mischief. For,

One of the lands Gulliver visits on his travels is Lilliput, where he becomes a favorite of the court, a satirical version of the court of George I of England.

your mouths lying flat with your faces, you can hardly bite each other to any purpose, unless by consent. Then as to the claws upon your feet before and behind, they are so short and tender, that one of our Yahoos would drive a dozen of yours before him. And therefore, in recounting the numbers of those who have been killed in battle, I cannot but think you have said the thing which is not."

I could not forbear shaking my head, and smiling a little at his ignorance. And being no stranger to the art of war, I gave him a description of cannons, culverins, muskets, carabines, pistols, bullets, powder, swords, bayonets, battles, sieges, retreats, attacks, undermines, countermines, bombardments, sea fights, ships sunk with a thousand men, twenty thousand killed on each side, dying groans, limbs flying in the air, smoke, noise, confusion, trampling to death under horses' feet, flight, pursuit, victory; fields strewed with carcases, left for food to dogs and wolves and birds of prey; plundering, stripping, ravishing, burning, and destroying. And to set forth the valor of my own dear countrymen, I assured him, "that I had seen them blow up a hundred enemies at once in a siege, and as many in a ship, and beheld the dead bodies drop down in pieces from the clouds, to the great diversion of the spectators."

I was going on to more particulars, when my master commanded me silence. He said, "whoever understood the nature of Yahoos, might easily believe it possible for so vile an animal to be capable of every action I had named, if their strength and cunning equaled their malice. But as my discourse had increased his abhorrence of the whole species, so he found it gave him a disturbance in his mind to which he was wholly a stranger before. He thought his ears, being used to such abominable words, might, by degrees, admit them with less detestation: that although he hated the Yahoos of this country, yet he no more blamed them for their odious qualities, than he did a gnnayh (a bird of prey) for its cruelty, or a sharp stone for cutting his hoof. But when a creature pretending to reason could be capable of such enormities, he dreaded lest the corruption of that faculty might be worse than brutality itself. He seemed therefore confident, that, instead of reason we were only possessed of some quality fitted to increase our natural vices; as the reflection from a troubled stream returns the image of an ill-shapen body, not only larger but more distorted."

"Fly from the wrath to come"
Jonathan Edwards, Enfield, Connecticut, 8 July 1741

This is the best known of the Puritan New England sermons, a fire and brimstone speech delivered by Jonathan Edwards (1703–1758), a Calvinist preacher, in his church at Enfield, Connecticut. He was leader of a US religious revival movement known as "The Great Awakening," which took hold in the 1730s. For Edwards, God was a vengeful, vicious deity who believed that every Christian was born a sinner, and who, without repentance, must rightly expect all manner of eternal physical and mental torments.

Obviously, Edwards's aim is to petrify his audience into agreeing with him; he melodramatically lists a series of disasters that will befall anyone who does not mend their wicked ways and adopt the word of God. There is no hint of the view (expressed by St. John, among many others) that "God is love."

However, the view that God is actually a merciful, not a vengeful, manifestation, was becoming more popular. In 1750 Edwards's parishioners, tiring of what may be described as his excessive negativity, dismissed him.

The God that holds you over the pit of hell, much as one holds a spider or some loathsome insect over the fire, abhors you, and is dreadfully provoked; his wrath towards you burns like fire; he looks upon you as worthy of nothing else, but to be cast into the fire; he is of purer eyes than to bear to have you in his sight; you are ten thousand times so abominable in his eyes, as the most hateful and venomous serpent is in ours. You have offended him infinitely more than ever a stubborn rebel did his prince: and yet it is nothing but his hand that holds you from falling into the fire every moment. 'Tis ascribed to nothing else, that you did not go to hell the last night; that you were suffered to awake again in this world after you closed your eyes to sleep; and there is no other reason to be given why you have not dropped into hell since you arose in the morning, but that God's hand has held you up. There is no other reason to be given why you haven't gone to hell since you have sat here in the house of God, provoking his pure eyes by your sinful wicked manner of attending his solemn worship. Yea, there is nothing else that is to be given as a reason why you don't this very moment drop down into hell.

Oh sinner... it is a great furnace of wrath, a wide and bottomless pit, full of the fire of wrath, that you are held over in the hand of that God whose

wrath is provoked and incensed as much against you as against many of the damned in hell; you hang by a slender thread, with the flames of divine wrath flashing about it, and ready every moment to singe it and burn it asunder, and you have...nothing to lay hold of to save yourself, nothing to keep off the flames of wrath, nothing of your own, nothing that you have ever done, nothing that you can do to induce God to spare you one moment...

It would be dreadful to suffer this fierceness and wrath of Almighty God one moment; but you must suffer it to all eternity: there will be no end to this exquisite, horrible misery: when you look forward you shall see along forever a boundless duration before you, which will swallow up your thoughts, and amaze your soul; and you will absolutely despair of ever having any deliverance, any end, any mitigation, any rest at all; you will know certainly that you must wear out long ages, millions of millions of ages in wrestling and conflicting with this almighty, merciless vengeance; and then when you have so done, when so many ages have actually been spent by you in this manner, you will know that all is but a point to what remains, so that your punishment will indeed be infinite...

...it would be a wonder, if some that are now present should not be in hell in a very short time, even before this year is out. And it would be no wonder if some persons that now sit here, in some seats of this meeting-house, in health quiet and secure, should be there before tomorrow morning...

And let every one that is yet out of Christ and hanging over the pit of hell, whether they be old men and women or middle-aged or young people or little children, now hearken to the loud calls of God's word and providence. This acceptable year of the Lord that is a day of such great favor to some will doubtless be a day of as remarkable vengeance to others. Now undoubtedly it is as it was in the days of John the Baptist, the axe is in an extraordinary manner laid at the root of the trees, that very tree that bringeth not forth good fruit may be hewn down and cast into the fire.

Therefore let every one that is out of Christ now awake and fly from the wrath to come. The wrath of Almighty God is now undoubtedly hanging over a great part of his congregation. Let every one fly out of Sodom. "Haste and escape for your lives, look not behind you, escape to the mountain, lest ye be consumed."

Listeners sometimes fled from Edwards's sermons in terror; one may admire the quality of his florid and violent descriptions of the grotesque fate that awaits the unbeliever.

Speech against the *Stamp Act*
William Pitt, House of Commons, London, 14 January 1766

William Pitt the Elder (1708–1778), was a powerful figure in the British House of Commons and an ally of Britons living in America during the events that led to the American Revolution. He had resigned from the Cabinet in 1761, and was absent from the House when the *Stamp Act*, which compelled British residents in America to pay taxes to Britain, was passed. Although he firmly agreed with Parliament's right to legislate for America and other colonies, he also agreed with the Americans that this right did not extend to taxation.

This address to the Parliament is regarded as one of the most magnificent speeches in parliamentary history. It helped secure the repeal of the *Stamp Act*, and King George III subsequently invited Pitt to form a government entirely on his own conditions. He also became a hero in America, where towns, battleships, and babies were named for him.

...A great deal has been said without doors of the power, of the strength of America. It is a topic that ought to be cautiously meddled with. In a good cause, on a sound bottom, the force of this country can crush America to atoms. I know the valor of your troops. I know the skill of your officers. There is not a company of foot that has served in America out of which you may not pick a man of sufficient knowledge and experience to make him governor of a colony there. But on this ground, on the *Stamp Act*, when so many here will think a crying injustice, I am one who will lift up my hands against it.

In such a cause, your success would be hazardous. America, if she fell, would fall like a strong man. She would embrace the pillars of the state, and pull down the constitution along with her. Is this your boasted peace? Not to sheathe the sword in its scabbard, but to sheathe it in the bowels of your countrymen? Will you quarrel with yourselves, now the whole House of Bourbon is united against you...

The Americans have not acted in all things with prudence and temper. They have been wronged. They have been driven to madness by injustice. Will you punish them for the madness you have occasioned? Rather let prudence and temper come first from this side. I will undertake for America, that she will follow the example. There are two lines in a ballad of Prior's, of a man's behavior to his wife, so applicable to you and your colonies, that I cannot help repeating them:

Be to her faults a little blind
Be to her virtues very kind.

Upon the whole, I will beg leave to tell the House what is really my opinion. It is, that the *Stamp Act* be repealed absolutely, totally, and immediately; that the reason for the repeal should be assigned, because it was founded on an erroneous principle. At the same time, let the sovereign authority of this country over the colonies be asserted in as strong terms as can be devised, and be made to extend every point of legislation whatsoever: that we may bind their trade, confine their manufactures, and exercise every power whatsoever — except that of taking money out of their pockets without their consent.

British officials flee from rioting colonists, enraged by the proposed *Stamp Act*.

"Give me liberty, or give me death!"
Patrick Henry, St. John's church, Richmond, Virginia, United States, 23 March 1775

Patrick Henry urges Virginia's House of Burgesses to vote in favor of military action against the invading British.

A staunch advocate of republicanism, Patrick Henry (1736–1799) was a prominent figure in the American War of Independence. He inspired popular agitation against the *Stamp Act*, which forced British residents in America to pay taxes to England, and was elected Governor of Virginia for the periods 1776–79 and 1784–86. He is perhaps best known for this speech, made in the House of Burgesses, the Virginia colonial legislature, urging its members to take military action against the invading British forces.

His speech, a triumph of rhetoric, uses loaded questions and scornful answers to emphasize his point: "...what have we to oppose to them? Shall we try argument? Sir, we have been trying that for the last ten years..." He also uses repetition of synonyms in the active voice: "...we have remonstrated; we have supplicated; we have prostrated ourselves..." and lists the failures of the British in the passive voice: "...our supplications have been disregarded; and we have been spurned, with contempt..."

In the following speech, Henry implores the 122 delegates to vote in favor. He spoke without any notes — at least none have been found — in a voice that became progressively louder, climaxing in a passionate crescendo with the now famous final words. Following his speech, the vote was taken; his resolutions were passed by a margin of five, and Virginia entered the American Revolution.

No man thinks more highly than I do of the patriotism, as well as abilities, of the very worthy gentlemen who have just addressed the House. But different men often see the same subject in different lights; and, therefore, I hope that it will not be thought disrespectful to those gentlemen, if, entertaining as I do opinions of a character very opposite to theirs, I shall speak forth my sentiments freely and without reserve.

This is no time for ceremony. The question before the House is one of awful moment to this country. For my own part I consider it as nothing less than a question of freedom or slavery; and in proportion to the magnitude of the subject ought to be the freedom of the debate. It is only in this way that we can hope to arrive at truth, and fulfil the great responsibility which we hold to God and our country. Should I keep back my opinions at such a time, through fear of giving offence, I should consider myself as guilty of treason towards my country, and of an act of disloyalty towards the majesty of heaven, which I revere above all earthly kings.

Mr President, it is natural to man to indulge in the illusions of hope. We are apt to shut our eyes against a painful truth, and listen to the song of that siren, till she transforms us into beasts. Is this the part of wise men, engaged in a great and arduous struggle for liberty? Are we disposed to be of the number of those who, having eyes, see not, and having ears, hear not, the things which so nearly concern their temporal salvation?

For my part, whatever anguish of spirit it may cost, I am willing to know the whole truth — to know the worst and to provide for it. I have but one lamp by which my feet are guided; and that is the lamp of experience.

FAMOUS LAST WORDS

"Do not hack me as you did my Lord Russell."
James Scott, Duke of Monmouth and illegitimate son of Charles II of England, to his executioner after a failed rebellion against James II, 1685

"Why are you weeping? Did you imagine that I was immortal?" and "Has God forgotten everything I have done for him?"
Louis XIV, French king, to his servants, 1715

"I feel nothing, apart from a certain difficulty in continuing to exist."
Bernard de Fontenelle, French philosopher, on his deathbed, 1757

"I only regret that I have but one life to lose for my country."
Nathan Hale, America's first spy (in the War of Independence), before the British executed him by hanging, 1776

"*Pardonnez-moi, monsieur. Je ne l'ai pas fait exprès.*
Pardon me, sir. I did not do it on purpose."
Marie Antoinette (pictured), the wife of King Louis XVI of France, after she stepped on the foot of her executioner as she approached the guillotine to be executed for treason, 1793

"Only from the cold, my friend."
Jean Sylvain Bailly, on being asked why he was shivering, shortly before he was guillotined during the French Revolution, 1793

"Thou wilt show my head to the people: it is worth showing."
George Jacques Danton (1759–1794), to his executioner, 1794, also during the revolution

I know of no way of judging of the future but by the past. And judging by the past, I wish to know what there has been in the conduct of the British ministry for the last ten years, to justify those hopes with which gentlemen have been pleased to solace themselves and the House?

Is it that insidious smile with which our petition has been lately received? Trust it not, sir; it will prove a snare to your feet. Suffer not yourselves to be betrayed with a kiss. Ask yourselves how this gracious reception of our petition comports with these war-like preparations which cover our waters and darken our land. Are fleets and armies necessary to a work of love and reconciliation? Have we shown ourselves so unwilling to be reconciled that force must be called in to win back our love? Let us not deceive ourselves, sir. These are the implements of war and subjugation — the last arguments to which kings resort. I ask gentlemen, sir, what means this martial array, if its purpose be not to force us to submission? Can gentlemen assign any other possible motives for it? Has Great Britain any enemy, in this quarter of the world, to call for all this accumulation of navies and armies?

No, sir, she has none. They are meant for us; they can be meant for no other. They are sent over to bind and rivet upon us those chains which the British ministry have been so long forging. And what have we to oppose to them? Shall we try argument? Sir, we have been trying that for the last ten years. Have we anything new to offer on the subject? Nothing.

We have held the subject up in every light of which it is capable; but it has been all in vain. Shall we resort to entreaty and humble supplication? What terms shall we find which have not been already exhausted? Let us not, I beseech you, sir, deceive ourselves longer.

Sir, we have done everything that could be done to avert the storm which is now coming on. We have petitioned; we have remonstrated; we have supplicated; we have prostrated ourselves before the throne, and have implored its interposition to arrest the tyrannical hands of the ministry and Parliament.

Our petitions have been slighted; our remonstrances have produced additional violence and insult; our supplications have been disregarded; and we have been spurned, with contempt, from the foot of the throne. In vain, after these things, may we indulge the fond hope of peace and reconciliation. There is no longer any room for hope.

If we wish to be free — if we mean to preserve inviolate those inestimable privileges for which we have been so long contending — if we mean not basely to abandon the noble struggle in which we have been so long engaged, and which we have pledged ourselves never to abandon until the glorious object of our contest shall be obtained, we must fight! I repeat it, sir, we must fight! An appeal to arms and to the God of Hosts is all that is left us!

They tell us, sir, that we are weak — unable to cope with so formidable an adversary. But when shall we be stronger? Will it be the next week, or the next year? Will it be when we are totally disarmed, and when a British guard shall be stationed in every house? Shall we gather strength by irresolution and inaction? Shall we acquire the means of effectual resistance, by lying supinely on our backs, and hugging the delusive phantom of hope, until our enemies shall have bound us hand and foot?

Sir, we are not weak, if we make a proper use of the means which the God of nature hath placed in our power. Three millions of people, armed in the holy cause of liberty, and in such a country as that which we possess, are invincible by any force which our enemy can send against us. Besides, sir, we shall not fight our battles alone. There is a just God who presides over the destinies of nations, and who will raise up friends to fight our battles for us.

The battle, sir, is not to the strong alone; it is to the vigilant, the active, the brave. Besides, sir, we have no election. If we were base enough to desire it, it is now too late to retire from the contest. There is no retreat but in submission and slavery! Our chains are forged! Their clanking may be heard on the plains of Boston! The war is inevitable — and let it come! I repeat it, sir, let it come!

It is in vain, sir, to extenuate the matter. Gentlemen may cry, "Peace! Peace!" — but there is no peace. The war is actually begun! The next gale that sweeps from the north will bring to our ears the clash of resounding arms! Our brethren are already in the field! Why stand we here idle? What is it that gentlemen wish? What would they have? Is life so dear, or peace so sweet, as to be purchased at the price of chains and slavery? Forbid it, Almighty God! I know not what course others may take; but as for me, give me liberty, or give me death!

The Newburgh Address
George Washington, Newburgh, New York, 15 March 1783

After the successful completion of the American War of Independence against the British (1775–83), some of General Washington's army officers met in Newburgh, New York, to discuss their grievances and consider a possible military revolt against the rule of Congress.

They were furious about Congress's failure to honor promises to the army regarding salary, bounties, and pensions. The officers had heard that the government was going broke, and that they might receive no compensation for their war service.

On 10 March 1783, an anonymous letter did the rounds at Washington's main camp, addressing their complaints and calling for a meeting to consider possible military solutions to the problem of the government's financial difficulties. Washington forbade the officers to meet, instead suggesting they discuss the matter a few days later at the regular officers' meeting.

But on 15 March, the General's officers gathered in a church building in Newburgh, effectively holding the fate of American democracy in their hands. Washington turned up unexpectedly; he was not entirely welcomed by his men, but they reluctantly allowed him to address them.

The officers cast a unanimous vote agreeing to the rule of Congress. Thus the democratic government was preserved, and a military takeover — with all its devastating implications — was averted.

Gentlemen: By an anonymous summons, an attempt has been made to convene you together; how inconsistent with the rules of propriety! how unmilitary! and how subversive of all order and discipline, let the good sense of the Army decide.

In the moment of this Summons, another anonymous production was sent into circulation, addressed more to the feelings and passions, than to the reason and judgment of the Army. The author of the piece is entitled to much credit for the goodness of his Pen and I could wish he had as much credit for the rectitude of his Heart, for, as Men see through different Optics, and are induced by the reflecting faculties of the Mind, to use different means, to attain the same end, the Author of the Address should have had more charity than to mark for Suspicion the Man who should recommend moderation and longer forbearance, or, in other words, who

should not think as he thinks, and act as he advises. But he had another plan in view, in which candor and liberality of Sentiment, regard to justice, and love of Country, have no part; and he was right, to insinuate the darkest suspicion, to effect the blackest designs...

Thus much, Gentlemen, I have thought it incumbent on me to observe to you, to show upon what principles I opposed the irregular and hasty meeting which was proposed to have been held on Tuesday last: and not because I wanted a disposition to give you every opportunity consistent with your own honor, and the dignity of the army, to make known your grievances. If my conduct heretofore, has not evinced to you, that I have been a faithful friend to the Army, my declaration of it at this moment would be equally unavailing and improper. But as I was among the first who embarked in the cause of our common Country. As I have never left your side one moment, but when called from you on public duty. As I have been the constant companion and witness of your Distresses, and not among the last to feel, and acknowledge your Merits. As I have ever considered my own Military reputation as inseparably connected with that of the Army. As my Heart has ever expanded with joy, when I have heard its praises, and my indignation has arisen, when the mouth of detraction has been opened against it, it can scarcely be supposed, at this late stage of the War, that I am indifferent to its interests. But, how are they to be promoted? The way is plain, says the anonymous Addresser. If War continues, remove into the unsettled Country; there establish yourselves, and leave an ungrateful Country to defend itself. But how are they to defend? Our Wives, our Children, our Farms, and other property which we leave behind us. Or, in this state of hostile separation, are we to take the two first (the latter cannot be removed), to perish in a Wilderness, with hunger, cold and nakedness? If Peace takes place, never sheath your Swords says he until you have obtained full and ample justice; this dreadful alternative, of either deserting our Country in the extremest hour of her distress, or turning our Arms against it (which is the apparent object, unless Congress can be compelled into instant compliance) has something so shocking in it, that humanity revolts at the idea...Some Emissary, perhaps from New York, plotting the ruin of both, by sowing the seeds of discord and separation between the Civil and Military powers of the Continent?...

For myself (and I take no merit in giving the assurance, being induced to it from principles of gratitude, veracity, and justice), a grateful sense of the confidence you have ever placed in me, a recollection of the cheerful

At one point in his address, Washington stopped reading his speech and took out a pair of reading glasses, saying: "Gentlemen, you will permit me to put on my spectacles, for I have not only grown gray but almost blind in the service of my country."

assistance and prompt obedience I have experienced from you, under every vicissitude of Fortune, and the sincere affection I feel for an Army I have so long had the honor to Command, will oblige me to declare, in this public and solemn manner, that, in the attainment of compleat justice for all your toils and dangers, and in the gratification of every wish, so far as may be done consistently with the great duty I owe my Country, and those powers we are bound to respect, you may freely command my Services to the utmost of my abilities.

While I give you these assurances, and pledge myself in the most unequivocal manner, to exert whatever ability I am possessed of, in your favor, let me entreat you, Gentlemen, on your part, not to take any measures, which viewed in the calm light of reason, will lessen the dignity, and sully the glory you have hitherto maintained; let me request you to rely on the plighted faith of your Country, and place a full confidence in the purity of the intentions of Congress; that, previous to your dissolution as an Army they will cause all your Accounts to be fairly liquidated, as directed in their resolutions, which were published to you two days ago, and that they will adopt the most effectual measures in their power, to render ample justice to you, for your faithful and meritorious Services. And let me conjure you, in the name of our common Country, as you value your own sacred honor, as you respect the rights of humanity, and as you regard the Military and National character of America, to express your utmost horror and detestation of the Man who wishes, under any specious pretences, to overturn the liberties of our Country, and who wickedly attempts to open the flood Gates of Civil discord, and deluge our rising Empire in Blood. By thus determining, and thus acting, you will pursue the plain and direct road to the attainment of your wishes. You will defeat the insidious designs of our Enemies, who are compelled to resort from open force to secret Artifice. You will give one more distinguished proof of unexampled patriotism and patient virtue, rising superior to the pressure of the most complicated sufferings; and you will, by the dignity of your Conduct, afford occasion of Posterity to say, when speaking of the glorious example you have exhibited to Mankind, "had this day been wanting, the World had never seen the last stage of perfection to which human nature is capable of attaining."

FREDERICK II

Frederick II of Prussia (1712–1786) is remembered as one of the more enlightened eighteenth century European despots. A great admirer of US president George Washington, he corresponded with the philosopher Voltaire (among many others), and strongly opposed the hard-line theories of Niccoló Machiavelli.

"The cavalry regiment that does not on this instant, on orders given, dash full plunge into the enemy, I will, directly after the battle, unhorse and make it a garrison regiment. The infantry battalion which, meet with what it may, shows the least sign of hesitancy, loses its colors and its sabers, and I cut the trimmings from its uniform! Now, goodnight, gentlemen: shortly we have either beaten the enemy, or we never see one another again."
Frederick gives his generals a motivational talk before the Battle of Leuthen, 1757.

"All religions must be tolerated...for every man must get to heaven in his own way."

"I begin by taking. I shall find scholars later to demonstrate my perfect right."

"If my soldiers were to begin to think, not one of them would remain in the army."

"My people and I have come to an agreement which satisfied us both. They are to say what they please, and I am to do what I please."

"Religion is the idol of the mob; it adores everything it does not understand."

"The greatest and noblest pleasure which men can have in this world is to discover new truths; and the next is to shake off old prejudices."

"We must dare, dare again, always dare"
Georges Jacques Danton, French National Assembly, Paris, 2 September 1792

Like many tyrants, Georges Jacques Danton (1759–1794) masqueraded as a supporter of the masses in order to attain power. The Parisian lawyer was a leading figure in the initial stages of the French Revolution, and when he made this speech, France was in convoluted turmoil; the new revolutionary government had declared war on Austria, whose cause was being supported by counter-revolutionary forces of the overthrown government. The country was riddled with spies, double agents, and opportunists of all colors, and a general atmosphere of paranoia and suspicion prevailed.

Danton had established his patriotic credentials by leading the attack on the Tuileries the previous month, resulting in the overthrow of the Bourbon monarchy and the establishment of the Revolutionary Tribunal. He made this speech as the new republic was under threat from the invading Austrian and Prussian armies, which had — contrary to Danton's assertion — already captured the north-eastern town of Verdun.

Shortly afterwards he was named minister of justice, going on to become the predominant member of the Executive Committee.

But after two years of massacres, which Danton did little to try to prevent, the voters dumped him from the committee, and the leadership of the Revolution passed on to the militant Maximilien Robespierre (see page 92), who had Danton guillotined on 5 April 1794 for anti-revolutionary activity.

Danton's legacy is disputed; he appears to have been regarded less as a principled radical than as an unruly, opportunistic individualist, whose personality and eloquence enabled him to achieve great personal power. Remarkably, he never used speaking notes.

It is gratifying to the ministers of a free people to have to announce to them that their country will be saved. All are stirred, all are excited, all burn to fight. You know that Verdun is not yet in the power of our enemies. You know that its garrison swears to immolate the first who breathes a proposition of surrender.

One portion of our people will proceed to the frontiers, another will throw up entrenchments, and the third with pikes will defend the hearts of our cities. Paris will second these great efforts. The commissioners of the Commune will solemnly proclaim to the citizens the invitation to arm and

Danton was president of the Cordeliers Club, one of the many clubs that advocated "popular sovereignty."

march to the defence of the country. At such a moment you can proclaim that the capital deserves well of all France.

At such a moment this National Assembly becomes a veritable committee of war. We ask that you concur with us in directing this sublime movement of the people, by naming commissioners who will second us in these great measures. We ask that any one refusing to give personal service or to furnish arms shall be punished with death. We ask that a set of instructions be drawn up for the citizens to direct their movements. We ask that couriers be sent to all the departments to notify them of the decrees that you proclaim here. The tocsin we are about to ring is not an alarm signal; it sounds the charge on the enemies of our country. To conquer them we must dare, dare again, always dare, and France is saved!

The Cult of the Supreme Being
Maximilien Robespierre, Paris, 7 May 1794

French lawyer and magistrate Maximilien Robespierre (1758–1794), one of the leaders of the French Revolution, is infamous for his involvement in the Reign of Terror that followed.

At the start of the revolution, Robespierre was leader of the powerful Jacobin Club, which advocated exile or death for France's nobility. In 1792, after Paris mobs seized power from King Louis XVI and Queen Marie Antoinette, Robespierre helped organize a new quasi-government, the Paris Commune. He demanded the execution of the king and queen, which was duly carried out.

He was then elected to The Committee of Public Safety, which ruled as a dictatorship designed to secure internal stability and protect against hostile would-be-invaders such as Austria, Prussia, and Holland, which were encircling France's borders, hoping to feast on the spoils of the revolution. The Committee instituted the three-year "Reign of Terror," during which numerous royalists and various unsympathetic elements were guillotined without trial.

Robespierre became intoxicated with power and created many enemies on all sides. Soon after he made this speech he was arrested by his political enemies. On 28 July 1794 he was guillotined, leading to the collapse of the Reign of Terror.

The day forever fortunate has arrived, which the French people have consecrated to the Supreme Being. Never has the world which He created offered to Him a spectacle so worthy of His notice. He has seen reigning on the earth tyranny, crime, and imposture. He sees at this moment a whole nation, grappling with all the oppressions of the human race, suspend the course of its heroic labors to elevate its thoughts and vows towards the great Being who has given it the mission it has undertaken and the strength to accomplish it.

Is it not He whose immortal hand, engraving on the heart of man the code of justice and equality, has written there the death sentence of tyrants? Is it not He who, from the beginning of time, decreed for all the ages and for all peoples liberty, good faith, and justice?

He did not create kings to devour the human race. He did not create priests to harness us, like vile animals, to the chariots of kings and to give

FIGHTING WORDS

"There never was a good war or a bad peace."
US diplomat, war hero, inventor, and writer
Benjamin Franklin (1706–1790), pictured,
was responsible for many famous and
enduring aphorisms, including:
"In this world nothing can be said to be
certain, except death and taxes."

"Among the calamities of war may be jointly
numbered the diminution of the love of truth,
by the falsehoods which interest dictates and
credulity encourages."
Samuel Johnson (1709–1784), British
essayist, poet, biographer, and lexicographer
as well as a great wit, in *The Idler* (1758)

"An army of asses led by a lion is better than an army
of lions led by an ass."
George Washington (1732–1799), who was elected first
American president in 1789, after leading the American army to victory
over Britain in the American War of Independence

"You must consider every man your enemy who speaks ill of your king:
and...you must hate a Frenchman as you hate the devil."
Lord Nelson (1758–1805) is remembered for his famous and brilliant
victory over the French and Spanish fleets at the Battle of Trafalgar
in 1805. Sadly, he was killed by a sniper's bullet when victory had been
all but secured.

"From my earliest youth I have regarded the connection between Great Britain
and Ireland as the curse of the Irish nation, and felt convinced that, while it
lasted, this country could never be free nor happy."
Wolf Tone (1763–1798) was an Irish patriot who was court-martialed for his
part in the Irish Rebellion of 1798. As he made this statement in court, he
asked that he be granted a soldier's death — by firing squad — but was
refused. He committed suicide before he could be hung from the gallows.

to the world examples of baseness, pride, perfidy, avarice, debauchery, and falsehood. He created the universe to proclaim His power. He created men to help each other, to love each other mutually, and to attain to happiness by the way of virtue.

It is He who implanted in the breast of the triumphant oppressor remorse and terror, and in the heart of the oppressed and innocent calmness and fortitude. It is He who impels the just man to hate the evil one, and the evil man to respect the just one. It is He who adorns with modesty the brow of beauty, to make it yet more beautiful. It is He who makes the mother's heart beat with tenderness and joy. It is He who bathes with delicious tears the eyes of the son pressed to the bosom of his mother. It is He who silences the most imperious and tender passions before the sublime love of the fatherland. It is He who has covered nature with charms, riches, and majesty. All that is good is His work, or is Himself. Evil belongs to the depraved man who oppresses his fellow man or suffers him to be oppressed.

The Author of Nature has bound all mortals by a boundless chain of love and happiness. Perish the tyrants who have dared to break it!

Republican Frenchmen, it is yours to purify the earth which they have soiled, and to recall to it the justice that they have banished! Liberty and virtue together came from the breast of Divinity. Neither can abide with mankind without the other.

O generous People, would you triumph over all your enemies? Practice justice, and render the Divinity the only worship worthy of Him. O People, let us deliver ourselves today, under His auspices, to the just transports of a pure festivity. Tomorrow we shall return to the combat with vice and tyrants. We shall give to the world the example of republican virtues. And that will be to honor Him still.

The monster which the genius of kings had vomited over France has gone back into nothingness. May all the crimes and all the misfortunes of the world disappear with it! Armed in turn with the daggers of fanaticism and the poisons of atheism, kings have always conspired to assassinate humanity. If they are able no longer to disfigure Divinity by superstition, to associate it with their crimes, they try to banish it from the earth, so that they may reign there alone with crime.

O People, fear no more their sacrilegious plots! They can no more snatch the world from the breast of its Author than remorse from their own hearts. Unfortunate ones, uplift your eyes towards heaven! Heroes

Robespierre meets his fate under the guillotine blade.

of the fatherland, your generous devotion is not a brilliant madness. If the satellites of tyranny can assassinate you, it is not in their power entirely to destroy you. Man, whoever thou mayest be, thou canst still conceive high thoughts for thyself. Thou canst bind thy fleeting life to God, and to immortality. Let nature seize again all her splendor, and wisdom all her empire! The Supreme Being has not been annihilated.

It is wisdom above all that our guilty enemies would drive from the Republic. To wisdom alone it is given to strengthen the prosperity of empires. It is for her to guarantee to us the rewards of our courage. Let us associate wisdom, then, with all our enterprises. Let us be grave and discreet in all our deliberations, as men who are providing for the interests of the world. Let us be ardent and obstinate in our anger against conspiring tyrants, imperturbable in dangers, patient in labors, terrible in striking back, modest and vigilant in successes. Let us be generous towards the good, compassionate with the unfortunate, inexorable with the evil, just towards every one. Let us not count on an unmixed prosperity, and on triumphs without attacks, nor on all that depends on fortune or the perversity of others. Sole, but infallible guarantors of our independence, let us crush the impious league of kings by the grandeur of our character, even more than by the strength of our arms.

Frenchmen, you war against kings; you are therefore worthy to honor Divinity. Being of Beings, Author of Nature, the brutalized slave, the vile instrument of despotism, the perfidious and cruel aristocrat, outrages Thee by his very invocation of Thy name. But the defenders of liberty can give themselves up to Thee, and rest with confidence upon Thy paternal bosom. Being of Beings, we need not offer to Thee unjust prayers. Thou knowest Thy creatures, proceeding from Thy hands. Their needs do not escape Thy notice, more than their secret thoughts. Hatred of bad faith and tyranny burns in our hearts, with love of justice and the fatherland. Our blood flows for the cause of humanity. Behold our prayer. Behold our sacrifices. Behold the worship we offer Thee.

FIGHTING SONG
La Marseillaise

Allons enfants de la Patrie
Le jour de gloire est arrivé.
Contre nous, de la tyrannie,
L'étandard sanglant est levé,
L'étandard sanglant est levé,
Entendez-vous, dans la compagnes.
Mugir ces farouches soldats
Ils viennent jusque dans nos bras
Egorger vos fils,
vos compagnes.

Aux armes citoyens!
Formez vos bataillons,
Marchons, marchons!
Qu'un sang impur
Abreuve nos sillons.

Amour sacré de la Patrie,
Conduis, soutiens nos bras vengeurs,
Liberté, liberté cherie,
Combats avec tes defénseurs;
Combats avec tes défenseurs.
Sous drapeaux, que la victoire
Acoure à tes mâles accents;
Que tes ennemis expirants
Voient ton triomphe et notre gloire!

Ye sons of France, awake to glory!
Hark! Hark! the people bid you rise!
Your children, wives, and grandsires hoary
Behold their tears and hear their cries!
Behold their tears and hear their cries!
Shall hateful tyrants, mischief breeding,
With hireling hosts a ruffian band
Affright and desolate the land
While peace and liberty lie bleeding?

To arms, to arms, ye brave!
Th'avenging sword unsheathe!
March on, march on, all hearts resolved
On liberty or death.

Oh liberty can man resign thee,
Once having felt thy gen'rous flame?
Can dungeons, bolts, and bar confine thee?
Or whips thy noble spirit tame?
Or whips thy noble spirit tame?
Too long the world has wept bewailing
That falsehood's dagger tyrants wield;
But freedom is our sword and shield
And all their arts are unavailing.

To arms, to arms, ye brave!
Th'avenging sword unsheathe!
March on, march on, all hearts resolved
On liberty or death.

"La Marseillaise," the national anthem of France, was written in 1792 (at
the height of the French Revolution) by Claude Joseph Rouget de Lisle. It
was originally called "War Song for the Army of the Rhine." This English
translation is not literal, but is widely used in English-speaking schools.

Part 4

NEW NATIONS FORGED IN BATTLE

"

The Nineteenth Century

"I am going to my cold and silent grave"
Robert Emmet, Dublin, 19 September 1803

In 1803 Irish patriot Robert Emmet (1778–1803) led a poorly organized rebellion against the occupying British government, during which the chief justice, Lord Kilwarden, was murdered. Emmet was found guilty of treason and executed. He made this speech after the court asked him whether there was any reason why he should not be sentenced to death. Defiant to the last, he makes no claims for mitigation, and makes it clear that he is happy to be judged by God, the highest arbiter.

I am asked what have I to say why sentence of death should not be pronounced on me, according to law. I have nothing to say that can alter your predetermination, nor that it will become me to say, with any view to the mitigation of that sentence which you are to pronounce, and I must abide by. But I have that to say which interests me more than life, and which you have labored to destroy. I have much to say why my reputation should be rescued from the load of false accusation and calumny which has been cast upon it…

…Were I only to suffer death, after being adjudged guilty by your tribunal, I should bow in silence, and meet the fate that awaits me without a murmur; but the sentence of the law which delivers my body to the executioner will, through the ministry of the law, labor in its own vindication to consign my character to obloquy; for there must be guilt somewhere; whether in the sentence of the court, or in the catastrophe, time must determine. A man in my situation has not only to encounter the difficulties of fortune, and the force of power over minds which it has corrupted or subjugated, but the difficulties of established prejudice. The man dies, but his memory lives. That mine may not perish, that it may live in the respect of my countrymen, I seize upon this opportunity to vindicate myself from some of the charges alleged against me...

I appeal to the immaculate God — I swear by the throne of Heaven, before which I must shortly appear — by the blood of the murdered patriots who have gone before me — that my conduct has been, through all this peril, and through all my purposes, governed only by the conviction which I have uttered, and by no other view than that of the emancipation of my country from the super-inhuman oppression under which she has so long and too patiently travailed; and I confidently hope that, wild and chimerical as it may appear, there is still union and strength in Ireland to accomplish this noblest of enterprises…

…My lords, it may be a part of the system of angry justice to bow a man's mind by humiliation to the proposed ignominy of the scaffold; but worse to me than the purposed shame or the scaffold's terrors would be the shame of such foul and unfounded imputations as have been laid against me in this court. You, my lord, are a judge; I am the supposed culprit. I am a man; you are a man also. By a revolution of power we might change places, though we never could change characters. If I stand at the bar of this court and dare not vindicate my character, what a farce is your justice! If I stand at this bar and dare not vindicate my character, how dare you calumniate it? Does the sentence of death, which your unhallowed policy inflicts on my body, condemn my tongue to silence and my reputation to reproach? Your executioner may abridge the period of my existence; but while I exist, I shall not forbear to vindicate my character and motives from your aspersions; and, as a man, to whom fame is dearer than life, I will make the last use of that life in doing justice to that reputation which is to live after me, and which is the only legacy I can leave to those I honor and love, and for whom I am proud to perish. As men, my lords, we must appear on the great day at one common tribunal; and it will then remain for the Searcher of All Hearts to show a collective universe who was engaged in the most virtuous actions, or swayed by the purest motive — my country's oppressors, or…[interruption by the court]

I am charged with being an emissary of France. An emissary of France! and for what end? It is alleged that I wish to sell the independence of my country; and for what end? Was this the object of my ambition? And is this the mode by which a tribunal of justice reconciles contradiction? No, I am no emissary; and my ambition was to hold a place among the deliverers of my country, not in power nor in profit, but in the glory of the achievement. Sell my country's independence to France! and for what? Was it a change of masters? No, but for ambition. O my country! was it personal ambition that could influence me? Had it been the soul of my actions, could I not by my education and fortune, by the rank and consideration of my family, have placed myself amongst the proudest of your oppressors? My country was my idol! To it I sacrificed every selfish, every endearing sentiment; and for it I now offer up myself, O God! No, my lords; I acted as an Irishman, determined on delivering my country from the yoke of a foreign and unrelenting tyranny, and the more galling yoke of a domestic

This wreath of clover, known as the Fenian banner, is a tribute to Irish patriots such as Robert Emmet.

THE FENIAN BANNER.

" But the Harp, that so long hath been silent and weeping,   When the voice of the brave with its echoes shall mingle,
Resigned by its master in gloom and despair,   In the clangor of arms, or the transport of glee,
Shall again be brought forth from the shrine where 'tis sleeping,   For the millions who love it will shortly assemble,
And with glad notes of freedom enliven the air;   To proclaim that their nation again shall be free

faction, which is its joint partner and perpetrator in the patricide, from the ignominy existing with an exterior of splendor and a conscious depravity. It was the wish of my heart to extricate my country from this doubly riveted despotism — I wished to place her independence beyond the reach of any power on earth. I wished to exalt her to that proud station in the world. Connection with France was, indeed, intended, but only as far as mutual interest would sanction or require. Were the French to assume any authority inconsistent with the purest independence, it would be the signal for their destruction. We sought their aid — and we sought it as we had assurance we should obtain it — as auxiliaries in war, and allies in peace. Were the French to come as invaders or enemies, uninvited by the wishes of the people, I should oppose them to the utmost of my strength. Yes! my countrymen, I should advise you to meet them upon the beach with a sword in one hand and a torch in the other. I would meet them with all the destructive fury of war. I would animate my countrymen to immolate them in their boats, before they had contaminated the soil of my country. If they succeeded in landing, and if forced to retire before superior discipline, I would dispute every inch of ground, burn every blade of grass, and the last entrenchment of liberty should be my grave...But it was not as an enemy that the succors of France were to land. I looked, indeed, for the assistance of France; but I wished to prove to France and to the world that Irishmen deserved to be assisted; that they were indignant at slavery, and ready to assert the independence and liberty of their country. I wished to procure for my country the guarantee which Washington procured for America; to procure an aid which, by its example, would be as important as its valor; disciplined, gallant, pregnant with science and experience; that of a people who would perceive the good, and polish the rough points of our character...

What, my lord, shall you tell me, on the passage to the scaffold, which that tyranny (of which you are only the intermediary executioner) has erected for my murder, that I am accountable for all the blood that has been and will be shed in this struggle of the oppressed against the oppressor — shall you tell me this, and must I be so very a slave as not to repel it? I do not fear to approach the Omnipotent Judge to answer for the conduct of my whole life; and am I to be appalled and falsified by a mere remnant of mortality here? By you, too, although, if it were possible to collect all the innocent blood that you have shed in your unhallowed ministry in one great reservoir, your lordship might swim in it.

Let no man dare, when I am dead, to charge me with dishonor; let no man attaint my memory, by believing that I could have engaged in any cause but that of my country's liberty and independence; or that I could have become the pliant minion of power, in the oppression and misery of my country. The proclamation of the provisional government speaks for our views; no inference can be tortured from it to countenance barbarity or debasement at home, or subjection, humiliation, or treachery from abroad. I would not have submitted to a foreign oppressor, for the same reason that I would resist the foreign and domestic oppressor. In the dignity of freedom, I would have fought upon the threshold of my country, and its enemy should enter only by passing over my lifeless corpse. And am I, who lived but for my country, and who have subjected myself to the dangers of the jealous and watchful oppressor, and the bondage of the grave, only to give my countrymen their rights, and my country her independence — am I to be loaded with calumny, and not suffered to resent it? No; God forbid!

If the spirits of the illustrious dead participate in the concerns and cares of those who were dear to them in this transitory life, O, ever dear and venerated shade of my departed father! look down with scrutiny upon the conduct of your suffering son, and see if I have, even for a moment, deviated from those principles of morality and patriotism which it was your care to instil into my youthful mind, and for which I am now about to offer up my life. My lords, you are impatient for the sacrifice. The blood which you seek is not congealed by the artificial terrors which surround your victim — it circulates warmly and unruffled through the channels which God created for noble purposes, but which you are now bent to destroy for purposes so grievous that they cry to heaven. Be yet patient! I have but a few more words to say — I am going to my cold and silent grave...the grave opens to receive me, and I sink into its bosom. I have but one request to ask at my departure from this world; it is — the charity of its silence. Let no man write my epitaph; for, as no man who knows my motives dares now vindicate them, let not prejudice or ignorance asperse them. Let them and me rest in obscurity and peace, and my tomb remain uninscribed, and my memory in oblivion, until other times and other men can do justice to my character. When my country takes her place among the nations of the earth, then, and not till then, let my epitaph be written. I have done.

"You have got our country, but you are not satisfied"
Chief Red Jacket (Sagoyewatha), Buffalo Creek, New York, United States, 1805

A New York-born Seneca chief of the Iroquois confederacy, Sagoyewatha (c. 1758–1830) worked as a messenger for his British allies during the American Revolution. After the British defeat, many Indians faced competition for their homelands as post-war territorial negotiations took place, and Sagoyewatha became a valuable mediator in relations with the new US government.

Sagoyewatha suffered from alcoholism and lost most of his children to illness. When asked if he had any children, he replied sadly: "Red Jacket was once a great man, and in favor with the Great Spirit. He was a lofty pine among the smaller trees of the forest. But, after years of glory, he degraded himself by drinking the firewater of the white man. The Great Spirit has looked upon him in anger, and his lightning has stripped the pine of its branches."

In 1805 Reverend Cram of the Boston Missionary Society asked his permission to conduct mission work among the Iroquois in northern New York State. Red Jacket's eloquent and logical reply, in which he defended his native religion, resulted in Cram refusing the proffered handshake; he announced that no fellowship could exist between the religion of God and the works of the devil.

Friend and Brother: It was the will of the Great Spirit that we should meet together this day. He orders all things and has given us a fine day for our council. He has taken his garment from before the sun, and caused it to shine with brightness upon us. Our eyes are opened, that we see clearly; our ears are unstopped, that we have been able to hear distinctly the words you have spoken. For all these favors we thank the Great Spirit; and him only.

Brother, this council fire was kindled by you. It was at your request that we came together at this time. We have listened with attention to what you have said. You requested us to speak our minds freely. This gives us great joy, for we now consider that we stand upright before you, and can speak what we think. All have heard your voice, and all speak to you now as one man. Our minds are agreed.

Brother, you say you want an answer to your talk before you leave this place. It is right you should have one, as you are a great distance from home, and we do not wish to detain you. But we will first look back a little, and tell you what our fathers have told us, and what we have heard from the white people.

Brother, listen to what we say. There was a time when our forefathers owned this great island. Their seats extended from the rising to the setting of the sun. The Great Spirit had made for the use of the Indians. He had created the buffalo, the deer, and other animals for food. He'd made the bear and the deer, and their skins served us for clothing. He had scattered them over the country, and had taught us how to take them. He had caused the earth to produce corn for bread. All this He had done for his red children, because He loved them. If we had any disputes about hunting grounds, they were generally settled without the shedding of much blood.

But an evil day came upon us. Your forefathers crossed the great waters and landed on this island. Their numbers were small. They found friends and not enemies. They told us they had fled from their own country for fear of wicked men, and had come here to enjoy their religion. They asked for a small seat. We took pity on them, granted their request, and they sat down amongst us. We gave them corn and meat; they gave us poison in return.

The white people had now found our country. Tidings were carried back, and more came amongst us. Yet we did not fear them. We took them to be friends. They called us brothers. We believed them, and gave them a large seat. At length their numbers had greatly increased. They wanted more land; they wanted our country. Our eyes were opened, and our minds became uneasy. Wars took place. Indians were hired to fight against Indians, and many of our people were destroyed. They also brought strong liquors among us. It was strong and powerful and has slain thousands.

Brother, our seats were once large, and yours very small. You have now become a great people, and we have scarcely a place left to spread our blankets. You have got our country, but you are not satisfied; you want to force your religion upon us.

Brother, continue to listen. You say that you are sent to instruct us how to worship the Great Spirit agreeable to His mind. And if we do not take hold of the religion which you white people teach, we shall be unhappy hereafter. You say that you are right, and we are lost. How do you know this to be true? We understand that your religion is written in a book. If it was intended for us as well as for you, why has not the Great Spirit given it to us, and not only to us, but why did He not give to our forefathers knowledge of that book, with the means of understanding it rightly? We

RED JACKET.

SENECA WAR CHIEF.

only know what you tell us about it. How shall we know when to believe, being so often deceived by the white man?

Brother, you say there is but one way to worship and serve the Great Spirit. If there is but one religion, why do you white people differ so much about it? Why not all agree, as you can all read the book?

Brother, we do not understand these things. We are told that your religion was given to your forefathers and has been handed down — father to son. We also have a religion, which was given to our forefathers, and has been handed down to us, their children. We worship that way. It teaches us to be thankful for all the favors we receive; to love each other, and to be united. We never quarrel about religion.

Brother, the Great Spirit has made us all, but He has made a great difference between his white and red children. He has given us a different complexion and different customs. To you He has given the arts. To these He has not opened our eyes. We know these things to be true. Since He has made so great a difference between us in other things, why may we not conclude that He has given us a different religion according to our understanding? The Great Spirit does right. He knows what is best for his children; we are satisfied.

Brother, we do not wish to destroy your religion, or to take it from you. We only want to enjoy our own.

Brother, you say you have not come to get our land or our money, but to enlighten our minds. I will now tell you that I have been at your meetings, and saw you collecting money from the meeting. I cannot tell what this money was intended for, but suppose it was for your minister, and if we should conform to your way of thinking, perhaps you may want some from us.

Brother, we are told that you have been preaching to the white people in this place. These people are our neighbors. We are acquainted with them. We will wait a little while, and see what effect your preaching has upon them. If we find it does them good, and makes them honest, and less disposed to cheat Indians, we will then consider again what you have said.

Brother, you have now heard our answer to your talk, and this is all we have to say at present. As we are going to part, we will come and take you by the hand, and hope the Great Spirit will protect you on your journey, and return you safe to your friends.

Sagoyewatha's English name, Chief Red Jacket, came from his practice of wearing red coats provided by the British.

—⟩ 「」 ⟨—

Maiden speech to the House of Lords
**Lord George Byron, House of Lords, London,
27 February 1812**

George Gordon Byron (1788–1824), commonly known as Lord Byron, was an English romantic poet and politician whose best known works include the long narrative poems *Childe Harold's Pilgrimage* and *Don Juan*. His fame rests not only on his writings but also on his exotic and scandalous life, including many love affairs and allegations of homosexuality.

Byron took his seat in the House of Lords in 1811. This, his maiden speech to the House, was delivered during the war against Napoleon's France, at a time when the Industrial Revolution was rapidly impoverishing the working class. Large, efficient weaving frames had recently been introduced, with the result that unemployed weavers were resorting to desperate measures, including sabotage. Byron's speech opposes the introduction of legislation calling for the death penalty for the saboteurs. He was not successful; the *Frame-Breaking Act* was passed, although most of the death penalties were commuted to transportation to the colonies.

Byron traveled to Greece, where he lent his assistance to the cause of Greek freedom against the Ottoman occupiers. He used his riches to refit the Greek navy and employ military experts, intending to attack the Ottoman stronghold of Lepanto in the Gulf of Corinth, but he died of fever in 1824 before he could fulfil his plan.

The last line of the speech refers to Judge George Jeffreys, who was renowned for his malice, bias, and loathing of the working class.

...The rejected workmen, in the blindness of their ignorance, instead of rejoicing at these improvements in arts so beneficial to mankind, conceived themselves to be sacrificed to improvements in mechanism. In the foolishness of their hearts they imagined that the maintenance and well-doing of the industrious poor were objects of greater consequence than the enrichment of a few individuals by any improvement, in the implements of trade, which threw the workmen out of employment, and rendered the laborer unworthy of his hire. And it must be confessed that although the adoption of the enlarged machinery in that state of our commerce which the country once boasted might have been beneficial to the master without being detrimental to the servant; yet, in the present situation of our manufactures, rotting in warehouses, without a prospect of exportation, with the demand for work and workmen equally diminished, frames of this description tend materially to aggravate the distress and discontent of the disappointed sufferers. But the real cause of these distresses and consequent disturbances lies deeper. When we are told that these men are leagued together not only for the destruction of their own comfort, but of their very means of subsistence, can we forget that it is the bitter policy, the destructive warfare of the last eighteen years, which has destroyed their comfort, your comfort, all men's comfort? That policy, which, originating with "great statesmen now no more," has survived the dead to become a curse on the living, unto the third and fourth generation! These men never destroyed their looms till they were become useless, worse than useless; till they were become actual impediments to their exertions in obtaining their daily bread...

It has been stated that the persons in the temporary possession of frames connive at their destruction; if this be proved upon inquiry, it were necessary that such material accessories to the crime should be principals in the punishment. But I did hope, that any measure proposed by his Majesty's government for your Lordships" decision, would have bad conciliation for its basis; or, if that were hopeless, that some previous inquiry, some deliberation, would have been deemed requisite; not that we should have been called at once, without examination and without cause, to pass sentences by wholesale, and sign death warrants, blindfold. But, admitting that these men had no cause of complaint; that the grievances of them and their employers were alike groundless; that they deserved the worst; what inefficiency, what imbecility has been evinced in the method chosen to reduce them!...

At present the country suffers from the double infliction of an idle military and a starving population. In what state of apathy have we been plunged so long, that now for the first time the House has been officially apprised of these disturbances? All this has been transacting within 130 miles of London; and yet we, "good easy men, have deemed full sure our greatness was a-ripening," and have sat down to enjoy our foreign triumphs in the midst of domestic calamity. But all the cities you have taken, all the armies which have retreated before your leaders, are but paltry subjects of self-congratulation, if your land divides against itself, and your dragoons and your executioners must be let loose against your fellow citizens. You call these men a mob, desperate, dangerous and ignorant; and seem to think that the only way to quiet the "*Bellua multorum capitum*" [a many-headed beast] is to lop off a few of its superfluous heads. But

Weaving, once a cottage industry, became mechanized during the Industrial Revolution, which began in the late eighteenth century.

reduced to reason by a mixture even a mob may be better of conciliation and firmness, than by additional irritation and redoubled penalties...

You may call the people a mob; but do not forget that a mob too often speaks the sentiments of the people. And here I must remark, with what alacrity you are accustomed to fly to the succor of your distressed allies, leaving the distressed of your own country to the care of Providence or the parish. When the Portuguese suffered under the retreat of the French, every arm was stretched out, every hand was opened, from the rich man's largesse to the widow's mite, all was bestowed, to enable them to rebuild their villages and replenish their granaries. And at this moment, when thousands of misguided but most unfortunate fellow countrymen are struggling with the extremes of hardships and hunger, as your charity began abroad it should end at home...

I have traversed the seat of war in the Peninsula, I have been in some of the most oppressed provinces of Turkey; but never under the most despotic of infidel governments did I behold such squalid wretchedness as I have seen since my return in the very heart of a Christian country. And what are your remedies? After months of inaction, and months of action worse than inactivity, at length comes forth the grand specific, the never-failing nostrum of all state physicians, from the days of Draco to the present time. After feeling the pulse and shaking the head over the patient, prescribing the usual course of warm water and bleeding, the warm water of your mawkish police, and the lancers of your military, these convulsions must terminate in death, the sure consummation of the prescriptions of all political Sangrados...

Will you erect a gibbet in every field, and hang up men like scarecrows? Or will you proceed (as you must to bring this measure into effect) by decimation? Place the country under martial law? Depopulate and lay waste all around you and restore Sherwood Forest as an acceptable gift to the crown, in its former condition of a royal chase and an asylum for outlaws? Are these the remedies for a starving and desperate populace? Will the famished wretch who has braved your bayonets be appalled by your gibbets? When death is a relief, and the only relief it appears that you will afford him, will he be dragooned into tranquillity? Will that which could not be effected by your grenadiers be accomplished by your executioners?...

When a proposal is made to emancipate or relieve, you hesitate, you deliberate for years, you temporize and tamper with the minds of men; but a death-bill must be passed off-hand, without a thought of the consequences. Sure I am, from what I have heard, and from what I have seen, that to pass the Bill under all the existing circumstances, without inquiry, without deliberation, would only be to add injustice to irritation, and barbarity to neglect. The framers of such a bill must be content to inherit the honors of that Athenian law-giver whose edicts were said to be written not in ink but in blood. But suppose it passed; suppose one of these men, as I have seen them, meagre with famine, sullen with despair, careless of a life which your Lordships are perhaps about to value at something less than the price of a stocking-frame; suppose this man surrounded by the children for whom he is unable to procure bread at the hazard of his existence, about to be torn forever from a family which he lately supported in peaceful industry, and which it is not his fault that he can no longer so support; suppose this man, and there are ten thousand such from whom you may select your victims dragged into court, to be tried for this new offence, by this new law; still, there are two things wanting to convict and condemn him and these are, in my opinion, twelve butchers for a jury, and a Jeffreys for a judge!

Farewell to the Old Guard

Napoleon Bonaparte, Château de Fontainebleau, Paris, 20 April 1814

A general in the French Revolution of 1789–99, Napoleon Bonaparte (1769–1821) seized political power in 1799 and crowned himself Emperor of France in 1804. By 1808 he had achieved military victories over much of Europe and beyond, including Russia. When the Russians refused to cooperate in France's military blockade of Britain in 1812, an enraged Napoleon decided to invade Russia instead. But he made the mistake of underestimating both Russia's strength and the difficulties of maintaining a campaign throughout the brutal Russian winter, and his army was completely routed by a coalition of Austria, Russia, Prussia, Sweden, and the United Kingdom. Perhaps half a million French troops died. (More than a century later, German dictator Adolf Hitler failed to heed the lesson, and made the same disastrous blunder in World War II, with similar results; see page 228.)

Forced to abdicate after his defeat, Napoleon was banished to the small island of Elba in the Mediterranean in 1814.

But he managed to escape in February 1815, returning to France, where he cobbled together an "Old Guard" army of soldiers who had retained their allegiance to him. He regained power for about 100 days, but was again forced to abdicate following his defeat by the English and Prussian armies in the Battle of Waterloo in June 1815. He was then imprisoned by the British and exiled to the island of St. Helena, in the middle of the South Atlantic Ocean, where he died in 1821.

Napoleon believed in government "for" the people, but not "by" them. Under his rule, France was a police and military dictatorship with an extensive network of secret agents and domestic spies. The press was controlled by the state and all criticism of the government was banned. He did, however, institute many progressive reforms in the fields of education, legislation, and government, and many of his battle strategies are regarded as exemplary models of military genius.

This speech was made a few weeks after Napoleon's first abdication, following the Russian fiasco, and the subsequent capture of Paris by Russian allies England, Austria, and Prussia. Napoleon bids farewell to the remaining faithful officers of the Old Guard, who presumably believed his patently ridiculous, conceited claim: "I have sacrificed all of my interests to those of the country..."

Soldiers of my Old Guard: I bid you farewell. For twenty years I have constantly accompanied you on the road to honor and glory. In these latter times, as in the days of our prosperity, you have invariably been models of courage and fidelity. With men such as you our cause could not be lost; but the war would have been interminable; it would have been civil war, and that would have entailed deeper misfortunes on France.

I have sacrificed all of my interests to those of the country.

I go, but you, my friends, will continue to serve France. Her happiness was my only thought. It will still be the object of my wishes. Do not regret my fate; if I have consented to survive, it is to serve your glory. I intend to write the history of the great achievements we have performed together. Adieu, my friends. Would I could press you all to my heart.

Napoleon in exile on board the French ship *Bellerophon*, which took him to Plymouth in 1815.

NAPOLEON BONAPARTE

Napoleon Bonaparte was a general in the French Revolution and installed himself as Emperor of France in 1804 (see also page 114). He fought a series of wars against Britain, Russia, Austria, and other European countries, with mixed success. He is responsible for numerous *bon mots*, including: "An army marches on its stomach."

"More glorious to merit a scepter than to possess one."

"A great people may be killed, but they cannot be intimidated."

"Soldiers: Behold your colors! These eagles will always be your rallying point! They will always be where your Emperor may think them necessary for the defence of his throne and of his people. Swear to sacrifice your lives to defend them, and by your courage to keep them constantly in the path of victory. Swear!"
Napoleon addressing his troops on presenting the colors, 3 December 1804

"Soldiers: This is the battle you have so much desired. The victory depends upon you! It is now necessary to us. It will give us abundance of good winter quarters, and a prompt return to our country. Behave as at Austerlitz, at Friedland, at Witepsk, at Smolensk, and let the latest posterity recount with pride your conduct on this day; let them say of you, 'He was at the battle under the walls of Moscow.'"
From Napoleon's address to his troops before the Battle of Borodino, 7 September 1812

"Ain't I a woman?"
Sojourner Truth, Akron, Ohio, United States, 1851

Anti-slavery and women's rights activist Isabella Baumfree (1797–1883) was born into slavery in Swartekill, New York. Following New York's emancipation of slaves in 1827, and a religious epiphany in 1843, she took on the name "Sojourner Truth" and quit her job as a servant to become a traveling preacher or "sojourner."

Her usual themes were slavery and the religious life, but she delivered her best known speech, on the theme of feminism, in 1851 at the Ohio Women's Rights Convention. She uses a conversational style, repetition ("...ain't I a woman?") and rhetorical questions to persuade her audience. Although illiterate, this mother of thirteen was appointed "Counselor to the Freedmen of the Capital" by President Abraham Lincoln during the American Civil War. She continued to agitate for social justice, particularly feminism, desegregation, and women's suffrage until her death at home in 1883, in Battle Creek, Michigan.

Well, children, where there is so much racket there must be something out of kilter. I think that "twixt the Negroes of the South and the women at the North, all talking about rights, the white men will be in a fix pretty soon. But what's all this here talking about?

That man over there says that women need to be helped into carriages, and lifted over ditches, and to have the best place everywhere. Nobody ever helps me into carriages, or over mud-puddles, or gives me any best place! And ain't I a woman? Look at me! Look at my arm! I have ploughed and planted, and gathered into barns, and no man could head me! And ain't I a woman? I could work as much and eat as much as a man — when I could get it — and bear the lash as well! And ain't I a woman? I have borne thirteen children, and seen most all sold off to slavery, and when I cried out with my mother's grief, none but Jesus heard me! And ain't I a woman?

Then they talk about this thing in the head; what's this they call it? [member of audience whispers "intellect"] That's it, honey. What's that got to do with women's rights or Negroes' rights? If my cup won't hold but a pint, and yours holds a quart, wouldn't you be mean not to let me have my little half measure full?

Then that little man in black there, he says women can't have as much rights as men, 'cause Christ wasn't a woman! Where did your Christ come

Truth's second owners beat her fiercely; it was then that she sought comfort in religion and social activism.

from? Where did your Christ come from? From God and a woman! Man had nothing to do with Him.

If the first woman God ever made was strong enough to turn the world upside down all alone, these women together ought to be able to turn it back, and get it right side up again! And now they is asking to do it, the men better let them.

Obliged to you for hearing me, and now old Sojourner ain't got nothing more to say.

"To arms, all — all of you!"
Giuseppe Garibaldi, Naples, Italy, 1860

Giuseppe Garibaldi (1807–1882) was an Italian patriot who helped end the occupation of a divided Italy by Britain, France, Austria, and other loose coalitions of vested interests. In 1860 he took Sicily from the British with a small band of volunteers. He then moved north into Italy, gathering more "red shirt" volunteers along the way as he secured a series of brilliant victories.

In August 1860 he and his army conquered Naples. Garibaldi turned the city over to King Victor Emmanuel II, then retired to the island of Caprera. A year later the independent kingdom of Italy was finally proclaimed.

This speech is an eloquent appeal to his soldiers in Naples just before their successful campaign. He uses frequent repetition, and invokes great Italian victories of the past to inspire his charges.

...Yes, young men...You have conquered and you will conquer still, because you are prepared for the tactics that decide the fate of battles. You are not unworthy of the men who entered the ranks of a Macedonian phalanx, and who contended not in vain with the proud conquerors of Asia. To this wonderful page in our country's history another more glorious still will be added, and the slave shall show at last to his free brothers a sharpened sword forged from the links of his fetters.

To arms, then, all of you! all of you! And the oppressors and the mighty shall disappear like dust. You, too, women, cast away all the cowards from your embraces; they will give you only cowards for children, and you who are the daughters of the land of beauty must bear children who are noble and brave. Let timid doctrinaires depart from among us to carry their servility and their miserable fears elsewhere. This people is its own master. It wishes to be the brother of other peoples, but to look on the insolent with a proud glance, not to grovel before them imploring its own freedom. It will no longer follow in the trail of men whose hearts are foul. No! No! No!

Providence has presented Italy with Victor Emmanuel. Every Italian should rally round him. By the side of Victor Emmanuel every quarrel should be forgotten, all rancor depart. Once more I repeat my battle cry: "To arms, all — all of you!" If March, 1861, does not find one million of Italians in arms, then alas for liberty, alas for the life of Italy. Ah, no, far be from me a thought which I loathe like poison. March of 1861, or if need be February, will find us all at our post — Italians of Calatafimi, Palermo,

Garibaldi learnt guerrilla tactics as a freedom fighter in the 1840s, leading the Italian Legion in the Uruguayan Civil War. His military successes in South America and Italy resulted in the epithet, "Hero of Two Worlds."

Ancona, the Volturno, Castelfidardo, and Isernia, and with us every man of this land who is not a coward or a slave. Let all of us rally round the glorious hero of Palestro and give the last blow to the crumbling edifice of tyranny. Receive, then, my gallant young volunteers, at the honored conclusion of ten battles, one word of farewell from me.

I utter this word with deepest affection and from the very bottom of my heart. Today I am obliged to retire, but for a few days only. The hour of battle will find me with you again, by the side of the champions of Italian liberty. Let those only return to their homes who are called by the imperative duties which they owe to their families, and those who by their glorious wounds have deserved the credit of their country. These, indeed, will serve Italy in their homes by their counsel, by the very aspect of the scars which adorn their youthful brows. Apart from these, let all others remain to guard our glorious banners. We shall meet again before long to march together to the redemption of our brothers who are still slaves of the stranger. We shall meet again before long to march to new triumphs.

As Garibaldi and his soldiers marched into Naples, they were greeted by crowds singing the national anthem, now known as "Garibaldi's Hymn."

Gettysburg Address

Abraham Lincoln, Gettysburg, Pennsylvania, 19 November 1863

Following Lincoln's election as US president in 1860, largely on an anti-slavery ticket, many of the southern states refused to accept the result. They formed a rebel government, and the American Civil War broke out in April 1861. After more than 600 000 were killed, the war ended in April 1865 with victory to Lincoln and the North. The result was the abolition of slavery in the United States, and the reunification of the northern (Yankee) and southern (Confederate) states.

Lincoln (1809–1865) made this speech as he opened and dedicated a military cemetery for recently slain soldiers at Gettysburg, Pennsylvania. It is his most famous speech, and one of the most often quoted in US history. "Four score and seven years ago…" refers to the successful American War of Independence against Britain (1775–83) and, in particular, the 1776 US Declaration of Independence. In just two minutes, Lincoln emphasizes the tenets of human equality, and defines the Civil War as a struggle not just for the United States, but also for the very principles of democracy and freedom.

How wrong he was when he said: "The world will little note, nor long remember what we say here…"

Four score and seven years ago our fathers brought forth on this continent a new nation, conceived in Liberty, and dedicated to the proposition that all men are created equal.

Now we are engaged in a great civil war, testing whether that nation, or any nation so conceived and so dedicated, can long endure. We are met on a great battlefield of that war. We have come to dedicate a portion of that field, as a final resting place for those who here gave their lives that that nation might live. It is altogether fitting and proper that we should do this.

But, in a larger sense, we cannot dedicate, we cannot consecrate, we cannot hallow this ground. The brave men, living and dead, who struggled here, have consecrated it, far above our poor power to add or detract. The world will little note, nor long remember what we say here, but it can never forget what they did here. It is for us the living, rather, to be dedicated here to the unfinished work which they who fought here have thus far so nobly advanced. It is rather for us to be here dedicated to the great task remaining before us, that from these honored dead we take

increased devotion to that cause for which they gave the last full measure of devotion, that we here highly resolve that these dead shall not have died in vain, that this nation, under God, shall have a new birth of freedom, and that government of the people, by the people, for the people, shall not perish from the earth.

Lincoln delivers his Gettysburg Address, regarded as one of the greatest speeches in American history.

FIGHTING WORDS

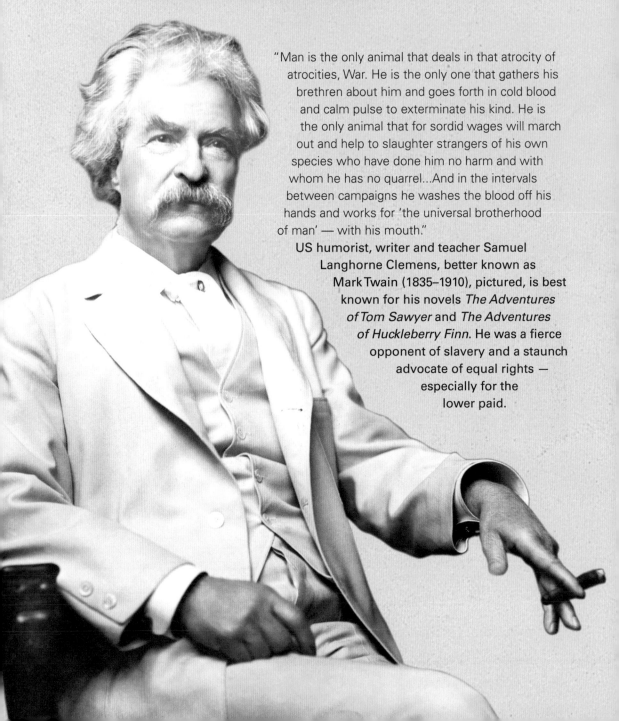

"Man is the only animal that deals in that atrocity of atrocities, War. He is the only one that gathers his brethren about him and goes forth in cold blood and calm pulse to exterminate his kind. He is the only animal that for sordid wages will march out and help to slaughter strangers of his own species who have done him no harm and with whom he has no quarrel...And in the intervals between campaigns he washes the blood off his hands and works for 'the universal brotherhood of man' — with his mouth."

US humorist, writer and teacher Samuel Langhorne Clemens, better known as Mark Twain (1835–1910), pictured, is best known for his novels *The Adventures of Tom Sawyer* and *The Adventures of Huckleberry Finn*. He was a fierce opponent of slavery and a staunch advocate of equal rights — especially for the lower paid.

"A diplomat who says 'yes' means 'maybe'; a diplomat who says 'maybe' means 'no' and a diplomat who says 'no' is no diplomat."
Charles de Talleyrand (1754–1838), who served as a French envoy under Napoleon and a series of French monarchs, is widely regarded as one of the most resourceful and influential diplomats in European history.

"War is an ugly thing, but not the ugliest of things. The decayed and degraded state of moral and patriotic feeling which thinks that nothing is worth war is much worse. The person who has nothing for which he is willing to fight, nothing which is more important than his own personal safety, is a miserable creature and has no chance of being free unless made and kept so by the exertions of better men than himself."
John Stuart Mill (1806–1873) was a British philosopher and member of parliament who taught the ethical theory of utilitarianism.

"It is well that war is so terrible. We should grow too fond of it."
Robert E. Lee (1807–1870) was the Confederate general in the American Civil War. He allegedly said this in December 1862 after the Battle of Fredericksburg, in which the Union army under Ambrose E. Burnside suffered more than twice as many casualties as the Confederates.

"There is many a boy here today who looks on war as all glory, but, boys, it is all hell."
William T. Sherman (1820–1891), an educator, author, and soldier, was a brilliant Union general in the American Civil War (1861–65). This famous quote was made during an address to the graduating class of the Michigan Military Academy on 19 June 1879.

"As soon as war is looked upon as wicked, it will always have its fascination. When it is looked upon as vulgar, it will cease to be popular."
Oscar Wilde (1854–1900), Irish playwright, satirist, poet, and author, one of the most successful playwrights of the late Victorian era, was known for his acerbic wit.

Last speech
Abraham Lincoln, White House, Washington, DC, 11 April 1865

Two days after the surrender of Confederate general Robert E. Lee's army, and with the end of the American Civil War imminent, Lincoln made this speech in front of a jubilant crowd outside the White House. *Sacramento Daily Union* reporter Noah Brooks wrote: "Outside was a vast sea of faces, illuminated by the lights that burned in the festal array of the White House, and stretching far out into the misty darkness. It was a silent, intent, and perhaps surprised, multitude. Within stood the tall, gaunt figure of the President, deeply thoughtful, intent upon the elucidation of the generous policy which should be pursued toward the South. That this was not the sort of speech which the multitude had expected is tolerably certain."

Lincoln appeared at the window over the building's main door. Brooks held a light while the president read his speech, addressing the theme of post-war reconstruction. For the first time in public, Lincoln expressed his support of black suffrage, which so enraged John Wilkes Booth, a white supremacist who was in the audience, that he vowed: "That is the last speech he will make." Three days later Booth assassinated Lincoln, shooting him from behind while the president and his wife watched the farce *Our American Cousin* at Ford's Theater in New York. Eight people were convicted of conspiring in the assassination. Four were hanged, including Mary Surratt, the first woman executed by the US government.

Lincoln's speech is remarkably free of triumphalism; rather it suggests ways to rebuild the war-ravaged country and redress past injustices.

A contemporary portrait of Abraham Lincoln.

...By these recent successes the re-inauguration of the national authority — reconstruction — which has had a large share of thought from the first, is pressed much more closely upon our attention. It is fraught with great difficulty. Unlike the case of a war between independent nations, there is no authorized organ for us to treat with. No one man has authority to give up the rebellion for any other man. We simply must begin with, and mould from, disorganized and discordant elements. Nor is it a small additional embarrassment that we, the loyal people, differ among ourselves as to the mode, manner, and means of reconstruction. As a general rule, I abstain from reading the reports of attacks upon myself, wishing not to be provoked by that to which I cannot properly offer an answer. In spite of this

precaution, however, it comes to my knowledge that I am much censured for some supposed agency in setting up, and seeking to sustain, the new State Government of Louisiana. In this I have done just so much as, and no more than, the public knows. In the Annual Message of December 1863 and accompanying Proclamation, I presented a plan of re-construction (as the phrase goes) which, I promised, if adopted by any State, should be acceptable to, and sustained by, the Executive government of the nation. I distinctly stated that this was not the only plan which might possibly be acceptable; and I also distinctly protested that the Executive claimed no right to say when, or whether members should be admitted to seats in Congress from such States. This plan was, in advance, submitted to the then Cabinet, and distinctly approved by every member of it...

The Message went to Congress, and I received many commendations of the plan, written and verbal; and not a single objection to it, from any professed emancipationist, came to my knowledge, until after the news reached Washington that the people of Louisiana had begun to move in accordance with it...

I have been shown a letter on this subject, supposed to be an able one, in which the writer expresses regret that my mind has not seemed to be definitely fixed on the question whether the seceded States, so called, are in the Union or out of it. It would perhaps add astonishment to his regret, were he to learn that since I have found professed Union men endeavoring to make that question, I have purposely forborne any public expression upon it. As appears to me that question has not been, nor yet is, a practically material one, and that any discussion of it, while it thus remains practically immaterial, could have no effect other than the mischievous one of dividing our friends. As yet, whatever it may hereafter become, that question is bad, as the basis of a controversy, and good for nothing at all — a merely pernicious abstraction.

We all agree that the seceded States, so called, are out of their proper practical relation with the Union; and that the sole object of the government, civil and military, in regard to those States is to again get them into that proper practical relation. I believe it is not only possible, but in fact, easier, to do this, without deciding, or even considering, whether these States have ever been out of the Union, than with it. Finding themselves safely at home, it would be utterly immaterial whether they had ever been abroad. Let us all join in doing the acts necessary to restoring the proper practical relations between these States and the Union; and each forever after, innocently indulge his own opinion whether, in doing the acts, he brought the States from without, into the Union, or only gave them proper assistance, they never having been out of it...

Some twelve thousand voters in the heretofore slave-state of Louisiana have sworn allegiance to the Union, assumed to be the rightful political power of the State, held elections, organized a State government, adopted a free-state constitution, giving the benefit of public schools equally to black and white, and empowering the Legislature to confer the elective franchise upon the colored man. Their Legislature has already voted to ratify the constitutional amendment recently passed by Congress, abolishing slavery throughout the nation. These twelve thousand persons are thus fully committed to the Union, and to perpetual freedom in the State — committed to the very things, and nearly all the things the nation wants — and they ask the nation's recognition, and its assistance to make good their committal. Now, if we reject and spurn them, we do our utmost to disorganize and disperse them. We in effect say to the white men "You are worthless, or worse — we will neither help you, nor be helped by you." To the blacks we say "This cup of liberty which these, your old masters, hold to your lips, we will dash from you, and leave you to the chances of gathering the spilled and scattered contents in some vague and undefined when, where and how." If this course, discouraging and paralysing both white and black, has any tendency to bring Louisiana into proper practical relations with the Union, I have, so far, been unable to perceive it. If, on the contrary, we recognize and sustain the new government of Louisiana the converse of all this is made true. We encourage the hearts, and nerve the arms of the twelve thousand to adhere to their work, and argue for it, and proselyte for it, and fight for it, and feed it, and grow it, and ripen it to a complete success. The colored man too, in seeing all united for him, is inspired with vigilance, and energy, and daring, to the same end. Grant that he desires the elective franchise, will he not attain it sooner by saving the already advanced steps toward it, than by running backward over them?

In favor of a 16th Amendment
Elizabeth Cady Stanton, Washington, DC, 1868

An American social activist, slavery abolitionist, and pioneering figure in the fledgling women's movement, Elizabeth Cady Stanton (1815–1902) worked to achieve voting rights for American women, and also against prevailing social and political norms that excluded women from many rights and privileges. She agitated for women's rights in the fields of parenthood and custody, property, employment and income, divorce law, the economic health of the family, and birth control.

She gave this compelling speech in 1868 at a Women's Suffrage Convention in Washington, DC. America had recently passed the 14th and 15th amendments to the Constitution, which she claimed granted suffrage to African-American men, not to women (either black or white). Here she proposes a 16th amendment to clarify her viewpoint and enshrine it in Law. Women eventually achieved full suffrage in 1920.

I urge a sixteenth amendment, because "manhood suffrage," or a man's government, is civil, religious, and social disorganisation. The male element is a destructive force, stern, selfish, aggrandising, loving war, violence, conquest, acquisition, breeding in the material and moral world alike discord, disorder, disease, and death...

The male element has held high carnival thus far; it has fairly run riot from the beginning, overpowering the feminine element everywhere, crushing out all the diviner qualities in human nature, until we know but little of true manhood and womanhood, of the latter comparatively nothing, for it has scarce been recognized as a power until within the last century. Society is but the reflection of man himself, untempered by woman's thought; the hard iron rule we feel alike in the church, the state and the home. No one need wonder at the disorganisation, at the fragmentary condition of everything, when we remember that man, who represents but half a complete being, with but half an idea on every subject, has undertaken the absolute control of all sublunary matters.

People object to the demands of those whom they choose to call the strong-minded, because they say "the right of suffrage will make the women masculine." That is just the difficulty in which we are involved today. Though disfranchised, we have few women in the best sense; we have simply so many reflections, varieties and dilutions of the masculine

In 1848 Stanton presented a "Declaration of Sentiments" paper at Seneca Falls, New York, at a convention marking the beginning of the US women's rights movement.

gender. The strong, natural characteristics of womanhood are repressed and ignored in dependence, for so long as man feeds woman she will try to please the giver and adapt herself to his condition. To keep a foothold in society, woman must be as near like man as possible, reflect his ideas, opinions, virtues, motives, prejudices, and vices. She must respect his statutes, though they strip her of every inalienable right, and conflict with that higher law written by the finger of God on her own soul.

She must look at everything from its dollar-and-cent point of view, or she is a mere romancer. She must accept things as they are and make the best of them. To mourn over the miseries of others, the poverty of the poor, their hardships in jails, prisons, asylums, the horrors of war, cruelty, and brutality in every form, all this would be mere sentimentalising. To protest against the intrigue, bribery and corruption of public life, to desire that her sons might follow some business that did not involve lying, cheating, and a hard, grinding selfishness, would be arrant nonsense.

In this way man has been moulding woman to his ideas by direct and positive influences, while she, if not a negation, has used indirect means to control him, and in most cases developed the very characteristics both in him and herself that needed repression. And now man himself stands appalled at the results of his own excesses, and mourns in bitterness that falsehood, selfishness, and violence are the law of life. The need of this hour is not territory, gold mines, railroads, or specie payments but a new evangel of womanhood, to exalt purity, virtue, morality, true religion, to lift man up into the higher realms of thought and action.

We ask for woman's enfranchisement as the first step towards the recognition of that essential element in government that can only secure the health, strength, and prosperity of the nation. Whatever is done to lift woman to her true position will help to usher in a new day of peace and perfection for the race.

In speaking of the masculine element...I refer to those characteristics, though often marked in woman, that distinguish what is called the stronger sex. For example, the love of acquisition and conquest, the very pioneers of civilisation, when expended on the earth, the sea, the elements, the riches, and forces of nature, are powers of destruction when used to subjugate one man to another or to sacrifice nations to ambition.

Here that great conservator of woman's love, if permitted to assert itself, as it naturally would in freedom against oppression, violence, and war, would hold all these destructive forces in check, for woman knows

the cost of life better than man does, and not with her consent would one drop of blood ever be shed, one life sacrificed in vain.

With violence and disturbance in the natural world, we see a constant effort to maintain an equilibrium of forces. Nature, like a loving mother, is ever trying to keep land and sea, mountain and valley, each in its place, to hush the angry winds and waves, balance the extremes of heat and cold, of rain and drought, that peace, harmony, and beauty may reign supreme. There is a striking analogy between matter and mind, and the present disorganisation of society warns us that in the dethronement of woman we have let loose the elements of violence and ruin that she only has the power to curb. If the civilisation of the age calls for an extension of the suffrage, surely a government of the most virtuous educated men and women would better represent the whole and protect the interests of all...

The National Women's Suffrage Association in session during a political convention in Chicago in 1880.

FAMOUS LAST WORDS

"Kiss me Hardy (or Kismet Hardy)" or "Thank God I have done my duty" or "Drink drink, fan fan, rub rub"
Horatio Nelson, British vice-admiral (pictured), 1805
Debate raged over Lord Nelson's alleged last words, uttered after he was hit by a bullet while leading the successful Battle of Trafalgar against the Spanish Navy. As he lay dying he probably said "Kiss me, Hardy" to his close friend and flag captain Thomas Hardy, but not as his last words. Later accounts claimed he said "Kismet Hardy" (*kismet* is Turkish for "fate"), but this seems unlikely, as the word was not "borrowed" by English until at least twenty-five years later. The euphemism was probably devised later in a prudish attempt to hide the homoerotic imagery of men kissing. But platonic kissing between men was not uncommon (or condemned) at the time, lending more credence to the "Kiss me" camp. In any case, Nelson's surgeon William Beatty claimed that the last words were "Thank God I have done my duty," repeated several times until he could speak no more. And Nelson's chaplain, Alexander Scott, and purser Walter Burke recorded the last words as "Drink drink, fan fan, rub rub." This was a demand to assuage his symptoms of thirst, heat, and pain.

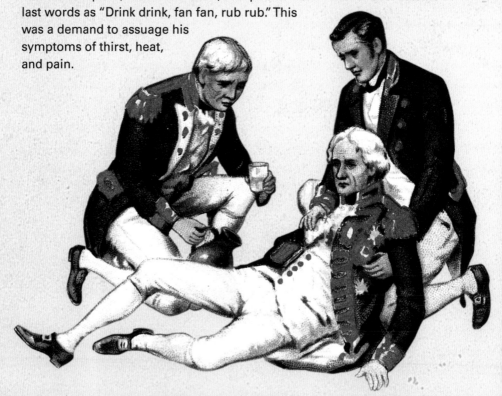

"Don't give up the ship."
James Lawrence, American naval captain, after being mortally wounded in battle during the War of 1812 (actually 1812–15) against Britain, 1813

"*France, armée, Joséphine*...France, army, Josephine."
Napoleon Bonaparte, French military and political leader, summarizes his priorities on his deathbed, 1821

"This is the last of earth! I am content."
John Quincy Adams, abolitionist and the sixth president of the United States, suffered a stroke in the House of Representatives and died two days later, 1848.

"Nonsense, they couldn't hit an elephant at this distance."
John Sedgwick, US general, upon being advised to keep his head below the parapet during the Battle of the Wilderness in the American Civil War — a sharpshooter's bullet killed him a few seconds later, 1864

"They won't think anything about it."
Abraham Lincoln, US president, assuring his wife that it would be all right to hold hands in the theater, moments before assassin John Wilkes Booth shot him, 1865

"Ah well, I suppose it has come to this. Such is life."
Ned Kelly, Australian bushranger, murderer, and folk anti-hero, allegedly before his execution by hanging, 1880

"Go on, get out. Last words are for fools who haven't said enough."
Karl Marx, German political and social theorist, after his housekeeper asked him what his last words would be, 1883

"Shoot straight, you b******s! Don't make a mess of it!"
Harry "Breaker" Morant instructs his firing squad (see page 140), 1902

Women's right to vote
Susan Brownell Anthony, New York, 1873

Susan B. Anthony (1820–1906) was a prominent US civil rights leader who, along with Elizabeth Cady Stanton, played a critical role in the women's rights movement. She traveled the United States and Europe, making speeches in favor of the abolition of slavery and other issues. She also petitioned Congress and state legislatures, and published a feminist newspaper.

Anthony asked excellent questions. In 1859, at the Ninth National Women's Rights convention, she had asked: "Where, under our Declaration of Independence, does the Saxon man get his power to deprive all women and Negroes of their inalienable rights?" In this speech she notes that the US Constitution grants rights to "the people of the United States" and asks, reasonably, whether women are people. She made the speech after her arrest in Albany, New York, for casting an illegal vote in the 1872 presidential election. She was tried and fined $100 with costs after the judge ordered the jury to find her guilty, but she refused to pay. She was not imprisoned, probably a ploy by the government to deny her the right to appeal the verdict, thus denying her the inevitable attendant publicity for her cause.

In 1979 Anthony was honored as the first American woman to appear on a circulating US coin.

...I stand before you tonight under indictment for the alleged crime of having voted at the last presidential election, without having a lawful right to vote. It shall be my work this evening to prove to you that in thus voting, I not only committed no crime, but, instead, simply exercised my citizen's rights, guaranteed to me and all United States citizens by the National Constitution, beyond the power of any State to deny.

The preamble of the Federal Constitution says: "We, the people of the United States, in order to form a more perfect Union, establish justice, ensure domestic tranquillity, provide for the common defence, promote the general welfare, and secure the blessings of liberty to ourselves and our posterity, do ordain and establish this Constitution for the United States of America."

It was we, the people; not we, the white male citizens; nor yet we, the male citizens; but we, the whole people, who formed the Union. And we formed it, not to give the blessings of liberty, but to secure them; not to the half of ourselves and the half of our posterity, but to the whole

A rather unflattering political portrait of Susan B. Anthony in costume in the 1890s.

people — women as well as men. And it is a downright mockery to talk to women of their enjoyment of the blessings of liberty while they are denied the use of the only means of securing them provided by this democratic-republican government — the ballot.

For any State to make sex a qualification that must ever result in the disfranchisement of one entire half of the people, is to pass a bill of attainder, or an *ex post facto* law, and is therefore a violation of the supreme law of the land. By it the blessings of liberty are forever withheld from women and their female posterity.

To them this government has no just powers derived from the consent of the governed. To them this government is not a democracy. It is not a republic. It is an odious aristocracy; a hateful oligarchy of sex; the most hateful aristocracy ever established on the face of the globe; an oligarchy of wealth, where the rich govern the poor. An oligarchy of learning, where the educated govern the ignorant, or even an oligarchy of race, where the Saxon rules the African, might be endured; but this oligarchy of sex, which makes father, brothers, husband, sons, the oligarchs over the mother and sisters, the wife and daughters, of every household — which ordains all men sovereigns, all women subjects, carries dissension, discord, and rebellion into every home of the nation.

Webster, Worcester, and Bouvier all define a citizen to be a person in the United States, entitled to vote and hold office.

The only question left to be settled now is: Are women persons? And I hardly believe any of our opponents will have the hardihood to say they are not. Being persons, then, women are citizens; and no State has a right to make any law, or to enforce any old law, that shall abridge their privileges or immunities. Hence, every discrimination against women in the constitutions and laws of the several States is today null and void, precisely as is every one against Negroes.

"I will fight no more forever"
Chief Joseph, Montana, United States, 5 October 1877

Joseph, otherwise known as "Thunder Traveling to the Loftier Mountain Heights" (1840–1904), was chief of the Nez Perce Native American tribe of north-western Oregon. After a series of negotiations, in 1877 the tribe was ordered by the invading US army to relocate to a reservation. Chief Joseph agreed, but some young men of the tribe killed four white men — an act of war. In an attempt to escape to freedom in Canada, Joseph led about 800 of his people across Oregon, Washington, Idaho, Wyoming, and Montana. En route they fought some 2000 US army troops, impressing US General Howard with their effective use of advance and rear guards, pincer and diversionary tactics, and field fortifications.

After a journey of more than 990 miles, the remaining 431 Nez Perce were finally trapped just 40 miles from the Canadian border. At the end of a five-day battle in the Bear Paw Mountains, Montana, in freezing conditions with no food or blankets, Joseph finally and formally surrendered. This is the speech he made.

Tell General Howard I know his heart. What he told me before, I have it in my heart. I am tired of fighting. Our chiefs are killed; Looking Glass is dead, Ta-Hul-Hul-Shote is dead. The old men are all dead. It is the young men who say yes or no. He who led on the young men is dead. It is cold, and we have no blankets; the little children are freezing to death. My people, some of them, have run away to the hills, and have no blankets, no food. No one knows where they are — perhaps freezing to death. I want to have time to look for my children, and see how many of them I can find. Maybe I shall find them among the dead. Hear me, my chiefs! I am tired; my heart is sick and sad. From where the sun now stands, I will fight no more forever.

FIGHTING POEMS AND SONGS
In prison cell I sadly sit

In prison cell I sadly sit,
A d—d crestfallen chappy,
And own to you I feel a bit —
A little bit — unhappy.

It really ain't the place nor time
To reel off rhyming diction;
But yet we'll write a final rhyme
While waiting crucifixion.

No matter what "end" they decide —
Quick-lime? or "b'iling ile?" sir —
We'll do our best when crucified
To finish off in style, sir?

But we bequeath a parting tip
For sound advice of such men
Who come across in transport ship
To polish off the Dutchmen.

If you encounter any Boers
You really must not loot 'em,
And, if you wish to leave these shores,
For pity's sake, don't shoot 'em.

And if you'd earn a D.S.O.,
Why every British sinner
Should know the proper way to go
Is: Ask the Boer to dinner.

Let's toss a bumper down our throat
Before we pass to heaven,
And toast: "The trim-set petticoat
We leave behind in Devon."

Harry "Breaker" Morant (1864–1902) was an Australian folk hero and poet who fought on the side of the British in the Second Boer War. In 1902 he was one of several men court-martialed for murder. Morant and another Australian were executed by the British Army on 27 February, but their British co-accused merely received dishonorable discharges from the army. He wrote this sardonic poem the night before his execution.

The Star-Spangled Banner

...And where is that band who so vauntingly swore,
That the havoc of war and the battle's confusion,
A home and a country they'd leave us no more?
Their blood hath washed out their foul footsteps' pollution;
No refuge could save the hireling and slave
From the terror of flight, or the gloom of the grave:
And the star-spangled banner in triumph doth wave
O'er the land of the free and the home of the brave!

Oh! thus be it ever, when freemen shall stand
Between their loved home and the war's desolation!
Blessed with victory and peace, may the heav'n-rescued land
Praise the Power that hath made and preserved us a nation.
Then conquer we must, for our cause it is just,
And this be our motto, "In God is our trust."
And the star-spangled banner in triumph shall wave
O'er the land of the free and the home of the brave!

This song has been the US national anthem since 3 March 1931. The lyrics
come from the 1814 poem by Francis Scott Key (1779–1843); they were later
set to the tune of a popular British drinking song. Although the song has four
verses, only the first is generally sung. Verses 3 and 4 are printed here.

Part 5

THE FIRST GLOBAL WAR

The Early Twentieth Century

"I am here as a soldier"
Emmeline Pankhurst, Hartford, Connecticut, US, 13 November 1913

Emmeline Pankhurst (1848–1928) was one of the founders of the Women's Social and Political Union (WSPU), a British suffragist movement whose aim was to achieve equality for women, in particular the right to vote. In the previous year she had been jailed twelve times, undergoing several hunger strikes (and violent force-feeding by authorities) in order to publicize her situation. The WSPU favored direct action, including publicity stunts. In June 1913, at the English Derby, fellow activist Emily Davison ran onto Epsom racecourse and attempted to grab the bridle of King George V's horse Anmer. The collision resulted in a fractured skull for Davison, and she died without regaining consciousness.

Pankhurst gained the cooperation of the British government during World War I by suspending her enfranchisement activism and encouraging the war effort. All suffragists were released from jail to aid the war effort, and Pankhurst urged women to assist by taking over jobs previously undertaken by men now at war.

In 1918 the British government granted voting rights to women over the age of 30, with a property qualification. In 1928, just three weeks after Pankhurst died, women finally achieved complete suffrage equality.

This speech was made during a fundraising tour of the United States, which Pankhurst undertook after her release from prison in England. She had been serving a sentence for "incitement to violence," but her hunger strike, and the resulting publicity and public outcry, forced the government to release her early. Here she explains why she is regarded as a "dangerous person," and sounds a call to arms in the fight for women's suffrage.

I do not come here as an advocate, because whatever position the suffrage movement may occupy in the United States of America, in England it has passed beyond the realm of advocacy and it has entered into the sphere of practical politics. It has become the subject of revolution and civil war, and so tonight I am not here to advocate woman suffrage. American suffragists can do that very well for themselves.

I am here as a soldier who has temporarily left the field of battle in order to explain — it seems strange it should have to be explained — what civil war is like when civil war is waged by women. I am not only here as a soldier temporarily absent from the field of battle; I am here — and that, I think, is the strangest part of my coming — I am here as a person who, according to the law courts of my country, it has been decided, is of no value to the community at all; and I am adjudged because of my life to be a dangerous person, under sentence of penal servitude in a convict prison.

...It is about eight years since the word militant was first used to describe what we were doing. It was not militant at all, except that it provoked militancy on the part of those who were opposed to it. When women asked questions in political meetings and failed to get answers,

Pankhurst makes an open-air speech from a carriage.

they were not doing anything militant. In Great Britain it is a custom, a time-honored one, to ask questions of candidates for parliament and ask questions of members of the government. No man was ever put out of a public meeting for asking a question. The first people who were put out of a political meeting for asking questions were women; they were brutally ill-used; they found themselves in jail before twenty-four hours had expired. We were called militant, and we were quite willing to accept the name. We were determined to press this question of the enfranchisement of women to the point where we were no longer to be ignored by the politicians.

...When you have warfare things happen; people suffer; the non-combatants suffer as well as the combatants. And so it happens in civil war. When your forefathers threw the tea into Boston Harbor, a good many women had to go without their tea. It has always seemed to me an extraordinary thing that you did not follow it up by throwing the whisky overboard; you sacrificed the women; and there is a good deal of warfare for which men take a great deal of glorification which has involved more practical sacrifice on women than it has on any man. It always has been so. The grievances of those who have got power, the influence of those who have got power commands a great deal of attention; but the wrongs and the grievances of those people who have no power at all are apt to be absolutely ignored. That is the history of humanity right from the beginning.

Well, in our civil war people have suffered, but you cannot make omelettes without breaking eggs; you cannot have civil war without damage to something. The great thing is to see that no more damage is done than is absolutely necessary, that you do just as much as will arouse enough feeling to bring about peace, to bring about an honorable peace for the combatants; and that is what we have been doing...

If you are dealing with an industrial revolution, if you get the men and women of one class rising up against the men and women of another class, you can locate the difficulty; if there is a great industrial strike, you know exactly where the violence is and how the warfare is going to be waged; but in our war against the government you can't locate it. We wear no mark; we belong to every class; we permeate every class of the community from the highest to the lowest; and so you see in the woman's civil war the dear men of my country are discovering it is absolutely impossible to deal with it: you cannot locate it, and you cannot stop it...

I have seen men smile when they heard the words "hunger strike," and yet I think there are very few men today who would be prepared to adopt a "hunger strike" for any cause. It is only people who feel an intolerable sense of oppression who would adopt a means of that kind. It means you refuse food until you are at death's door, and then the authorities have to choose between letting you die, and letting you go; and then they let the women go...

It has come to a battle between the women and the government as to who shall yield first, whether they will yield and give us the vote, or whether we will give up our agitation.

Well, they little know what women are. Women are very slow to rouse, but once they are aroused, once they are determined, nothing on earth and nothing in heaven will make women give way; it is impossible. And so this "Cat and Mouse Act" which is being used against women today has failed. There are women lying at death's door, recovering enough strength to undergo operations who have not given in and won't give in, and who will be prepared, as soon as they get up from their sick beds, to go on as before. There are women who are being carried from their sick beds on stretchers into meetings. They are too weak to speak, but they go amongst their fellow workers just to show that their spirits are unquenched, and that their spirit is alive, and they mean to go on as long as life lasts.

Now, I want to say to you who think women cannot succeed, we have brought the government of England to this position, that it has to face this alternative: either women are to be killed or women are to have the vote. I ask American men in this meeting, what would you say if in your State you were faced with that alternative, that you must either kill them or give them their citizenship? Well, there is only one answer to that alternative, there is only one way out — you must give those women the vote.

You won your freedom in America when you had the revolution, by bloodshed, by sacrificing human life. You won the Civil War by the sacrifice of human life when you decided to emancipate the Negro. You have left it to women in your land, the men of all civilized countries have left it to women, to work out their own salvation. That is the way in which we women of England are doing it. Human life for us is sacred, but we say if any life is to be sacrificed it shall be ours; we won't do it ourselves, but we will put the enemy in the position where they will have to choose between giving us freedom or giving us death.

Intention to declare war on Germany
Woodrow Wilson, US president, 2 April 1917

This speech was made by Democrat president Woodrow Wilson (1856–1924) to a Special Session of the US Congress. He had already been unsuccessful in negotiating a peace in Europe. Here he stresses that it is moral principle — as opposed to selfish or nationalist ambition — that requires the United States to reluctantly declare war upon Germany, which had recently initiated a program of submarine attacks against US commercial and other non-military vessels. His final sentence invokes and echoes the moral certainty of religious reformer Martin Luther, who said in his famous speech to the Diet of Worms in 1521: "Here, I stand. I can do nothing else. God help me. Amen."

Four days later, on 6 April, Congress passed the War Resolution, which brought the United States into World War I.

...I have called the Congress into extraordinary session because there are serious, very serious, choices of policy to be made, and made immediately, which it was neither right nor constitutionally permissible that I should assume the responsibility of making.

On the third of February last I officially laid before you the extraordinary announcement of the Imperial German Government that on and after the first day of February it was its purpose to put aside all restraints of law or of humanity and use its submarines to sink every vessel that sought to approach either the ports of Great Britain and Ireland or the western coasts of Europe or any of the ports controlled by the enemies of Germany within the Mediterranean. That had seemed to be the object of the German submarine warfare earlier in the war, but since April of last year the Imperial Government had somewhat restrained the commanders of its undersea craft in conformity with its promise then given to us that passenger boats should not be sunk and that due warning would be given to all other vessels which its submarines might seek to destroy, when no resistance was offered or escape attempted, and care taken that their crews were given at least a fair chance to save their lives in their open boats...

Even hospital ships and ships carrying relief to the sorely bereaved and stricken people of Belgium, though the latter were provided with safe conduct through the proscribed areas by the German Government itself and were distinguished by unmistakable marks of identity, have been sunk with the same reckless lack of compassion or of principle...

I am not now thinking of the loss of property involved, immense and serious as that is, but only of the wanton and wholesale destruction of the lives of non-combatants, men, women, and children, engaged in pursuits which have always, even in the darkest periods of modern history, been deemed innocent and legitimate. Property can be paid for; the lives of peaceful and innocent people cannot be. The present German submarine warfare against commerce is a warfare against mankind.

It is a war against all nations. American ships have been sunk, American lives taken...but the ships and people of other neutral and friendly nations have been sunk and overwhelmed in the waters in the same way. There has been no discrimination. The challenge is to all mankind. Each nation must decide for itself how it will meet it. The choice we make for ourselves must be made with a moderation of counsel and a temperateness of judgment befitting our character and our motives as a nation. We must put excited feeling away. Our motive will not be revenge or the victorious assertion of the physical might of the nation, but only the vindication of right, of human right, of which we are only a single champion...

Our object now, as then, is to vindicate the principles of peace and justice in the life of the world as against selfish and autocratic power and to set up amongst the really free and self-governed peoples of the world such a concert of purpose and of action as will henceforth ensure the observance of those principles. Neutrality is no longer feasible or desirable where the peace of the world is involved and the freedom of its peoples, and the menace to that peace and freedom lies in the existence of autocratic governments backed by organized force which is controlled wholly by their will, not by the will of their people. We have seen the last of neutrality in such circumstances. We are at the beginning of an age in which it will be insisted that the same standards of conduct and of responsibility for wrong done shall be observed among nations and their governments that are observed among the individual citizens of civilized states.

We have no quarrel with the German people. We have no feeling towards them but one of sympathy and friendship. It was not upon their impulse that their Government acted in entering this war. It was not with their previous knowledge or approval. It was a war determined upon as wars used to be determined upon in the old, unhappy days when peoples were nowhere consulted by their rulers and wars were provoked and waged in the interest of dynasties or of little groups of ambitious men who were accustomed to use their fellow men as pawns and tools...

We are accepting this challenge of hostile purpose because we know that in such a government, following such methods, we can never have a friend; and that in the presence of its organized power, always lying in wait to accomplish we know not what purpose, there can be no assured security for the democratic governments of the world. We are now about to accept gage of battle with this natural foe to liberty and shall, if necessary, spend the whole force of the nation to check and nullify its pretensions and its power. We are glad, now that we see the facts with no veil of false pretence about them, to fight thus for the ultimate peace of the world and for the liberation of its peoples, the German peoples included: for the rights of nations great and small and the privilege of men everywhere to choose their way of life and of obedience. The world must be made safe for democracy. Its peace must be planted upon the tested foundations of political liberty. We have no selfish ends to serve. We desire no conquest, no dominion. We seek no indemnities for ourselves, no material compensation for the sacrifices we shall freely make. We are

On 2 April 1917, Woodrow Wilson addresses a Special Session of the US Congress. Four days later the United States declared war on Germany.

but one of the champions of the rights of mankind. We shall be satisfied when those rights have been made as secure as the faith and the freedom of nations can make them.

Just because we fight without rancor and without selfish object, seeking nothing for ourselves but what we shall wish to share with all free peoples, we shall, I feel confident, conduct our operations as belligerents without passion and ourselves observe with proud punctilio the principles of right and of fair play we profess to be fighting for...

We enter this war only where we are clearly forced into it because there are no other means of defending our rights. It will be all the easier for us to conduct ourselves as belligerents in a high spirit of right and fairness because we act without animus, not in enmity towards a people or with the desire to bring any injury or disadvantage upon them, but only in armed opposition to an irresponsible government which has thrown aside all considerations of humanity and of right and is running amuck. We are, let me say again, the sincere friends of the German people, and shall desire nothing so much as the early re-establishment of intimate relations of mutual advantage between us — however hard it may be for them, for the time being, to believe that this is spoken from our hearts...

It is a distressing and oppressive duty, gentlemen of the Congress, which I have performed in thus addressing you. There are, it may be, many months of fiery trial and sacrifice ahead of us. It is a fearful thing to lead this great peaceful people into war, into the most terrible and disastrous of all wars, civilisation itself seeming to be in the balance. But the right is more precious than peace, and we shall fight for the things which we have always carried nearest our hearts — for democracy, for the right of those who submit to authority to have a voice in their own governments, for the rights and liberties of small nations, for a universal dominion of right by such a concert of free peoples as shall bring peace and safety to all nations and make the world itself at last free. To such a task we can dedicate our lives and our fortunes, everything that we are and everything that we have, with the pride of those who know that the day has come when America is privileged to spend her blood and her might for the principles that gave her birth and happiness and the peace which she has treasured. God helping her, she can do no other.

The "Four Minute Men"
Volunteer speeches during World War I, 1917–18

In a 1925 memoir, *Twenty-Five Years: 1892–1916*, Sir Edward Grey, British foreign secretary from 1906 to 1916, described the pre-World War I arms build-up thus:

> One nation increases its army and makes strategic railways towards the frontiers of neighboring countries. The second nation makes counter-strategic railways and increases its army in reply. The first nation says this is very unreasonable because its own military preparations were only precautions; the second nation says that its preparations were also only precautions…and so it goes on, till the whole continent is an armed camp covered by strategic railways…

He may well have used similar words to describe the situation in Europe after the mid-1930s as the Nazis (purely for defensive, peaceful purposes, of course) devoted Germany's entire industrial production to the manufacture of war hardware, sparking off a worldwide (defensive, peaceful) arms build-up.

One detects Grey's impression of absurdity at the twisted logic that leads nations to prepare for war in the name of maintaining peace.

By mid-1914, European and other countries had committed to a complicated, often contradictory maze of industrial and military treaties, both secret and open. Traditional enemies Britain and France had signed an *entente cordiale* agreement in 1904, agreeing to settle their colonial disputes. Russia became the third signatory in 1907. Serbia had increased its territory and power during the two Balkan wars of 1912 and 1913, largely at the expense of the Turkish Ottoman Empire. The "victorious" Balkan states of Greece, Montenegro, Serbia, and Romania were squabbling over the spoils of victory in an atmosphere of mutual mistrust and resentment; each state believed the peace settlement treated them unfairly. Bulgaria was humiliated, while a furious Turkey was determined to regain lost territory.

France and Britain agreed that the French navy would protect the Mediterranean, while Britain would defend the British Channel. But Britain was secretly concerned at the potential and growing power of its ally Russia, in particular the possibility that it may gain access to the Mediterranean through the Turk-controlled Dardanelles strait. Meanwhile, of course, the arms race continued in earnest, creating a powder keg of suspicion.

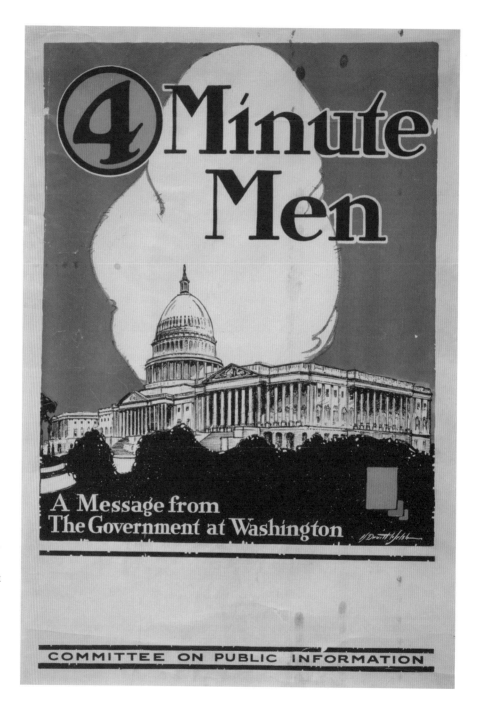

4 Minute Men

A Message from
The Government at Washington

COMMITTEE ON PUBLIC INFORMATION

The Four Minute Men were so called because they delivered their speeches in the four minutes it took to change the reels in a movie theater. Creel (see page 156) hired some of the best artists in the country to design the posters.

France maintained a lingering hatred of Germany over the Franco-Prussian War of 1870–71, which resulted in Germany seizing the French border states of Alsace and Lorraine.

Britain had long been threatened by leaders of dominant European countries (Napoleon Bonaparte; King Louis XIV) and so was wary of allowing any country — in this case the burgeoning Germany, which was greatly increasing its naval capacity in particular— from attaining too much centralized power.

What started as just another European skirmish between Serbia and Austria somehow gradually turned into a worldwide conflagration. On 28 July 1914, Austria declared war on Serbia. On 1 August, Germany declared war on Serbia's ally Russia, then on France on 3 August. The next day Germany invaded neutral Belgium, causing Britain (along with Australia a few days later) to declare war on Germany.

Japan declared war on Germany on 23 August.

In November Russia declared war on Turkey. Italy joined the Allies in June 1915, and on 6 April 1917, the United States declared war on Germany. We now had our first fully-fledged world war.

When the fighting ended on 11 November 1918, at the eleventh hour of the eleventh day of the eleventh month, Germany signed an armistice with the Allies and the haggling over peace treaties began. Large tracts of Europe had been laid to waste and four empires had fallen; perhaps nine million people had been killed and over twice as many injured. America had risen to prominence as an economic power, and new countries were taking shape in Europe and the Middle East. The aggressor states were ruined and the world had been irrevocably changed. Why? Since the Franco-Prussian War, Europe had managed to conduct a series of "minor" wars — that is, between only two countries — without a "domino" effect drawing in other countries. Historians still argue over the war's causes, but generally agree on one thing: each new participant, as it entered the war, was convinced of its own superiority and expected a rapid victory.

In June 1919 the Allies forced Germany to sign the Treaty of Versailles, which placed severe restrictions on its armed forces, and forced it to cede to the victors 13 percent of its national territory and all its overseas colonies. It was also forced to admit full responsibility for starting the war, and to make continuing financial reparations to the United States, Britain, France, and several other Allied states. Adolf Hitler took advantage of the German people's general resentment at the treaty's draconian terms in his bid to gain power.

During World War I, US president Woodrow Wilson established the Committee on Public Information (CPI), also known as the Creel Committtee, to control the release of news and solicit public support for the war. With the assistance of investigative journalist and newspaper editor George Creel, who was the committee's chairman, the CPI mass-produced national propaganda through assorted media, including paintings, cartoons, film, music, and posters.

Creel also organized the "Four Minute Men," an army of volunteers who gave brief pro-war speeches in movie theaters as well as churches, synagogues, and labor halls — in short, anywhere they could. Creel later claimed that 75 000 orators delivered at least 7.5 million speeches to more than 314 million people. The speakers were from diverse backgrounds and used a variety of languages, including Yiddish and Sioux.

CPI publications offered tips on developing and delivering a brief, effective "sound bite." Creel's comments on the need to avoid clichés, and to make every word count, are still pertinent today.

Reprinted here are some of his general suggestions for composers and speechmakers as well as a selection of the speeches (all anonymous) they produced.

GENERAL SUGGESTIONS TO SPEAKERS
The speech must not be longer than four minutes, which means there is no time for a single wasted word. Speakers should go over their speech time and time again until the ideas are firmly fixed in their mind and cannot be forgotten. This does not mean that the speech needs to be written out and committed (memorized), although most speakers, especially when limited in time, do best to commit.

Divide your speech carefully into certain divisions, say 15 seconds for final appeal; 45 seconds to describe the bond; 15 seconds for opening words, etc, etc. Any plan is better than none, and it can be amended every day in the light of experience.

There never was a speech yet that couldn't be improved. Never be satisfied with success. Aim to be more successful, and still more successful. So keep your eyes open. Read all the papers every day, to find a new slogan, or a new phraseology, or a new idea to replace something you have in your speech. For instance, the editorial page of the *Chicago Herald* of May 19 is crammed full of good ideas and phrases. Most of the article is a little above the average audience, but if the ideas

The British Army's 27th Division rejoices at the news of peace on 11 November 1918.

156

are good, you should plan carefully to bring them into the experience of your auditors. There is one sentence which says, "No country was ever saved by the other fellow; it must be done by you, by a hundred million yous, or it will not be done at all." Or again, Secretary (William) McAdoo says, "Every dollar invested in the Liberty Loan is a real blow for liberty, a blow against the militaristic system which would strangle the freedom of the world," and so on. Both the *Tribune* and the *Examiner*, besides the *Herald*, contain President Wilson's address to the nation in connection with the draft registration. The latter part is very suggestive and can be used effectively. Try slogans like "Earn the right to say, I helped to win the war," and "This is a Loyalty Bond as well as a Liberty Bond," or "A cause that is worth living for is worth dying for, and a cause that is worth dying for is worth fighting for." Conceive of your speech as a mosaic made up of five or six hundred words, each one of which has its function.

Get your friends to criticize you pitilessly. We all want to do our best and naturally like to be praised, but there is nothing so dangerous as "josh" and "jolly." Let your friends know that you want ruthless criticism. If their criticism isn't sound, you can reject it. If it is sound, wouldn't you be foolish to reject it?

Be sure to prepare very carefully your closing appeal, whatever it may be, so that you may not leave your speech hanging in the air.

Don't yield to the inspiration of the moment, or to applause to depart from your speech outline. This does not mean that you may not add a word or two, but remember that one can speak only 130, or 140, or 150 words a minute, and if your speech has been carefully prepared to fill four minutes, you cannot add anything to your speech without taking away something of serious importance.

Cut out "Doing your bit." "Business as usual." "Your country needs you." They are flat and no longer have any force or meaning.

Time yourself in advance on every paragraph and remember you are likely to speak somewhat more slowly in public than when you practice in your own room.

There are several good ideas and statements in the printed speech recently sent you. Look it up at once.

If you come across a new slogan, or a new argument, or a new story, or a new illustration, don't fail to send it to the Committee. We need your help to make the Four Minute Men the mightiest force for arousing patriotism in the United States.

I AM

I am the man who speaks throughout the length and breadth of our country.
I look east out past the Statue of Liberty towards the flaming battle line.
The sun sets in the Pacific as I work along our western shores.
The Southland hears my call, Canada knows I am her friend.
I am in the War Department, the Treasury, the cantonments, factories
and shipyards, in the busy city office, and in the country store beside the
cracker barrel.
I am on active duty every evening.
I see the city's dazzling lights and the country's twinkling lamps.
I am poor and rich, young and old.
I build morale and confidence in the right.
I defeat fear, mistrust, and ignorance.
Lies are cut down and fall naked before my sword.
False rumor flies before the searchlight of my truth as does the mist
at sunrise.
I make clear the issues so that all may know and understand.
It is my duty "to hold unbroken the inner lines," [and] "to inspire to
highest action and noblest sacrifice."
I am everywhere helping to win this greatest of wars and to save the
world for God and man.
I am here to stay on duty until the fight is won.
I am the Four Minute Man.

IT'S DUTY BOY

My boy must never bring disgrace to his immortal sires —
At Valley Forge and Lexington they kindled freedom's fires,
John's father died at Gettysburg, mine fell at Chancellorsville;
While John himself was with the boys who charged up San Juan Hill.
And John, if he was living now, would surely say with me,
"No son of ours shall e'er disgrace our grand old family tree
By turning out a slacker when his country needs his aid."
It is not of such timber that America was made.
I'd rather you had died at birth or not been born at all,
Than know that I had raised a son who cannot hear the call
That freedom has sent round the world, its previous rights to save —
This call is meant for you, my boy, and I would have you brave;
And though my heart is breaking, boy, I bid you do your part,

And show the world no son of mine is cursed with craven heart;
And if, perchance, you ne'er return, my later days to cheer,
And I have only memories of my brave boy, so dear,
I'd rather have it so, my boy, and know you bravely died
Than have a living coward sit supinely by my side.
To save the world from sin, my boy, God gave his only son —
He's asking for My boy, today, and may His will be done.

POEM
Attention, Mr Farmer Man, and listen now to me,
and I will try and show to you what I can plainly see.
Your Uncle Sam, the dear old man who's been so good to you,
is needing help and watching now to see what you will do.
Your Uncle's in the great world war and since he's entered in
it's up to every one of us to see that he shall win.
He's trying hard to "speed things up" and do it with a dash,
and so just now he's asking you to aid him with your cash.
Remember, all he asks of you is but a simple loan,
and every patriot comes across without a single moan.
Should Uncle Sammy once get mad (he will if you get lax),
he then will exercise his right, and make you pay a tax.
Should Kaiser Bill and all his hordes, once get across the Pond,
d'ye think he'll waste his time on you, and coax to take a bond?
Why no, siree. He'd grab and hold most everything he saw.
He'd take your farm, your stock and lands, your wife and babies all.
He'd make you work, he'd make you sweat, he'd squeeze you till you'd groan.
So be a man, and come across. Let Uncle have that loan.

FAMOUS LAST WORDS

"*Es ist gar nichts, es ist gar nichts*. It's nothing, it's nothing."
Franz Ferdinand, Archduke of Austria, whispered to Count Harrach as he
fell unconscious after being shot by an assassin, 1914. He died shortly
afterwards, sparking a chain of events that led to World War I.

"It is unbelievable."
Mata Hari (Margaretha Geertruida Zelle), pictured, an exotic
dancer, courtesan, and alleged German spy, before being
executed for espionage by firing squad, 1917

"Put out the light."
Theodore Roosevelt, the 26th US president, before
dying of a coronary embolism, 1919. On hearing
of his death, one of his sons telegraphed his siblings:
"The old lion is dead."

"Take a step forward lads — it'll be easier that way."
Robert Erskine Childers, Irish author, and nationalist,
to his firing squad during the Irish Civil War, 1922

"This time it will be a long one."
Georges Clemenceau, French prime minister during
World War I and one of the key players of the 1919
Paris Peace Conference, who drew up the Treaty of
Versailles, before dying of natural causes, 1929

"Bugger Bognor."
King George V of England, a heavy smoker
who was dying of multiple lung diseases,
after his doctor suggested that he recuperate
at his seaside palace in Bognor Regis, in
the south of England, 1936. But the diary
of his attending physician, Lord Dawson
of Penn, records George's last words,
after receiving a shot of morphine, as
"God damn you!"

Against Conscription and War
Emma Goldman, New York, 14 June 1917

Widely known as "Red Emma," Emma Goldman (1869–1940) was a Lithuanian-born anarchist who escaped Jewish pogroms in Russia, migrating to the United States with her family in 1886. Working in the textile industry, she became outraged by the working and social conditions in what she had expected to be a land of opportunity and freedom. She became an activist for women's rights, anti-conscription, and the violent overthrow of the government. She was arrested and jailed several times, then deported to the USSR in 1919 after assistant attorney-general J. Edgar Hoover referred to her as "one of the most dangerous anarchists in America."

Goldman returned to the United States in 1924 to work in urban slums. Among her more incendiary public statements was: "...Ask for work. If they do not give you work, ask for bread. If they do not give you work or bread, take bread." She published an autobiography, *Living My Life* (1931), and several anarchist works.

She made this speech in New York at a meeting of the No-Conscription League, ten weeks after the US entered World War I. Shortly afterwards she was fined $10 000 and jailed for two years for opposing conscription. Goldman, who had received a telephoned death threat warning her not to attend the meeting, was introduced by the Chairman as having "...more courage than half a dozen regiments."

[Introduced to great applause]
This is not the place to applaud or shout Hurrah for Emma Goldman. We have more serious things to talk about and some serious things to do...

Friends, tomorrow morning I am sure that you will read the report that a meeting took place on the East Side attended by foreigners, by workmen, and ill-kempt, poorly washed people of the East Side — foreigners who are being jeered at the present time in this country, foreigners who are being ridiculed because they have an idea. Well, friends, if the Americans are to wait until Americans wake up the country, they will have to resurrect the Indians who were killed in America and upon whose bodies this so-called democracy was established, because every other American, if you scratch him, you will find him to be an Englishman, Dutchman, Frenchman, Spaniard, a Jew, and a German and a hundred and one other nationalities who sent their young men and their women to this country in the foolish

In May 1916, Goldman speaks on birth control in Union Square Park in New York.

belief that liberty was awaiting them at the American Harbor, Liberty holding a torch. That torch has been burning dimly in the United States for a very long time. It is because the Goddess of Liberty is ashamed of the American people and what they have done in the name of liberty to liberty in the United States...

Evidently, America has to learn a salutary lesson and it is going to pay a terrible price. It is going to shed oceans of blood, it is going to heap mountains of human sacrifices of men of this country who are able to create and produce, to whom the future belongs. They are to be slaughtered in blood and in sacrifice in the name of a thing which has never yet existed in the United States of America, in the name of democracy and liberty...

The people were never asked whether they wanted war. Indeed, the people of America placed Mr Wilson in the White House and in the Chair of the Presidency because he told the people that he would keep them out of war, and as one of his political advertisements billposters were posted all over the city with the picture of a working woman and her children saying, "He has kept us out of war." He promised you heaven, he promised you everything if you would only place him in power. What made you place him in power. You expected peace and not war. The moment you placed him in power, however, he forgot his promises and he is giving you hell. War was imposed upon the people without the people getting a chance to say whether they wanted war or not, and war was imposed upon them, I say, because the gentlemen of power and those who back power want war...

I deny that the President or those who back the President have any right to tell the people that they shall take their sons and husbands and brothers and lovers and shall conscript them in order to ship them across the seas for the conquest of militarism and the support of wealth and power in the United States. You say that is a law. I deny your law. I don't believe in it.

The only law that I recognize is the law which ministers to the needs of humanity, which makes men and women finer and better and more humane, the kind of law which teaches children that human life is sacred, and that those who arm for the purpose of taking human life are going to be called before the bar of human justice and not before a wretched little court which is called your law of the United States. And so, friends, the people have not yet decided whether they want war and the people are going to say, ultimately, whether they want war or not...

If the framers of the Declaration of Independence, if Jefferson or Henry or the others, if they could look down upon the country and see what their offspring has done to it, how they have outraged it, how they have robbed it, how they have polluted it — why, my friends, they would turn in their graves. They would rise again and they would cleanse this country from its internal enemies, and that is the ruling class of the United States. There is a lesson you are going to learn and terrible as it is for us we nevertheless are glad that you will have to learn that lesson...

...to threaten anyone's life, to say that she will not come back from a meeting alive — how stupid. What is life unless you can live it in freedom and in beauty, and unless you can express yourself, unless you can be true to yourself what is life? I would rather than live the life of a dog to be compelled to sneak about and slink about, to worry that somebody is looking for you ready to take your life — Rather than that I would die the death of a lion any day...

Nothing but the human mind, nothing but human emotions, nothing but an intense passion for a great ideal, nothing but perseverance and devotion and strength of character — nothing else ever solved any problem...

I wish to say here, and I don't say it with any authority and I don't say it as a prophet, I merely tell you — I merely tell you the more people you lock up, the more will be the idealists who will take their place; the more of the human voice you suppress, the greater and louder and the profounder will be the human voice. At present it is a mere rumbling, but that rumbling is increasing in volume, it is growing in depth, it is spreading all over the country until it will be raised into a thunder and people of America will rise and say, we want to be a democracy, to be sure, but we want the kind of democracy which means liberty and opportunity to every man and woman in America.

FIGHTING WORDS

"War is a series of catastrophes that results in a victory."
"War is much too serious a matter to be entrusted to the military."
Georges Clemenceau (1841–1929), physician and journalist, served as
prime minister of France from 1906 to 1909 and from 1917 to 1920. Adolf
Hitler often spuriously quoted him out of context.

"You will be home before the leaves have fallen from the trees."
Wilhelm II (1859–1941), the German kaiser (emperor), addressing his
troops in August 1914, predicts a swift and successful end to World War I.

"I realise that patriotism is not enough. I must have no hatred or bitterness
towards anyone."
Edith Cavell (1865–1915), pictured opposite, a humanitarian and British
nurse in World War I, is celebrated for helping hundreds of Allied soldiers
to escape from Belgium. She helped German and Allied troops alike;
nonetheless, she was executed by the Germans on 11 October 1915,
the day after making this statement.

"…Enormous masses of ammunition, such as the human mind had never
imagined before the war, were hurled upon the bodies of men who passed a
miserable existence scattered about in mud-filled shell-holes…It was no longer
life at all. It was mere unspeakable suffering…"
Erich Ludendorff (1865–1937) was a general in the German army in World
War I. After the war, he briefly supported Hitler and the Nazi party, but once
Hitler came to power, he warned Paul von Hindenberg, prophetically as it
turned out, that "this evil man will plunge our Reich into the abyss." From
his book, *My War Memories, 1914–1918*.

"There will one day spring from the brain of science a machine or force so
fearful in its potentialities, so absolutely terrifying, that even man, the fighter,
who will dare torture and death in order to inflict torture and death, will be
appalled, and so abandon war forever."
Dutch-born American Thomas Edison (1847–1931) was a prolific inventor
and entrepreneur who produced numerous innovative devices, including
the light bulb and the phonograph. In this quote he correctly predicts the
advent of nuclear weapons, but we are yet to fulfil the rest of his prediction.

"Germany expected to find a lamb and found a lion"
David Lloyd George, 21 June 1917

In this speech to the British parliament, David Lloyd George (1863–1945), prime minister from 1916 to 1922, refutes the idea that Britain was responsible for the outbreak of World War I, and ridicules the Germans' propaganda efforts to paint England as the aggressor. In 1919 George represented Britain during negotiations over the Treaty of Versailles, successfully proposing that Germany should be forced to pay for the entire war as well as pay continuing reparations and pensions to the victors.

> It is a satisfaction for Britain in these terrible times that no share of the responsibility for these events rests on her.
>
> She is not the Jonah in this storm. The part taken by our country in this conflict, in its origin, and in its conduct, has been as honorable and chivalrous as any part ever taken in any country in any operation.

David Lloyd George at the 14th Army Corps headquarters with Sir Douglas Haig, the commander-in-chief of the British forces, and the French general, Joseph Joffre.

We might imagine from declarations which were made by the Germans, aye! and even by a few people in this country, who are constantly referring to our German comrades, that this terrible war was wantonly and wickedly provoked by England — never Scotland — never Wales — and never Ireland.

Wantonly provoked by England to increase her possessions, and to destroy the influence, the power, and the prosperity of a dangerous rival.

There never was a more foolish travesty of the actual facts. It happened three years ago, or less, but there have been so many bewildering events crowded into those intervening years that some people might have forgotten, perhaps, some of the essential facts, and it is essential that we should now and again restate them, not merely to refute the calumniators of our native land, but in order to sustain the hearts of her people by the unswerving conviction that no part of the guilt of this terrible bloodshed rests on the conscience of their native land.

What are the main facts? There were six countries which entered the war at the beginning. Britain was last, and not the first.

Before she entered the war Britain made every effort to avoid it; begged, supplicated, and entreated that there should be no conflict.

I was a member of the Cabinet at the time, and I remember the earnest endeavors we made to persuade Germany and Austria not to precipitate Europe into this welter of blood. We begged them to summon a European conference to consider.

Had that conference met arguments against provoking such a catastrophe that were so overwhelming there would never have been a war. Germany knew that, so she rejected the conference, although Austria was prepared to accept it. She suddenly declared war, and yet we are the people who wantonly provoked this war, in order to attack Germany.

We begged Germany not to attack Belgium, and produced a treaty, signed by the King of Prussia, as well as the King of England, pledging himself to protect Belgium against an invader, and we said, "If you invade Belgium we shall have no alternative but to defend it."

The enemy invaded Belgium, and now they say, "Why, forsooth, you, England, provoked this war."

It is not quite the story of the wolf and the lamb. I will tell you why — because Germany expected to find a lamb and found a lion.

VLADIMIR LENIN

Russian revolutionary and political leader Vladimir Ilyich Lenin (1870–1924) led the October 1917 revolution and became the first leader of the Soviet republic. He signed a peace treaty with Germany in March 1918 to remove Russia from World War I. Along with Josef Stalin, he set up a post-war state based on a system of mass terror, in which "counter-revolutionaries" — that is, opponents of the government — were subjected to penalties that included torture, maiming, imprisonment, and death. He was a revered figure in the Soviet Union until its demise in 1991; his status has declined considerably in recent years.

"While the State exists, there can be no freedom.
When there is freedom there will be no State."
From *State and Revolution*, 1919

"Communism is Soviet government plus the electrification of the whole country."
From *New External and Internal Position and the Problems of the Party*, 1920

"Germany wants revenge, and we want revolution. For the moment our aims are the same. When our ways part they will be our most ferocious and our greatest enemies. Time will tell whether a German hegemony or a Communist federation is to arise out of the ruins of Europe."
From a prophetic speech to his followers, 1920

"When we say 'the State,' the State is we, it is we, it is the proletariat, it is the advanced guard of the working class."
From a speech Lenin gave in 1922

"To hoard surpluses of grain and other food products at a time when the people in Petrograd, in Moscow and in dozens of non-agricultural *uyezds* [administrative subdivisions] are not only suffering from a shortage of bread, but are cruelly starving, is an enormous crime deserving the most ruthless punishment."
From *Collected Works*, Volume 42, 1923

Statement to the court
Mahatma Gandhi, Ahmedabad, India, 23 March 1922

Mohandas Karamchand Gandhi (1869–1948) was a major Indian political and spiritual leader. He introduced his *Satyagraha* policy of active — but non-violent — resistance to the British occupation of India in 1920, and traveled throughout India promoting it. As a result of three articles he wrote and published in *Young India* magazine in 1921 and 1922, he was charged with "bringing or attempting to excite disaffection towards His Majesty's Government established by law in British India, and thereby committing offences punishable under Section 124A of the Indian Penal Code." He proudly proclaimed his guilt, requested that the full force of the law be applied to him, and made this speech after the court invited him to make a statement on the question of his sentence. He was subsequently sentenced to six years' imprisonment.

Gandhi went on to lead India to independence from Britain, inspiring civil rights and freedom movements across the world before his assassination at the hands of a Hindu extremist in 1948. In India, Gandhi is officially accorded the honor of "Father of the Nation," and is known in India and throughout the world as Mahatma, "Great Soul."

Before I read this statement I would like to state that I entirely endorse the learned Advocate-General's remarks in connection with my humble self. I think that he has made, because it is very true and I have no desire whatsoever to conceal from this court the fact that to preach disaffection towards the existing system of Government has become almost a passion with me, and the Advocate-General is entirely in the right when he says that my preaching of disaffection did not commence with my connection with *Young India* but that it commenced much earlier, and in the statement that I am about to read, it will be my painful duty to admit before this court that it commenced much earlier than the period stated by the Advocate-General...

Non-violence is the first article of my faith. It is also the last article of my creed. But I had to make my choice. I had either to submit to a system which I considered had done an irreparable harm to my country, or incur the risk of the mad fury of my people bursting forth when they understood the truth from my lips. I know that my people have sometimes gone mad. I am deeply sorry for it and I am, therefore, here to submit not to a light penalty but to the highest penalty. I do not ask for mercy. I do not plead any extenuating act. I am here, therefore, to invite and cheerfully submit to the highest penalty that can be inflicted upon me for what in law is a deliberate crime, and what appears to me to be the highest duty of a citizen. The only course open to you, the Judge, is, as I am going to say in my statement, either to resign your post, or inflict on me the severest penalty if you believe that the system and law you are assisting to administer are good for the people. I do not except that kind of conversion. But by the time I have finished with my statement you will have a glimpse of what is raging within my breast to run this maddest risk which a sane man can run.

[Gandhi then read out the following statement.]

...I owe it perhaps to the Indian public and to the public in England, to placate which this prosecution is mainly taken up, that I should explain why from a staunch loyalist and cooperator, I have become an uncompromising disaffectionist and non-cooperator...

My public life began in 1893 in South Africa in troubled weather. My first contact with British authority in that country was not of a happy character. I discovered that as a man and an Indian, I had no rights. More correctly I discovered that I had no rights as a man because I was an Indian.

But I was not baffled. I thought that this treatment of Indians was an excrescence upon a system that was intrinsically and mainly good. I gave the Government my voluntary and hearty cooperation, criticising it freely where I felt it was faulty but never wishing its destruction.

Consequently when the existence of the Empire was threatened in 1899 by the Boer challenge, I offered my services to it, raised a volunteer ambulance corps and served at several actions that took place for the relief of Ladysmith. Similarly in 1906, at the time of the Zulu "revolt," I raised a stretcher bearer party and served till the end of the "rebellion." On both the occasions I received medals and was even mentioned in despatches...

When the war broke out in 1914 between England and Germany, I raised volunteer ambulance cars in London, consisting of the then resident Indians in London, chiefly students. Its work was acknowledged by the authorities to be valuable. Lastly, in India when a special appeal was made at the war Conference in Delhi in 1918 by Lord Chelmsford for recruits, I struggled at the cost of my health to raise a corps in Kheda, and the response was being made when the hostilities ceased and orders were received that no more recruits were wanted. In all these efforts at service, I was actuated by the belief that it was possible by such services to gain a status of full equality in the Empire for my countrymen...

I came reluctantly to the conclusion that the British connection had made India more helpless than she ever was before, politically and economically. A disarmed India has no power of resistance against any aggressor if she wanted to engage in an armed conflict with him. So much is this the case that some of our best men consider that India must take generations, before she can achieve Dominion Status. She has become so poor that she has little power of resisting famines. Before the British advent India spun and wove in her millions of cottages, just the supplement she needed for adding to her meagre agricultural resources. This cottage industry, so vital for India's existence, has been ruined by incredibly heartless and inhuman processes as described by English witnesses. Little do town dwellers know how the semi-starved masses of India are slowly sinking to lifelessness. Little do they know that their miserable comfort represents the brokerage they get for their work they do for the foreign exploiter, that the profits and the brokerage are sucked from the masses. Little do they realize that the Government established by law in British India is carried on for this exploitation of the masses...

My experience of political cases in India leads me to the conclusion, in nine out of every ten, the condemned men were totally innocent. Their crime consisted in the love of their country. In ninety-nine cases out of a hundred, justice has been denied to Indians as against Europeans in the courts of India. This is not an exaggerated picture. It is the experience of almost every Indian who has had anything to do with such cases. In my opinion, the administration of the law is thus prostituted, consciously or unconsciously, for the benefit of the exploiter...

The greater misfortune is that the Englishmen and their Indian associates in the administration of the country do not know that they are engaged in the crime I have attempted to describe. I am satisfied that many Englishmen and Indian officials honestly devised systems in the world, and that India is making steady, though, slow progress. They do not know, a subtle but effective system of terrorism and an organized display of force on the one hand, and the deprivation of all powers of retaliation or self-defence on the other, has emasculated the people and induced in them the habit of simulation. This awful habit has added to the ignorance and the self-deception of the administrators. Section 124A, under which I am happily charged, is perhaps the prince among the political sections of the Indian Penal Code designed to suppress

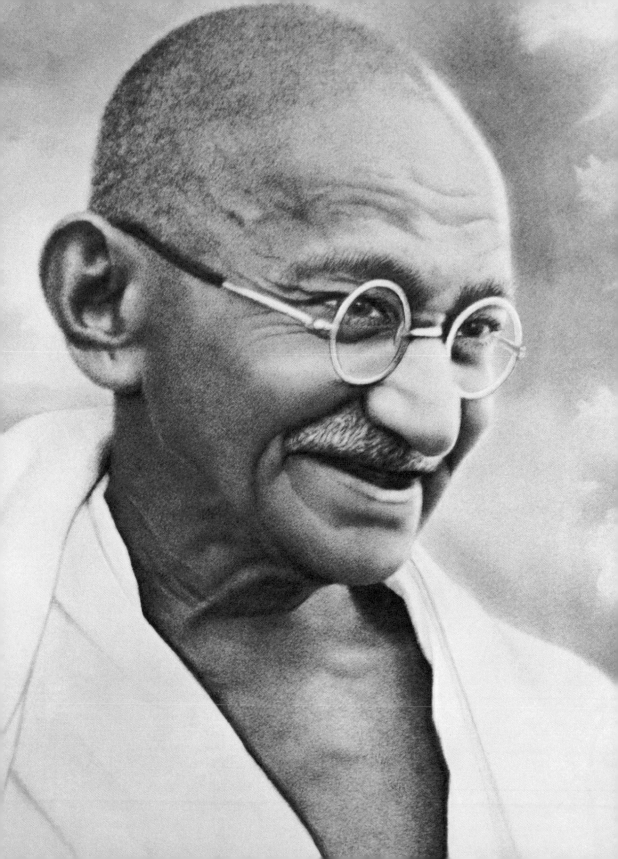

the liberty of the citizen. Affection cannot be manufactured or regulated by law. If one has no affection for a person or system, one should be free to give the fullest expression to his disaffection, so long as he does not contemplate, promote, or incite to violence. But the section under which [I am] charged is one under which mere promotion of disaffection is a crime. I have studied some of the cases tried under it; I know that some of the most loved of India's patriots have been convicted under it. I consider it a privilege, therefore, to be charged under that section. I have endeavored to give in their briefest outline the reasons for my disaffection. I have no personal ill will against any single administrator, much less can I have any disaffection towards the King's person. But I hold it to be a virtue to be disaffected towards a Government which in its totality has done more harm to India than any previous system. India is less manly under the British rule than she ever was before. Holding such a belief, I consider it to be a sin to have affection for the system. And it has been a precious privilege for me to be able to write what I have in the various articles tendered in evidence against me.

In fact, I believe that I have rendered a service to India and England by showing in non-cooperation the way out of the unnatural state in which both are living. In my opinion, non-cooperation with evil is as much a duty as is cooperation with good. But in the past, non-cooperation has been deliberately expressed in violence to the evil-doer. I am endeavoring to show to my countrymen that violent non-cooperation only multiplies evil, and that as evil can only be sustained by violence, withdrawal of support of evil requires complete abstention from violence. Non-violence implies voluntary submission to the penalty for non-cooperation with evil. I am here, therefore, to invite and submit cheerfully to the highest penalty that can be inflicted upon me for what in law is a deliberate crime, and what appears to me to be the highest duty of a citizen. The only course open to you, the Judge and the assessors, is either to resign your posts and thus dissociate yourselves from evil, if you feel that the law you are called upon to administer is an evil, and that in reality I am innocent, or to inflict on me the severest penalty, if you believe that the system and the law you are assisting to administer are good for the people of this country, and that my activity is, therefore, injurious to the common weal.

Gandhi lived simply, making his own clothes from cloth he wove himself.

FIGHTING POEMS

Australia to England

By all the deeds to Thy dear glory done,
By all the life blood spilt to serve Thy need,
By all the fettered lives Thy touch hath freed,
By all Thy dream in us anew begun;
By all the guerdon English sire to son
Hath given of highest vision, kingliest deed,
By all Thine agony, of God decreed
For trial and strength, our fate with Thine is one.

Still dwells Thy spirit in our hearts and lips,
Honor and life we hold from none but thee
And if we live Thy pensioners no more
But seek a nation's might of men and ships,
'Tis but that when the world is black with war
Thy sons may stand beside Thee strong and free.

Archibald T. Strong (1876–1930) was an Australian scholar, historian, and poet. He was rejected on medical grounds from serving in World War I, but was a strong supporter of the Allied cause. He addressed recruiting rallies, helped to raise war loans, and wrote numerous newspaper articles. This poem expresses his support for imperial ties between Australia ("Thy sons") and England.

Dulce et Decorum Est

Bent double, like old beggars under sacks,
Knock-kneed, coughing like hags, we cursed through sludge,
Till on the haunting flares we turned our backs
And towards our distant rest began to trudge.
Men marched asleep. Many had lost their boots
But limped on, blood-shod. All went lame; all blind;
Drunk with fatigue; deaf even to the hoots
Of tired, outstripped Five-Nines that dropped behind.
Gas! Gas! Quick, boys! — An ecstasy of fumbling,
Fitting the clumsy helmets just in time;
But someone still was yelling out and stumbling
And flound'ring like a man in fire or lime...
Dim, through the misty panes and thick green light,
As under a green sea, I saw him drowning.
In all my dreams, before my helpless sight,
He plunges at me, guttering, choking, drowning.
If in some smothering dreams you too could pace
Behind the wagon that we flung him in,
And watch the white eyes writhing in his face,
His hanging face, like a devil's sick of sin;
If you could hear, at every jolt, the blood
Come gargling from the froth-corrupted lungs,
Obscene as cancer, bitter as the cud
Of vile, incurable sores on innocent tongues,
My friend, you would not tell with such high zest
To children ardent for some desperate glory,
The old Lie: *Dulce et decorum est
Pro patria mori.*

Wilfred Owen (1893–1918) is generally regarded as the foremost poet
of World War I. His realistic poetry about the horrors of trench warfare
and chemical weapons was strongly influenced by his mentor and hero
Siegfried Sassoon, and stood in contrast to earlier, patriotic verse by poets
such as Rupert Brooke. Owen was killed a week before the Armistice, as
he led his men across a canal under heavy fire. His mother received the
telegram notifying her of his death as the Armistice church bells tolled.

Part 6

THE RISE & FALL OF FASCISM

The Mid-Twentieth Century

Speech to the Industry Club
Adolf Hitler, Dusseldorf, Germany, 27 January 1932

In early 1932, Adolf Hitler, leader of the German Nazi party, was preparing an electoral campaign to wrest power from German president Joseph von Hindenburg. But finances were a big problem; as Hitler's campaign organizer and propaganda guru Dr Joseph Goebbels said: "Money is wanting everywhere...Once you get the power you can get cash galore, but then you need it no longer. Without the power you need the money, but then you can't get it." (The same might be said today about applying for a bank loan.)

The Industry Club was an agglomeration of German leaders of industry, naturally conservative and hence sceptical about Hitler's radical agenda. But in this brilliant speech, Hitler paints himself as an economic conservative who believes that foreign policy plays too great a part in German life, and at the expense of industry, productivity, and profit. He dwells on the evils of communism (the communist party, like the Nazis, had recently been making large electoral gains) and the power of trade unions to stifle industry at the expense of the nation's prosperity. He mentions only two valid possible forms of government: democracy, whose outcome must be decay and mediocrity — "...the rule of stupidity, of mediocrity, of half-heartedness, of cowardice, of weakness, and of inadequacy..." — and authoritarianism, "because whatever man in the past has achieved — all human civilisations — is conceivable only if the supremacy of this principle is admitted." He quotes leaders and philosophers (selectively and out of context), his underlying message being that war is a natural and just response to exploitation by external forces, as measured by their detrimental (and obvious) effects on German industry.

The audience, cool and reserved at first, was soon eating out of Hitler's hand. His two-and-a-half-hour oration was received with loud applause and cheering. More importantly, the listeners' approval was confirmed by subsequent large donations to the Nazi campaign war chest. After a series of elections, and numerous devious machinations, Hitler was appointed chancellor on 30 January 1933, going on to achieve total power as führer (dictator) of Germany on 19 August 1934.

> ...If today the National Socialist Movement is regarded amongst widespread circles in Germany as being hostile to our business life, I believe the reason for this view is to be found in the fact that we adopted towards the events which determined the development leading to our present position an

attitude which differed from that of all the other organisations which are of any importance in our public life. Even now our outlook differs in many points from that of our opponents...

I regard it as of the first importance to break once and for all with the view that our destiny is conditioned by world events. It is not true that our distress has its final cause in a world crisis, in a world catastrophe: the true view is that we have reached a state of general crisis, because from the first certain mistakes were made. I must not say "According to the general view the Peace Treaty of Versailles is the cause of our misfortune."...

It is also in my view false to say that life in Germany today is solely determined by considerations of foreign policy, that the primacy of foreign policy governs today the whole of our domestic life. Certainly a people can reach the point when foreign relations influence and determine completely its domestic life. But let no one say that such a condition is from the first either natural or desirable. Rather the important thing is that a people should create the conditions for a change in this state of affairs.

If anyone says to me that its foreign politics is primarily decisive for the life of a people, then I must first ask: what then is the meaning of the term "politics"? There is a whole series of definitions. Frederick the Great said: "Politics is the art of serving one's state with every means." Bismarck's explanation was that "Politics is the art of the Possible," starting from the conception that advantage should be taken of every possibility to serve the state — and, in the later transformation of the idea of the State into the idea of nationalities, the nation. Another considers that this service rendered to the people can be effected by military as well as peaceful action, for Clausewitz says that war is the continuation of politics though with different means. Conversely, Clemenceau considers that today peace is nothing but the continuation of war and the pursuing of the war-aim, though again with other means...

It is therefore false to say that foreign politics shapes a people: rather, peoples order their relations to the world about them in correspondence with their inborn forces and according to the measure in which their education enables them to bring those forces into play. We may be quite convinced that if in the place of the Germany of today there had stood a different Germany, the attitude towards the rest of the world would also have been different, and then presumably the influences exercised by the rest of the world would have taken a different form. To deny this would mean that Germany's destiny can no longer be changed no matter what government rules in Germany...

The pomp and spectacular staging of Nazi rallies is evident at this May Day rally in Berlin on 1 May 1935.

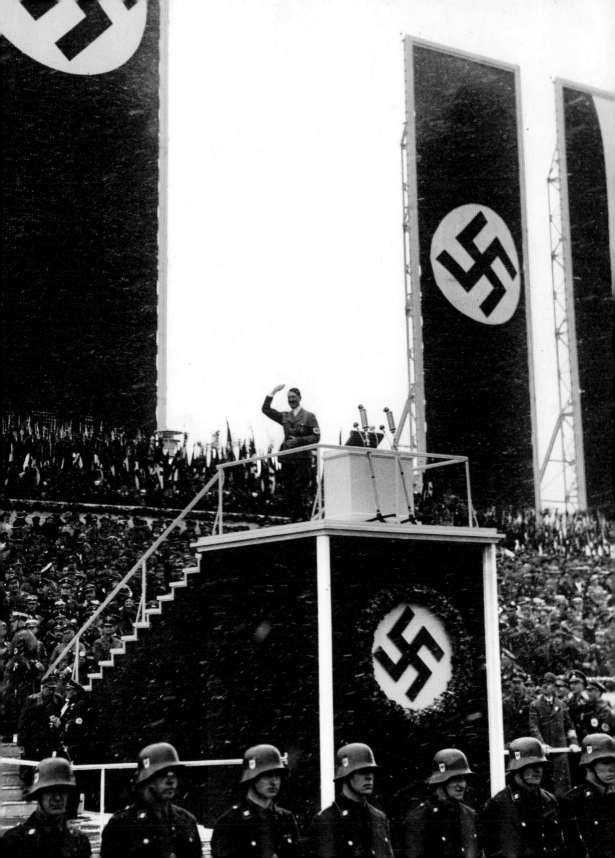

And as against this conception I am the champion of another standpoint: three factors, I hold, essentially determine a people's political life:

First, the inner value of a people which as an inherited sum and possession is transmitted again and again through the generations, a value which suffers any change when the people, the custodian of this inherited possession, changes itself in its inner blood-conditioned composition. It is beyond question that certain traits of character, certain virtues and certain vices always recur in peoples so long as their inner nature — their blood-conditioned composition — has not essentially altered. I can already trace the virtues and the vices of our German people in the writers of Rome just as clearly as I see them today. This inner value which determines the life of a people can be destroyed by nothing save only through a change in the blood causing a change in substance...

I said that this value can be destroyed. There are indeed in especial two other closely related factors which we can time and again trace in periods of national decline: the one is that for the conception of the value of personality there is substituted a leveling idea of the supremacy of mere numbers — democracy — and the other is the negation of the value of a people, the denial of any difference in the inborn capacity, the achievement, etc, of individual peoples. Thus both factors condition one another or at least influence each other in the course of their development. Internationalism and democracy are inseparable conceptions. It is but logical that democracy, which within a people denies the special value of the individual and puts in its place a value which represents the sum of all individualities — a purely numerical value — should proceed in precisely the same way in the life of peoples and should in that sphere result in internationalism. Broadly it is maintained: peoples have no inborn values, but, at the most, there can be admitted perhaps temporary differences in education. Between negroes, Aryans, Mongolians and redskins there is no essential difference in value. This view which forms the basis of the whole of the international thought-world of today and in its effects is carried to such lengths that in the end a negro can sit as president in the sessions of the League of Nations leads necessarily as a further consequence to the point that in a similar way within a people differences in value between the individual members of this people are denied. And thus naturally every special capacity, every fundamental value of a people, can practically be made of no effect. For the greatness of a people is the result not of the sum of all its achievements but in the last resort of the sum of its outstanding achievements...

So it is only natural that when the capable intelligences of a nation, which are always in a minority, are regarded only as of the same value as all the rest, then genius, capacity, the value of personality are slowly subjected to the majority and this process is then falsely named the rule of the people. For this is not rule of the people, but in reality the rule of stupidity, of mediocrity, of half-heartedness, of cowardice, of weakness, and of inadequacy...

Thus democracy will in practice lead to the destruction of a people's true values...

And thus in these conditions a people will gradually lose its importance not merely in the cultural and economic spheres but altogether, in a comparatively short time it will no longer, within the setting of the other peoples of the world, maintain its former value...

And to this there must be added a third factor: namely, the view that life in this world, after the denial of the value of personality and of the special value of a people, is not to be maintained through conflict. That is a conception which could perhaps be disregarded if it fixed itself only in

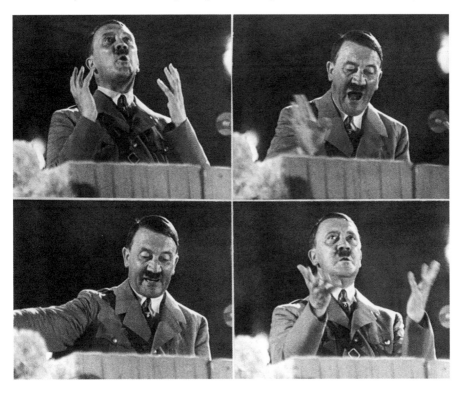

A gifted orator, Hitler practised in front of a mirror (like Churchill), concentrating on his hand and arm gestures.

the heads of individuals, but yet has appalling consequences because it slowly poisons an entire people. And it is not as if such general changes in men's outlook on the world remained only on the surface or were confined to their effects on men's minds. No, in the course of time they exercise a profound influence and affect all expressions of a people's life...

To sum up the argument: I see two diametrically opposed principles: the principle of democracy which, wherever it is allowed practical effect is the principle of destruction: and the principle of the authority of personality which I would call the principle of achievement, because whatever man in the past has achieved — all human civilisations — is conceivable only if the supremacy of this principle is admitted...

We have a number of nations which through their inborn outstanding worth have fashioned for themselves a mode of life which stands in no relation to the life-space — the *Lebensraum* — which, in their thickly populated settlements, they inhabit. We have the so-called white race which, since the collapse of ancient civilisation, in the course of some thousand years has created for itself a privileged position in the world. But I am quite unable to understand this privileged position, this economic supremacy, of the white race over the rest of the world if I do not bring it into close connection with a political conception of supremacy which has been peculiar to the white race for many centuries and has been regarded as in the nature of things: this conception it has maintained in its dealings with other peoples. Take any single area you like, take for example India. England did not conquer India by the way of justice and of law: she conquered India without regard to the wishes, to the views of the natives, or to their formulations of justice, and, when necessary, she has upheld this supremacy with the most brutal ruthlessness...

If I think away this attitude of mind which in the course of the last three or four centuries has won the world for the white race, then the destiny of this race would in fact have been no different from that, say, of the Chinese: an immensely congested mass of human beings crowded upon an extraordinarily narrow territory, an over-population with all its unavoidable consequences. If Fate allowed the white race to take a different path, that is only because this white race was convinced that it had the right to organize the rest of the world...

FIGHTING SONG
Lili Marlene

Underneath the lantern by the barrack gate,
Darling I remember
The way you used to wait,
'Twas there that you whispered tenderly,
That you loved me,
You'd always be,
My Lili of the lamplight,
My own Lili Marlene.

Time would come for roll call,
Time for us to part,
Darling I'd caress you and
Press you to my heart,
And there 'neath that far off lantern light,
I'd hold you tight,
We'd kiss good-night,
My Lili of the lamplight,
My own Lili Marlene.

Orders came for sailing
Somewhere over there,
All confined to barracks
Was more than I could bear;
I knew you were waiting in the street,
I heard your feet,
But could not meet,
My Lili of the lamplight,
My own Lili Marlene.

Resting in a billet
Just behind the line,
Even though we're parted
Your lips are close to mine,
You wait where that lantern softly gleams,
Your sweet face seems to haunt my dreams,
My Lili of the lamplight,
My own Lili Marlene.

"Lili Marlene" was originally a German song that was based on a poem written by German soldier Hans Leip in 1915. Norbert Schultze set the poem to music in 1938 and it was released just before World War II. It became an immediate favourite of German troops, and its immense popularity led to a hurried English re-write by Tommie Connor ("Till The Lights of London Shine Again"). Soon both sides were broadcasting both versions, intermingled with snippets of propaganda. Interestingly, both Lale Andersen and Marlene Dietrich — who began singing it in 1943 — were anti-Nazis.

The English version is even more sentimental than the original. Vera Lynn, pictured, performed the song at every concert she ever performed — both during the war and afterwards, at the numerous concerts she gave for British soldiers stationed in pre-NATO Germany.

"Before the gate of Germany stands the new German Army"

Adolf Hitler, Nuremberg, Germany, 14 September 1936

By 1936, when he had been dictator for three years, Hitler decided that world domination was achievable. To that end, he prepared to devote Germany's entire industrial complex to the exclusive production of military hardware. As always, the rationale was that peaceful Germany was being forced (reluctantly) to defend itself against hostile opportunists of various persuasions. The demons in this speech are bolshevism (communism) and democracy, with the occasional obligatory reference to Jews, who, he claimed, invented both ideologies. (In other speeches and writings, Hitler blamed Jews for creating the evils of the class war, modern art — especially Impressionism — jazz music, freedom of the press, social democracy, internationalism, parliamentarianism, capitalism, interest rates, venereal disease, and Christianity. He demonized Jews in every address and speech he ever made.)

Before the war, Hitler, who had been brought up and confirmed as a Catholic, rarely referred to God or Christianity in his speeches. To assert a religious principle too fervently would be to align himself with either the godless Soviets or the "degenerate" French, English, Americans, and so on, whose leaders frequently invoked God. One imagines Hitler was jealous of the adoration received by God, but he was wedged in by his crusades against Jewry and communism. (In a 1922 speech, he said: "My feelings as a Christian point me to my Lord and Savior as a fighter. It points me to the man who, once in loneliness, surrounded by a few followers, recognized these Jews for what they were and summoned men to fight against them and who, God's truth! was greatest not as a sufferer but as a fighter." This puts a completely new slant on Jesus as an anti-Semitic aggressor — an interpretation missed by most observers, but typical of Hitler's technique of mixing facts with fiction and arriving at an illogical, bigoted, and egotistical conclusion.)

"Democracy is the canal through which bolshevism lets its poisons flow" was probably news to everyone outside Germany (and many inside), but one may admire the seductively poetic polemic. This speech, as always, is full of Hitler's self-referential logic, whereby his own motives are sublimated into his attacks on his enemies. And who could disagree with: "That one should refuse to see a thing does not mean that it is not there..." or: "He who is undertaking such great economic and cultural tasks as we are and is so determined to carry them through can find his fairest memorial only in peace."?

This card shows Adolf Hitler at a Nuremberg rally in the 1930s. These rallies, masterpieces of propaganda, were held annually from 1923 to 1938.

...I can come to no terms with a *Weltanschauung* [world view] which everywhere as its first act after gaining power is — not the liberation of the working people — but the liberation of the scum of humanity, the asocial creatures concentrated in the prisons — and then the letting loose of these wild beasts upon the terrified and helpless world about them...

Bolshevism turns flourishing countrysides into sinister wastes of ruins; National Socialism transforms a Reich of destruction and misery into a healthy state and a flourishing economic life...

Russia planned a world revolution and German workmen would be used but as cannon fodder for bolshevist imperialism. But we National Socialists do not wish that our military resources should be employed to impose by force on other peoples what those peoples themselves do not want. Our army does not swear on oath that it will with bloodshed extend the National Socialist idea over other peoples, but that it will with its own blood defend the National Socialist idea and thereby the German Reich, its security and freedom, from the aggression of other peoples...

These are only some of the grounds for the antagonisms which separate us from communism. I confess, these antagonisms cannot be bridged. Here are really two worlds which do but grow further apart from each other and can never unite. When in an English newspaper a Parliamentarian complains that we wish to divide Europe into two parts, then unfortunately we are bound to inform this Robinson Crusoe living on his happy British island that — however unwelcome it may be — this division is already an accomplished fact...That one should refuse to see a thing does not mean that it is not there. For many a year in Germany I have been laughed to scorn as a prophet; for many a year my warnings and my prophecies were regarded as the illusions of a mind diseased...

Bolshevism has attacked the foundations of our whole human order, alike in state and society, the foundations of our conception of civilisation, of our faith and of our morals: all alike are at stake...

Unfortunately I cannot escape the impression that most of those who doubt the danger to the world of bolshevism come themselves from the East. As yet politicians in England have not come to know bolshevism in their own country; we know it already. Since I have fought against these Jewish Soviet ideas in Germany, since I have conquered and stamped out this peril, I fancy that I possess a better comprehension of its character than do men who have only at best had to deal with it in the field of literature... have won my successes simply because in the first place I endeavored to see things as they are and not as one would like them to be; secondly, when once I had formed my own opinion I never allowed weaklings to talk me out of it or to cause me to abandon it; and thirdly, because I was always determined in all circumstances to yield to a necessity when once it had been recognized..

...It is not necessary for me to strengthen the fame of the National Socialist Movement, far less that of the German Army, through military triumphs. He who is undertaking such great economic and cultural tasks as we are and is so determined to carry them through can find his fairest memorial only in peace...But this bolshevism which as we learned only a few months since intends to equip its army so that it may with violence, if necessary, open the gate to revolution amongst other peoples — this bolshevism should know that before the gate of Germany stands the new German Army...

It is with grave anxiety that I see the possibility in Europe of some such development as this: democracy may continuously disintegrate the European states, may make them internally ever more uncertain in their judgment of the dangers which confront them, may above all cripple all power for resolute resistance. Democracy is the canal through which bolshevism lets its poisons flow into the separate countries and lets them work there long enough for these infections to lead to a crippling of intelligence and of the force of resistance. I regard it as possible that then — in order to avoid something still worse — coalition governments, masked as popular fronts or the like, will be formed and that these will endeavor to destroy — and perhaps will successfully destroy — in these peoples the last forces which remain, either in organisation or in mental outlook, which could offer opposition to bolshevism.

The brutal mass slaughters of National Socialist fighters, the burning of the wives of National Socialist officers after petrol had been poured over them, the massacre of children and of babies of National Socialist parents, for example in Spain, are intended to serve as a warning to forces in other lands which represent views akin to those of National Socialism. Such forces are to be intimidated so that in a similar position they offer no resistance. If these methods are successful: if the modern Girondins are succeeded by Jacobins, if Kerensky's popular front gives place to the bolshevists, then Europe will sink into a sea of blood and mourning...

WAR CRIES

"*Tora, Tora, Tora!* Tiger, Tiger, Tiger!"
This was the coded radio signal indicating that the bombing attack on the US Navy at Pearl Harbor had been successful. It is not, strictly speaking, a war cry but is sometimes mistaken for one.

"*Ura!* Hurrah!"
Russian army battle cry, pronounced "Oo-rah" and probably derived from Turkish. In World War II a common Russian war cry was "*Ura Pobieda!* Victory!" Many cultures use a similar shout, although origins vary. US marines also shout "Oo-rah!" but the root is different. The US army shouts "Hoo-ah!" US navy teams yell "Hoo-YAH!" for inspiration. The Argentine navy shouts "*Ua! Ua! Ua!*", while the Greek army uses "*Aera!*" ("Wind!", as in "Blow them away like the...").

"*Banzai!* Ten thousand years!"
The battle cry of Japanese *kamikaze* (suicide) pilots. Adapted from the Chinese "*Wansui!*", this term has been used for over 1200 years to bless East Asian emperors and wish long life upon their dynasty. It can be used once or repeatedly — in China, it was traditional to say "*Wansui, wansui, wanwansui*" (the last indicating 100 million years). It is usually translated as "Long live!...", although it contains extra, non-English cultural undertones. "Ten thousand" in Chinese and Japanese has an implication of infinity, much like the Greek myriad. In 1956 Chinese chairman Mao Zedong said of this: "To chant '*Wansui!*' is to contradict natural laws. Everyone has to die sooner or later, whether they be killed by germs, crushed by a collapsing house, or blown to smithereens by an atom bomb. Anyway, one way or another everyone ends up dead..."

"Peace for our time"
Neville Chamberlain, London, 30 September 1938

Neville Chamberlain (1869–1940) was elected British prime minister in 1937. He is, perhaps unfairly, best remembered for his policy of "appeasement" with Germany and Italy leading up to World War II. Anxious to avoid the bloodshed of World War I, he refused to commit troops to fight against General Franco's fascist regime in Spain in 1936; and in 1938 he recognized Italy's sovereignty over recently invaded Ethiopia — in part to avert the need for Italy to align with Germany in order to further its own expansionist ambitions. He also had some sympathy for Germany, believing that the terms of the 1919 Versailles Treaty were too severe, and were to some extent responsible for Germany's desire to re-arm.

The signatories to the Munich Agreement (from left to right): Chamberlain, Daladier, Hitler, and Mussolini, with Ciano (Italian foreign minister).

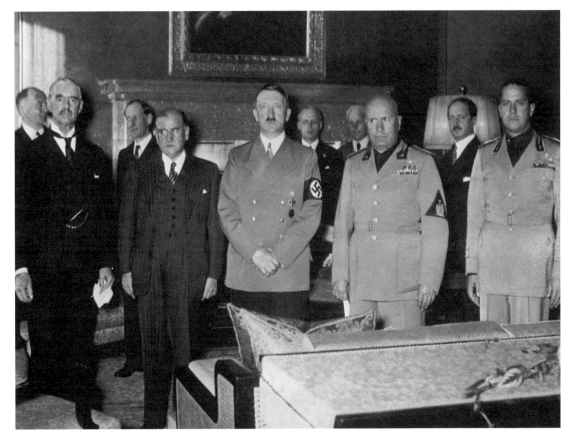

In September 1938, Chamberlain met with Hitler, Italian dictator Mussolini and French prime minister Édouard Daladier in Munich, where they agreed that Germany should annexe the Sudetenland region of Czechoslovakia. Hitler merely agreed not to make any further territorial claims but, as usual, already had quite different plans in train. In a rare flash of humor, Hitler later explained why he signed the Munich Agreement: "Chamberlain seemed such a nice old gentleman that I thought I would give him my autograph." Chamberlain apparently took Hitler's assurances at face value, and returned triumphantly to England on 30 September. How short-lived the triumph would prove to be.

On his return from Munich, waving the signed resolution in his hand, Chamberlain made the following statement on the tarmac of Heston Aerodrome.

We, the German Führer and Chancellor, and the British Prime Minister, have had a further meeting today and are agreed in recognising that the question of Anglo-German relations is of the first importance for the two countries and for Europe.

We regard the agreement signed last night and the Anglo-German Naval Agreement as symbolic of the desire of our two peoples never to go to war with one another again.

We are resolved that the method of consultation shall be the method adopted to deal with any other questions that may concern our two countries, and we are determined to continue our efforts to remove possible sources of difference, and thus to contribute to assure the peace of Europe.

Chamberlain later read the following statement to a cheering crowd in front of 10 Downing Street.

My good friends, for the second time in our history a British prime minister has returned from Germany bringing peace with honor. I believe it is peace for our time. Go home and get a nice quiet sleep.

"Nice quiet sleeps" would soon be in very short supply, in Britain and elsewhere.

3 SEPTEMBER 1939
WAR IS DECLARED

On 3 September 1939, the week after signing a non-aggression pact with the Soviets, Germany invaded Poland. Great Britain, France, Australia, and New Zealand immediately declared war on Germany. The following three speeches are the radio responses of the leaders of Australia, the United States, and Great Britain to this momentous event.

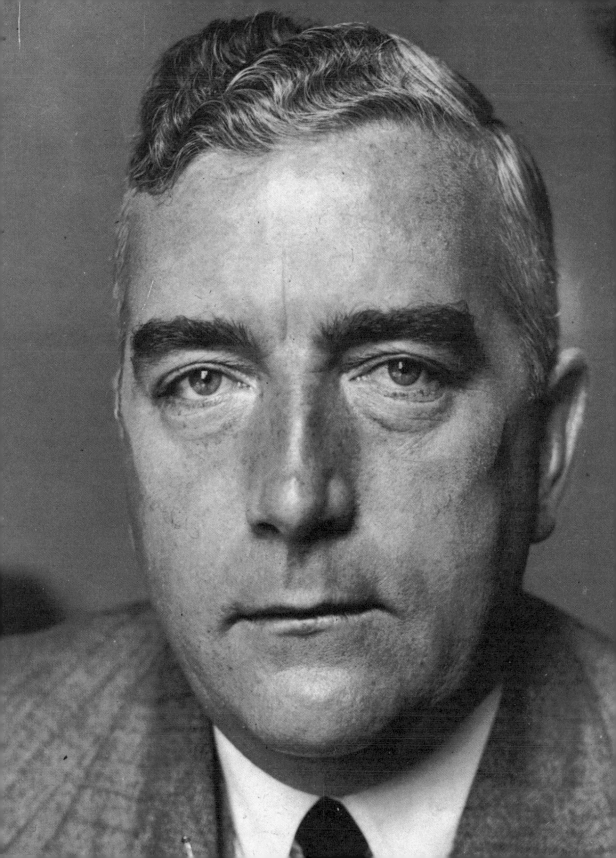

Declaration of war
Robert Menzies, radio speech (excerpts), 3 September 1939

The first sentence of this speech is part of Australian folklore, but it contains a misleading statement. When Prime Minister Menzies announces: "...Great Britain has declared war upon (Germany) and that, as a result, Australia is also at war," he implies that Australia was under some sort of obligation to support Britain, which was not the case; no such formal treaty existed. Nonetheless, the Australian parliament went on to unanimously accept Menzies's assumption that Britain's declaration of war against Germany required a similar declaration by Australia.

Menzies's war legacy was mixed. In 1938, as attorney-general and deputy prime minister, he had made an official visit to Germany and expressed admiration for the government. He also earned the epithet "Pig-Iron Bob" after an industrial battle in 1938 with waterside workers, who refused to load scrap iron being sold to Japan — on the grounds, *inter alia*, that it could be made into weapons and used against Australia. And during the war, despite assurances to the contrary, he failed to obtain a commitment from British prime minister Winston Churchill to come to Australia's aid in the event of an attack from the north, as occurred when Japan launched a series of bombing and submarine raids on Australian cities in February 1942.

By October 1941, the conservative Menzies government had disintegrated. Australians elected the Labor Party, led by John Curtin, to power. Menzies went on to found the Liberal Party, and subsequently served as prime minister from 1949 until his retirement in 1966.

Fellow Australians, it is my melancholy duty to inform you officially that in consequence of a persistence by Germany in her invasion of Poland, Great Britain has declared war upon her and that, as a result, Australia is also at war.

No harder task can fall to the lot of a democratic leader than to make such an announcement. Great Britain and France with the cooperation of the British Dominions have struggled to avoid this tragedy. They have, as I firmly believe, been patient. They have kept the door of negotiation open. They have given no cause for aggression.

But in the result their efforts have failed and we are therefore, as a great family of nations, involved in a struggle which we must at all costs win and which we believe in our hearts we will win...

Perhaps it was fitting that Menzies, a self-confessed monarchist, succeeded Churchill as Lord Warden of the Cinque Ports (1965–78).

... in the British government's communication of August 30, it informed the German Chancellor that it recognized the need for speed and that it also recognized the dangers which arose from the fact that two mobilized armies were facing each other on opposite sides of the Polish frontier, and that accordingly it strongly urged that both Germany and Poland should undertake that during the negotiations no aggressive military movements would take place. That being communicated to Poland, the Polish government on Thursday, August 31, categorically stated that it was prepared to give a formal guarantee that during negotiations Polish troops would not violate the frontiers, provided a corresponding guarantee was given by Germany. The German government made no reply whatever. My comments on these events need not be very long: the matter was admirably stated by the British Prime Minister to the House of Commons in these words: "It is plain, therefore, that Germany claims to treat Poland as in the wrong because she had not by Wednesday night entered upon discussions with Germany about a set of proposals of which she had never heard. Let me elaborate this a little. You can make an offer of settlement for two entirely different purposes. You may make your offer genuinely and hoping to have it accepted or discussed with a view to avoiding war. On the other hand, you may make it hoping to use it as "window dressing" and with no intention or desire to have it accepted. If I were to make an offer to my neighbor about a piece of land in dispute between us and, before he had had the faintest opportunity of dealing with my offer, I violently assaulted him, my offer would stand revealed as a fraud. If Germany had really desired a peaceful settlement of questions relating to Danzig and the Corridor she would have taken every step to see that her proposals were adequately considered by Poland and that there was proper opportunity for discussion. In other words, if Germany had wanted peace, does anybody believe that there would today be fighting on the Polish frontier, or that Europe would be plunged into war? Who wanted war? Poland? Great Britain? France?

I know that, in spite of the emotions we are all feeling, you will show that Australia is ready to see it through. May God in His mercy and compassion grant that the world may soon be delivered from this agony.

Fireside Chat on the war in Europe
Franklin D. Roosevelt, radio speech, 3 September 1939

Democrat leader Franklin Delano Roosevelt (1882–1945) was inaugurated US president in 1933. One of his methods of communicating with the population was by radio broadcasts, which he called "fireside chats." He used them to promote or defend policies, answer critics, or build up national morale.

This chat was broadcast a few hours after Great Britain and France declared war on Germany. Roosevelt stresses the neutrality of the United States, but provides implicit support for the Allies. He is also softening the audience for his 21 September proposal, which would successfully call on Congress to water down US neutrality laws to permit the selling of ready-made arms to Great Britain and France on a "lease-lend" basis. The United States was already supplying oil, raw materials, and other resources to Germany, the Soviet Union, Britain, France, and other countries gearing up for war.

...tonight my single duty is to speak to the whole of America.

Until 4.30 o'clock this morning I had hoped against hope that some miracle would prevent a devastating war in Europe and bring to an end the invasion of Poland by Germany.

For four long years a succession of actual wars and constant crises have shaken the entire world and have threatened in each case to bring on the gigantic conflict which is today unhappily a fact.

It is right that I should recall to your minds the consistent and at times successful efforts of your government in these crises to throw the full weight of the United States into the cause of peace. In spite of spreading wars I think that we have every right and every reason to maintain as a national policy the fundamental moralities, the teachings of religion, and the continuation of efforts to restore peace. Because some day, though the time may be distant, we can be of even greater help to a crippled humanity...

It is, of course, impossible to predict the future. I have my constant stream of information from American representatives and other sources throughout the world. You, the people of this country, are receiving news through your radios and your newspapers at every hour of the day.

You are, I believe, the most enlightened and the best informed people in all the world at this moment. You are subjected to no censorship of news, and I want to add that your government has no information which it withholds or which it has any thought of withholding from you.

President Roosevelt addresses the American people on radio, advocating neutrality in the face of the war in Europe, in September 1939.

At the same time...it is of the highest importance that the press and the radio use the utmost caution to discriminate between actual verified fact on the one hand, and mere rumor on the other...

It is easy for you and for me to shrug our shoulders and to say that conflicts taking place thousands of miles from the continental United States, and, indeed, thousands of miles from the whole American hemisphere, do not seriously affect the Americas — and that all the United States has to do is to ignore them and go about its own business. Passionately though we may desire detachment, we are forced to realize that every word that comes through the air, every ship that sails the sea, every battle that is fought, does affect the American future. Let no man or woman thoughtlessly or falsely talk of America sending its armies to European fields. At this moment there is being prepared a proclamation of American neutrality. This...proclamation is in accordance with international law and in accordance with American policy.

This will be followed by a proclamation required by the existing *Neutrality Act*. And I trust that in the days to come our neutrality can be made a true neutrality...

I myself cannot and do not prophesy the course of events abroad and the reason is that, because I have of necessity such a complete picture of what is going on in every part of the world, I do not dare to do so. And the other reason is that I think it is honest for me to be honest with the people of the United States.

I cannot prophesy the immediate economic effect of this new war on our nation, but I do say that no American has the moral right to profiteer at the expense either of his fellow citizens or of the men, the women and the children who are living and dying in the midst of war in Europe...

We have certain ideas and certain ideals of national safety, and we must act to preserve that safety today, and to preserve the safety of our children in future years.

That safety is and will be bound up with the safety of the Western Hemisphere and of the seas adjacent thereto. We seek to keep war from our own firesides by keeping war from coming to the Americas. For that we have historic precedent that goes back to the days of the administration of President George Washington. It is serious enough and tragic enough to every American family in every State in the Union to live in a world that is torn by wars on other continents. Those wars today affect every American home. It is our national duty to use every effort to keep those wars out of the Americas...

This nation will remain a neutral nation, but I cannot ask that every American remain neutral in thought as well. Even a neutral has a right to take account of facts. Even a neutral cannot be asked to close his mind or his conscience.

I have said not once, but many times, that I have seen war and that I hate war. I say that again and again.

I hope the United States will keep out of this war. I believe that it will. And I give you assurance and reassurance that every effort of your government will be directed towards that end.

As long as it remains within my power to prevent, there will be no black-out of peace in the United States.

Radio address to the German People
Neville Chamberlain, London, 4 September 1939

This speech was delivered when Chamberlain realized how spectacularly wrong was his statement that the 1938 Munich Agreement with Hitler meant "peace for our time." History has, by and large, judged Chamberlain as an "appeaser," who failed to observe Hitler's massive military build-up, and missed the opportunity to make a preemptive strike before Germany became too powerful. But Britain was far from alone in its lack of response to the growing German threat. In June 1941, after the German invasion of Russia, Winston Churchill referred to "the terrible military machine, which we and the rest of the civilized world so foolishly, so supinely, so insensately allowed the Nazi gangsters to build up."

Since the Munich Agreement, Britain had undergone a steep increase in military production, and introduced military conscription. Many historians believe that Chamberlain was quite aware of Hitler's aims, but was advised by his military chiefs that Britain would be at a severe disadvantage if it fought Germany over Czechoslovakia. Chamberlain's actions at Munich, rather than being a weak and uninformed concession, may have been a calculated tactic to buy Britain time so it could attain military parity or superiority.

Chamberlain resigned as prime minister in 1940, just before the evacuation of Allied troops at Dunkirk, and was succeeded by Winston Churchill. He died a month later.

> German people, your country and mine are at war. Your government has bombed and invaded the free and independent state of Poland, which this country is in honor bound to defend...God knows this country has done everything possible to prevent this calamity. But now that the invasion of Poland by Germany has taken place, it has become inevitable.
>
> You were told by your government that you are fighting because Poland rejected your leader's offer and resorted to force. What are the facts? The so-called "offer" was made to the Polish ambassador on Thursday evening, two hours before the announcement by your government that it had been "rejected." So far from having been rejected, there had been no time even to consider it. Your government had previously demanded that a Polish representative should be sent to Berlin within twenty-four hours to conclude an agreement. The Polish representative was expected to arrive within a fixed time to sign an agreement which he had not even seen. This

Prime Minister Chamberlain (left) with Alec Douglas-Home, at the time Chamberlain's parliamentary private secretary, outside 10 Downing Street on the day war was declared.

is not negotiation. This is a dictate. To such methods no self-respecting and powerful state could assent. Negotiations on a free and equal basis might well have settled the matter in dispute.

You may ask why Great Britain is concerned. We are concerned because we gave our word of honor to defend Poland against aggression. Why did we feel it necessary to pledge ourselves to defend this eastern power when our interests lie in the west? The answer is — and I regret to have to say it — that nobody in this country any longer places any trust in your leader's word.

He gave his word that he would respect the Locarno Treaty; he broke it. He gave his word that he neither wished nor intended to annex Austria; he broke it. He declared that he would not incorporate the Czechs in the Reich; he did so. He gave his word after Munich that he had no further territorial demands in Europe; he broke it. He has sworn for years that he was the mortal enemy of bolshevism; he is now its ally.

Can you wonder his word is, for us, not worth the paper it is written on?

The German–Soviet Pact was a cynical *volte-face*, designed to shatter the Peace Front against aggression. This gamble failed. The Peace Front stands firm. Your leader is now sacrificing you, the German people, to the still more monstrous gamble of a war to extricate himself from the impossible position into which he has led himself and you.

In this war we are not fighting against you, the German people, for whom we have no bitter feeling, but against a tyrannous and forsworn regime which has betrayed not only its own people but the whole of western civilisation and all that you and we hold dear.

May God defend the right!

The Non-Aggression Pact
Adolf Hitler, Reichstag, Berlin, 6 October 1939

This speech was made five weeks after the German invasion of Poland led to the onset of World War II. Hitler's main aim is to justify the Non-Aggression Pact Germany had signed with Russia on 23 August, after he had expended a great deal of energy over the previous twenty years vilifying communism and the Soviet people. He wanted to avoid the possibility of the Soviets allying with other European powers, should they come to Poland's defence. Stalin was already hoping for a long, wide-ranging European war that would weaken all sides to the extent that a neutral Soviet Union would be well placed to feast on the morsels once the dust had settled.

Hitler, with a long history of such subterfuges, was already planning to break the pact by invading the Soviet Union when the time was right. He intended to use the land as Germany's *Lebensraum* ("living room"), and did not expect the Soviet *Untermenschen* ("subhumans") to put up much resistance.

As well as provisions for non-aggression, the treaty included a secret agreement to divide Finland, Latvia, Lithuania, Estonia, Poland, and Romania into spheres of Nazi and Soviet influence. All were later invaded, occupied, or forced to yield territory by the Soviet Union, Germany, or both.

The pact lasted until 22 June 1941, when Germany invaded Russia.

As usual for Hitler, the scenario reflected in the speech is the exact opposite of the actual situation. Note the lack of irony in his references to "my conciliatory proposals" and the "appalling atrocities committed against German nationals in Poland."

...Villages with hundreds of German inhabitants are now left without men because they all have been killed. In others women were violated and murdered, girls and children outraged and killed. In 1598 an Englishman — Sir George Carew — wrote in his diplomatic reports to the English government that the outstanding features of Polish character were cruelty and lack of moral restraint.

Since that time this cruelty has not changed. Just as tens of thousands of Germans were slaughtered and sadistically tormented to death, so German soldiers captured in fighting were tortured and massacred.

This pet lapdog of the Western democracies cannot be considered a cultured nation at all...

To grant guarantees to this state and this government as was done could only lead to appalling disasters. Neither the Polish government, nor the small cliques supporting it, nor the Polish nation as such were capable of measuring the responsibilities which were implied in such guarantees in Poland's favor by half of Europe.

The passionate sentiment thus aroused, together with the sense of that security which had been unconditionally guaranteed to them, counted for the behavior of the Polish government...between April and August...

It was also the cause of the attitude they adopted towards my conciliatory proposals. The government rejected these proposals because they felt themselves protected, or even encouraged, by public opinion and public opinion protected them and encouraged them on their way because it had been left in ignorance by its government and particularly because in its every action it felt itself sufficiently protected from without.

All this led to an increase in the number of appalling atrocities committed against German nationals in Poland and to the rejection of all proposals for a solution and in the end to the steadily growing encroachments on actual Reich territory. It was quite comprehensible that such a state of mind interpreted German longsuffering as a weakness, that is, that every concession on Germany's part was regarded as proof of the possibility of some further aggressive steps...

The warning to suspend or at least to take steps against the unceasing cases of murder, ill treatment, and torture of German nationals in Poland had the effect of increasing these atrocities and of calling for more bloodthirsty harangues and provocative speeches from the Polish local administrative officials and military authorities.

The German proposals aiming at a last-minute agreement on a just and equitable basis were answered by a general mobilisation. The German request that an intermediary should be sent, founded on a proposal made by Great Britain, was not complied with and on the second day was answered by an offensive declaration...

Since they believed that this patience and longsuffering was a sign of weakness which would allow them to do anything, no other course remained than to show them their mistake by striking back with the weapons which they themselves had used for years.

Under these blows their state has crumbled to pieces in a few weeks and is now swept from the earth. One of the most senseless deeds perpetrated at Versailles is thus a thing of the past.

If this step on Germany's part has resulted in a community of interests with Russia, that is due not only to the similarity of the problems affecting the two states, but also to that of the conclusions which both states had arrived at with regard to their future relationship.

In my speech at Danzig I already declared that Russia was organized on principles which differ from those held in Germany. However, since it became clear that Stalin found nothing in the Russian–Soviet principles which should prevent him from cultivating friendly relations with states of a different political creed, National Socialist Germany sees no reason why she should adopt another criterion. The Soviet Union is the Soviet Union, National Socialist Germany is National Socialist Germany.

But one thing is certain: from the moment when the two states mutually agreed to respect each other's distinctive regime and principles, every reason for any mutually hostile attitude had disappeared. Long periods in the history of both nations have shown that the inhabitants of these two largest states in Europe were never happier than when they lived in friendship with each other. The Great War, which once made Germany and Russia enemies, was disastrous for both countries...

Months ago I stated in the Reichstag that the conclusion of the German–Russian non-aggression pact marked the turning point in the

Hitler at a rally in Dortmund, Germany, in the 1930s.

ADOLF HITLER

Hitler has achieved a gruesome kind of life after death, and has proven very useful to subsequent world leaders who regularly invoke his name in comparison with their enemy. Ho Chi Minh, Saddam Hussein, and Osama bin Laden are among many who have been compared to Hitler.

"Through clever and constant application of propaganda, people can be made to see paradise as hell, and also the other way round, to consider the most wretched sort of life as paradise."
Hitler reveals a trade secret in his autobiography, *Mein Kampf* (1926).

"The war against Russia will be such that it cannot be conducted in a knightly fashion. This struggle is one of ideologies and racial differences and will have to be conducted with unprecedented, unmerciful, and unrelenting harshness."
Hitler, in March 1941, to a conference of senior army officers, while he was still publicly denying his well advanced plans for the 22 June invasion of Russia

"Anyone who sees and paints a sky green and fields blue ought to be sterilised."
Hitler revealing his attitude to "degenerate" art forms — in this case, Impressionism. Although his wide-ranging "degenerate" list included anything composed by a Russian or a Jew, he gained inspiration by secretly listening to the works of Russian composer Dmitri Shostakovich, among others.

whole German foreign policy. The new pact of friendship and mutual interest since signed between Germany and the Soviet Union will ensure not only peace but a constant satisfactory cooperation for both states.

Germany and Russia together will relieve one of the most acute danger spots in Europe of its threatening character and will, each in her own sphere, contribute to the welfare of the peoples living there, thus aiding European peace in general. If certain circles today see in this pact either the breakdown of Russia or Germany — as suits them best — I should like to give them my answer.

For many years imaginary aims were attributed to Germany's foreign policy which at best might be taken to have arisen in the mind of a schoolboy.

At a moment when Germany is struggling to consolidate her own living space, which only consists of a few hundred thousand square kilometers, insolent journalists in countries which rule over forty million square kilometers state Germany is aspiring to world domination!

German–Russian agreements should prove immensely comforting to these worried sponsors of universal liberty, for do they not show most emphatically that their assertions as to Germany's aiming at the domination of the Urals, the Ukraine, Rumania, etc, are only excrescences of their own unhealthy war-lord fantasy?

In one respect it is true Germany's decision is irrevocable, namely in her intention to see peaceful, stable, and thus tolerable conditions introduced on her eastern frontiers; also it is precisely here that Germany's interests and desires correspond entirely with those of the Soviet Union. The two states are resolved to prevent problematic conditions arising between them which contain germs of internal unrest and thus also of external disorder and which might perhaps in any way unfavorably affect the relationship of these two great states with one another.

Germany and the Soviet Union have therefore clearly defined the boundaries of their own spheres of interest with the intention of being singly responsible for law and order and preventing everything which might cause injury to the other partner...

It is therefore essential for a far-sighted ordering of the life of Europe that a resettlement should be undertaken here so as to remove at least part of the material for European conflict. Germany and the Union of Soviet Republics have come to an agreement to support each other in this matter.

The German government will, therefore, never allow the residual Polish state of the future to become in any sense a disturbing factor for

WONDER HOW LONG THE HONEYMOON WILL LAST?

A cartoonist lampoons the Non-Aggression Pact between Germany and Russia.

the Reich itself and still less a source of disturbance between the German Reich and Soviet Russia.

As Germany and Soviet Russia undertake this work of re-establishment, the two states are entitled to point out that the attempt to solve this problem by the methods of Versailles has proved an utter failure. In fact it had to fail because these tasks cannot be settled sitting around a table or by simple decrees. Most of the statesmen who in Versailles had to decide on these complicated problems did not possess the slightest historical training, indeed they often had not even the vaguest idea of the nature of the task with which they were faced.

"I have nothing to offer but blood, toil, tears, and sweat."
Winston Churchill, House of Commons, London, 13 May 1940

British prime minister Winston Churchill overcame stammering and a lisp to become a brilliant and inspiring orator. Fond of using various literary and poetic devices to leaven his words, he often spent weeks preparing and rewriting his speeches, and practiced them at length, often in front of a mirror. Since his election into the House of Commons in 1901, he had made numerous extravagant speeches, which were often regarded as having more style than substance. But in the desperate situation confronting Britain early in World War II, Churchill's gifts found an environment in which they could prosper, and he became an inspirational leader, able to unite and rally the population in dire circumstances.

This speech was made three days after Winston Churchill took over from Neville Chamberlain as British prime minister, a position he held until 1945, and again from 1951 until his retirement in 1955.

France was about to surrender to the apparently all-powerful Germany, and the Battle of Britain was about to start. Churchill's main aim in the speech was to boost the morale of the British populace in its "...war against a monstrous tyranny, never surpassed in the dark, lamentable catalogue of human crime." He sets out his plans for Britain for the remainder of the war, using alliteration and repetition to emphasize the size and duration of the task ahead. At the time Churchill said privately to General Ismay, chief of his personal staff at the Ministry of Defence: "Poor people, poor people. They trust me, and I can give them nothing but disaster for quite a long time."

One line of the speech is often misquoted as: "I have nothing to offer but blood, sweat, and tears..."

On Friday evening last I received His Majesty's commission to form a new administration. It is the evident wish and will of parliament and the nation that this should be conceived on the broadest possible basis and that it should include all parties, both those who supported the late government and also the parties of the Opposition. I have completed the most important part of this task. A war cabinet has been formed of five members, representing, with the Opposition Liberals, the unity of the nation. The three party leaders have agreed to serve, either in the

War Cabinet or in high executive office. The three fighting services have been filled. It was necessary that this should be done in one single day, on account of the extreme urgency and rigor of events. A number of other positions, key positions, were filled yesterday, and I am submitting a further list to His Majesty tonight. I hope to complete the appointment of the principal ministers during tomorrow. The appointment of the other ministers usually takes a little longer, but I trust that, when parliament meets again, this part of my task will be completed, and that the administration will be complete in all respects...

To form an administration of this scale and complexity is a serious undertaking in itself, but it must be remembered that we are in the preliminary stage of one of the greatest battles in history, that we are in action at many other points in Norway and in Holland, that we have to be prepared in the Mediterranean, that the air battle is continuous and that many preparations have to be made here at home. In this crisis I hope I may be pardoned if I do not address the House at any length today. I hope that any of my friends and colleagues, or former colleagues, who are affected by the political reconstruction, will make allowance, all allowance, for any lack of ceremony with which it has been necessary to act. I would say to the House, as I said to those who have joined this government: "I have nothing to offer but blood, toil, tears, and sweat."

We have before us an ordeal of the most grievous kind. We have before us many, many long months of struggle and of suffering. You ask, what is our policy? I can say: it is to wage war, by sea, land, and air, with all our might and with all the strength that God can give us; to wage war against a monstrous tyranny, never surpassed in the dark, lamentable catalogue of human crime. That is our policy. You ask, what is our aim? I can answer in one word: it is victory, victory at all costs, victory in spite of all terror, victory, however long and hard the road may be; for without victory, there is no survival. Let that be realized; no survival for the British Empire, no survival for all that the British Empire has stood for, no survival for the urge and impulse of the ages, that mankind will move forward towards its goal. But I take up my task with buoyancy and hope. I feel sure that our cause will not be suffered to fail among men. At this time I feel entitled to claim the aid of all, and I say, "Come then, let us go forward together with our united strength."

Churchill arriving at Westminister Abbey for a Day of National Prayer service, 26 May 1940. His personal image was always supported by accessories such as a silk top hat and, often, a cigar.

"...we shall never surrender..."
Winston Churchill, House of Commons, London, 4 June, 1940

This is one of Churchill's most famous speeches, made in the House of Commons just after the successful evacuation of 338 000 Allied troops from Dunkerque (Dunkirk), France, to England, and in the face of a possible impending German invasion of Britain.

The *Blitzkrieg* of the German forces was carrying all before it, by now occupying most of Europe, including — most worryingly for Britain — France, Belgium and Holland, just across the English Channel. The secret withdrawal from Dunkirk was ultimately successful, despite some 30 000 Allied casualties. The prime minister's inspiring speech boosted the morale of the British populace, and made a powerful plea for assistance from the still neutral United States.

...From the moment when the defences at Sedan on the Meuse were broken at the end of the second week of May, only a rapid retreat to Amiens and the south could have saved the British and French armies who had entered Belgium at the appeal of the Belgian King.

This strategic fact was not immediately realized. The French High Command hoped it would be able to close the gap. The armies of the north were under their orders. Moreover, a retirement of that kind would have involved almost certainly the destruction of a fine Belgian Army of twenty divisions and abandonment of the whole of Belgium.

Therefore, when the force and scope of the German penetration was realized and when the new French Generalissimo, General Weygand, assumed command in place of General Gamelin, an effort was made by the French and British armies in Belgium to keep holding the right hand of the Belgians and give their own right hand to the newly created French Army which was to advance across the Somme in great strength.

However, the German eruption swept like a sharp scythe south of Amiens to the rear of the armies in the north — eight or nine armored divisions, each with about 400 armored vehicles of different kinds divisible into small self-contained units. This force cut off all communications between us and the main French Army. It severed our communications for food and ammunition. It ran first through Amiens, afterwards through Abbeville, and along the coast to Boulogne and Calais, almost to Dunkerque.

Behind this armored and mechanized onslaught came a number of German divisions in lorries, and behind them, again, plodded comparatively slowly the dull, brute mass of the ordinary German Army and German people, always ready to be led to the trampling down in other lands of liberties and comforts they never have known in their own...

When a week ago today I asked the House to fix this afternoon for the occasion of a statement, I feared it would be my hard lot to announce from this box the greatest military disaster of our long history...

I asked the House a week ago to suspend its judgment because the facts were not clear. I do not think there is now any reason why we should not form our own opinions upon this pitiful episode. The surrender of the Belgian Army compelled the British Army at the shortest notice to cover a flank to the sea of more than thirty miles' length which otherwise would have been cut off.

In doing this and closing this flank, contact was lost inevitably between the British and two of three corps forming the First French Army who were then further from the coast than we were. It seemed impossible that large numbers of Allied troops could reach the coast. The enemy attacked on all sides in great strength and fierceness, and their main power, air force, was thrown into the battle.

The enemy began to fire cannon along the beaches by which alone shipping could approach or depart. They sowed magnetic mines in the channels and seas and sent repeated waves of hostile aircraft, sometimes more than one hundred strong, to cast bombs on a single pier that remained and on the sand dunes.

Their U-boats, one of which was sunk, and motor launches took their toll of the vast traffic which now began. For four or five days the intense struggle raged. All armored divisions, or what was left of them, together with great masses of German infantry and artillery, hurled themselves on the ever narrowing and contracting appendix within which the British and French armies fought.

Meanwhile the Royal Navy, with the willing help of countless merchant seamen and a host of volunteers, strained every nerve and every effort and every craft to embark the British and Allied troops.

Over 220 light warships and more than 650 other vessels were engaged. They had to approach this difficult coast, often in adverse weather, under an almost ceaseless hail of bombs and increasing concentration of artillery fire. Nor were the seas themselves free from mines and torpedoes...

Hospital ships, which were plainly marked, were the special target for Nazi bombs, but the men and women aboard them never faltered in their duty.

Meanwhile the RAF, who already had been intervening in the battle so far as its range would allow it to go from home bases, now used a part of its main metropolitan fighter strength to strike at German bombers.

The struggle was protracted and fierce. Suddenly the scene has cleared. The crash and thunder has momentarily, but only for the moment, died away. The miracle of deliverance achieved by the valor and perseverance, perfect discipline, faultless service, skill, and unconquerable vitality is a manifesto to us all.

The enemy was hurled back by the British and French troops. He was so roughly handled that he dare not molest their departure seriously. The air force decisively defeated the main strength of the German Air Force and inflicted on them a loss of at least four to one...

How long it will be, how long it will last depends upon the exertions which we make on this island. An effort, the like of which has never been seen in our records, is now being made. Work is proceeding night and day. Sundays and weekdays. Capital and labor have cast aside their interests, rights, and customs and put everything into the common stock. Already the flow of munitions has leaped forward. There is no reason why we should not in a few months overtake the sudden and serious loss that has come upon us without retarding the development of our general program...

The French Army has been weakened, the Belgian Army has been lost, and a large part of those fortified lines upon which so much faith was reposed has gone, and many valuable mining districts and factories have passed into the enemy's possession.

The whole of the Channel ports are in his hands, with all the strategic consequences that follow from that, and we must expect another blow to be struck almost immediately at us or at France.

We were told that Hitler has plans for invading the British Isles. This has often been thought of before. When Napoleon lay at Boulogne for a year with his flat-bottomed boats and his Grand Army, someone told him there were bitter weeds in England. There certainly were and a good many more of them have since been returned. The whole question of defence against invasion is powerfully affected by the fact that we have for the time being in this island incomparably more military forces than we had in the last war. But this will not continue. We shall not be content with a defensive war. We have our duty to our Allies...

WINSTON CHURCHILL

"I cannot forecast to you the action of Russia. It is a riddle wrapped in a mystery inside an enigma..."
In a speech broadcast in October 1939

"If Hitler were to invade hell, I should find occasion to make a favourable reference to the Devil in the House of Commons."
Fervent anti-Communist and Stalin-hater Churchill explains why Britain will support the Soviet Union after the German invasion of June 1941.

"...You have committed every crime under the sun. Where you have been the least resisted there you have been the most brutal. It was you who began the indiscriminate bombing. We will have no truce or parley with you, or the grisly gang who work your wicked will. You do your worst — and we will do our best."
Churchill addresses Adolf Hitler in a speech to the London County Council on 14 July 1941.

"I hate nobody except Hitler — and that is professional."
Churchill to John Colville during World War II, quoted by Colville in his book *The Churchillians* (1981)

"You were given the choice between war and dishonour. You chose dishonour and you will have war."
Churchill on Neville Chamberlain and his appeasement policy, World War II

"Never give in — never, never, never, never...never give in except to convictions of honour and good sense."
In a speech given at Harrow School on 29 October 1941

Turning once again, and this time more generally, to the question of invasion, I would observe that there has never been a period in all these long centuries of which we boast when an absolute guarantee against invasion, still less against serious raids, could have been given to our people. In the days of Napoleon the same wind which would have carried his transports across the Channel might have driven away the blockading fleet. There was always the chance, and it is that chance which has excited and befooled the imaginations of many continental tyrants. Many are the tales that are told. We are assured that novel methods will be adopted, and when we see the originality of malice, the ingenuity of aggression, which our enemy displays, we may certainly prepare ourselves for every kind of novel stratagem and every kind of brutal and treacherous manoeuvre. I think that no idea is so outlandish that it should not be considered and viewed with a searching, but at the same time, I hope, with a steady eye. We must never forget the solid assurances of sea power and those which belong to air power if it can be locally exercised.

I have, myself, full confidence that if all do their duty, if nothing is neglected, and if the best arrangements are made, as they are being made, we shall prove ourselves once again able to defend our island home, to ride out the storm of war, and to outlive the menace of tyranny, if necessary for years, if necessary alone. At any rate, that is what we are going to try to do...

Even though large tracts of Europe and many old and famous states have fallen or may fall into the grip of the Gestapo and all the odious apparatus of Nazi rule, we shall not flag or fail. We shall go on to the end, we shall fight in France, we shall fight on the seas and oceans, we shall fight with growing confidence and growing strength in the air, we shall defend our island, whatever the cost may be, we shall fight on the beaches, we shall fight on the landing grounds, we shall fight in the fields and in the streets, we shall fight in the hills; we shall never surrender, and even if, which I do not for a moment believe, this island or a large part of it were subjugated and starving, then our Empire beyond the seas, armed and guarded by the British Fleet, would carry on the struggle, until, in God's good time, the New World, with all its power and might, steps forth to the rescue and the liberation of the old.

"This was their finest hour"
Winston Churchill, House of Commons, London, 18 June 1940

This speech was made a week after the French surrender to Germany — which now occupied the whole of Europe — and as Britain continued to face the very real prospect of invasion. Churchill correctly predicts that the German attack would be primarily from the air, and that the Royal Air Force (RAF) would "have the glory of saving their native land."

The Germans greatly underestimated the strength of the RAF, losing more than 1600 aeroplanes to Britain's 1087 during the four-month battle. British pilot deaths numbered 446; the Germans' perhaps twice as many. After failing to win the air war, in September Adolf Hitler ordered an all-out bombing attack on non-military targets, including London and other cities, in a misguided attempt to demoralize the population into surrender. Meanwhile, grateful for the unexpected breathing space, the British were building new aircraft and munitions at double the German rate.

Later, after Britain's successful repulsion of the German attack, Churchill would say of the RAF: "Never in the field of human conflict was so much owed by so many to so few."

...During the great battle in France, we gave very powerful and continuous aid to the French Army, both by fighters and bombers; but in spite of every kind of pressure we never would allow the entire metropolitan fighter strength of the Air Force to be consumed. This decision was painful, but it was also right, because the fortunes of the battle in France could not have been decisively affected even if we had thrown in our entire fighter force. That battle was lost by the unfortunate strategical opening, by the extraordinary and unforeseen power of the armored columns, and by the great preponderance of the German Army in numbers. Our fighter Air Force might easily have been exhausted as a mere accident in that great struggle, and then we should have found ourselves at the present time in a very serious plight. But as it is, I am happy to inform the House that our fighter strength is stronger at the present time relative to the Germans, who have suffered terrible losses, than it has ever been; and consequently we believe ourselves possessed of the capacity to continue the war in the air under better conditions than we have ever experienced before. I look forward confidently to the exploits of our fighter pilots,

these splendid men, this brilliant youth, who will have the glory of saving their native land, their island home and all they love, from the most deadly of all attacks.

...We do not yet know what will happen in France or whether the French resistance will be prolonged, both in France and in the French Empire overseas. The French government will be throwing away great opportunities and casting adrift their future if they do not continue the war in accordance with their treaty obligations, from which we have not felt able to release them. The House will have read the historic declaration in which, at the desire of many Frenchmen, and of our own hearts, we have proclaimed our willingness at the darkest hour in French history to conclude a union of common citizenship in this struggle. However matters may go in France or with the French government, or other French governments, we in this island and in the British Empire will never lose our sense of comradeship with the French people. If we are now called upon to endure what they have been suffering, we shall emulate their courage, and if final victory rewards our toils they shall share the gains, aye, and freedom shall be restored to all. We abate nothing of our just demands; not one jot or title do we recede. Czechs, Poles, Norwegians, Dutch, Belgians have joined their causes to our own. All these shall be restored.

What General Weygand called the Battle of France is over. I expect that the Battle of Britain is about to begin. Upon this battle depends the survival of Christian civilisation. Upon it depends our own British life and the long continuity of our institutions and our Empire. The whole fury and might of the enemy must very soon be turned on us now. Hitler knows that he will have to break us in this island or lose the war. If we can stand up to him, all Europe may be free and the life of the world may move forward into broad, sunlit uplands. But if we fail, then the whole world, including the United States, including all that we have known and cared for, will sink into the abyss of a new Dark Age, made more sinister, and perhaps more protracted, by the lights of perverted science. Let us therefore brace ourselves to our duties, and so bear ourselves that, if the British Empire and its Commonwealth last for a thousand years, men will still say, "This was their finest hour."

While inspecting coastal defences in the north-east of England, Churchill listens to a soldier explain how a Tommy gun works.

"We are merely interested in safeguarding peace"
Adolf Hitler, Reichstag, Berlin, 4 May 1941

As World War II approached, Hitler's use of the word "peace" became more and more a staple of his speeches. In the 1920s and early '30s he occasionally used the word to reproach his perceived enemies, but after 1936 it became an ever increasingly used mantra, a repetitive cloak to deceive, and conceal, his decidedly unpeaceful plans.

At the time of this speech, German troops already occupied Denmark, Norway, Poland, and most of Finland. Within two weeks they had invaded France, Belgium, Luxembourg, and the Netherlands, all of which surrendered within a matter of weeks.

Here Hitler masquerades as a humanitarian peace-lover in the face of fanatical, ignorant, and hostile opponents, and, as always, "the great international Jewish financial interests that control the banks...as well as the armament industry." Ironically, he points to Winston Churchill as "...proof of that perpetual blindness with which the gods afflict those whom they are about to destroy..."

Right idea; wrong person.

Deputies. Men of the German Reichstag:

At a time when only deeds count and words are of little importance, it is not my intention to appear before you, the elected representatives of the German people, more often than absolutely necessary. The first time I spoke to you was at the outbreak of the war when, thanks to the Anglo-French conspiracy against peace, every attempt at an understanding with Poland, which otherwise would have been possible, had been frustrated.

The most unscrupulous men of the present time had, as they admit today, decided as early as 1936 to involve the Reich, which in its peaceful work of reconstruction was becoming too powerful for them, in a new and bloody war and, if possible, to destroy it. They had finally succeeded in finding a state that was prepared for their interests and aims, and that state was Poland.

All my endeavors to come to an understanding with Britain were wrecked by the determination of a small clique which, whether from motives of hate or for the sake of material gain, rejected every German proposal for an understanding due to their resolve, which they never concealed, to resort to war, whatever happened.

The man behind this fanatical and diabolical plan to bring about war at whatever cost was Mr Churchill. His associates were the men who now form the British government.

These endeavors received most powerful support, both openly and secretly, from the so-called great democracies on both sides of the Atlantic. At a time when the people were more and more dissatisfied with their deficient statesmanship, the responsible men over there believed that a successful war would be the most likely means of solving problems that otherwise would be beyond their power to solve.

When delivering a speech, Hitler could work himself up into an almost apoplectic frenzy.

Behind these men there stood the great international Jewish financial interests that control the banks and the Stock Exchange as well as the armament industry. And now, just as before, they scented the opportunity of doing their unsavory business. And so, just as before, there was no scruple about sacrificing the blood of the peoples. That was the beginning of this war. A few weeks later the state that was the third country in Europe, Poland, but had been reckless enough to allow herself to be used for the financial interests of these warmongers, was annihilated and destroyed.

In these circumstances I considered that I owed it to our German people and countless men and women in the opposite camps...to make yet another appeal to the commonsense and the conscience of these statesmen. On October 6, 1939, I therefore once more publicly stated that Germany had neither demanded nor intended to demand anything either from Britain or from France, that it was madness to continue the war and, above all, that the scourge of modern weapons of warfare, once they were brought into action, would inevitably ravage vast territories.

But just as the appeal I made on September 1, 1939, proved to be in vain, this renewed appeal met with indignant rejection. The British and their Jewish capitalist backers could find no other explanation for this appeal, which I had made on humanitarian grounds, than the assumption of weakness on the part of Germany.

They assured the people of Britain and France that Germany dreaded the clash to be expected in the spring of 1940 and was eager to make peace for fear of the annihilation that would then inevitably result.

...On July 19, 1940, I then convened the German Reichstag for the third time in order to render that great account which you all still remember. The meeting provided me with the opportunity of expressing the thanks of the nation to its soldiers in a form suited to the uniqueness of the event. Once again I seized the opportunity of urging the world to make peace. And what I foresaw and prophesied at that time happened. My offer of peace was misconstrued as a symptom of fear and cowardice.

The European and American warmongers succeeded once again in befogging the sound commonsense of the masses, who can never hope to profit from this war, by conjuring up false pictures of new hope. Thus, finally, under pressure of public opinion, as formed by their press, they once more managed to induce the nation to continue this struggle.

Even my warnings against night bombings of the civilian population, as advocated by Mr Churchill, were interpreted as a sign of German impotence. He, the most bloodthirsty or amateurish strategist that history has ever known, actually saw fit to believe that the reserve displayed for months by the German Air Force could be looked upon only as proof of their incapacity to fly by night.

...As a German and as a soldier I consider it unworthy ever to revile a fallen enemy. But it seems to me to be necessary to defend the truth from the wild exaggerations of a man who as a soldier is a bad politician and as a politician is an equally bad soldier.

Mr Churchill, who started this struggle, is endeavoring, as with regard to Norway or Dunkirk, to say something that sooner or later might perhaps be twisted around to resemble success. I do not consider that honorable but in his case it is understandable.

The gift Mr Churchill possesses is the gift to lie with a pious expression on his face and to distort the truth until finally glorious victories are made out of the most terrible defeats...Churchill, one of the most hopeless dabblers in strategy...who in any other country would be court-martialed, gained fresh admiration as prime minister, this cannot be construed as an expression of magnanimity such as was accorded by Roman senators to generals honorably defeated in battle. It is merely proof of that perpetual blindness with which the gods afflict those whom they are about to destroy.

...Apart from the modest correction of its frontiers, which were infringed as a result of the outcome of the World War, the Reich has no special territorial interests in these parts. As far as politics are concerned we are merely interested in safeguarding peace in this region, while in the realm of economics we wish to see an order that will allow the production of goods to be developed and the exchange of products to be resumed in the interests of all. It is, however, only in accordance with supreme justice if those interests are also taken into account that are founded upon ethnographical, historical, or economic conditions.

I can assure you that I look into the future with perfect tranquillity and great confidence. The German Reich and its allies represent power, military, economic and, above all, in moral respects, which is superior to any possible coalition in the world. The German armed forces will always do their part whenever it may be necessary. The confidence of the German people will always accompany their soldiers.

Reaction to the German invasion of Russia
Vyacheslav Molotov, radio broadcast, 22 June 1941

A week before the German invasion of Poland, on 23 August 1939, Hitler and Stalin, through their intermediaries, foreign ministers Joachim von Ribbentrop and Vyacheslav Molotov, signed a non-aggression pact. Stalin kept his part of the deal, but on 22 June 1941, over three million German and other Axis troops invaded Russia through Romania, Ukraine, and Finland. This was perhaps the most costly mistake in military history.

Why did Germany invade the Soviet Union?

Hitler believed the Soviets were *Untermenschen*, literally "underpeople," subhumans. The Battle of Britain and the German bombing blitz had left Britain almost defenceless, ripe for invasion. The British arsenal of aeroplanes, ships, and most other ordinance was very depleted; factories hadn't been able to churn them out fast enough to replace those used or destroyed. But Hitler was unaware of this, due largely to the fact that the British Secret Service had cracked the Enigma code used by the German command, secret police, and internal and external espionage agencies. This meant that Britain knew almost everything about German troop activity, plans, strategies, and military strength. Britain concealed their knowledge of this by transmitting a constant stream of true and false information in the form of "secure" communications between its agencies, on which the Germans believed they were clandestinely eavesdropping. (To feed only misinformation would have revealed that they had cracked the code.) Part of the misinformation was that Allied strength, particularly in hardware, was much greater than was the case. They leaked continual misinformation about the British "Third Army" — which did not actually exist!

So brilliantly and effectively did Britain operate this deception that Germany did not discover Enigma had been cracked until the war was over. The Service knew when and where German spies would arrive in Britain, and intercepted all of them. Several became double agents to avoid being executed, providing extremely valuable misinformation to their German "spymasters." Perhaps the most effective deception occurred before the D-Day invasion of France, when Germany was led to believe that the impending invasion was to be centered around the town of Dieppe, rather than Normandy, further to the south. The element of surprise gave the Allies such an advantage that an inexorable momentum was created, from which Germany never recovered.

German soldiers enter the Citadel, a historic building in Kiev, Russia, on 20 October 1941.

How happy must the Allied command have been when Hitler decided not to invade a vulnerable Britain, but instead do a literal and figurative about-turn and take on the USSR, a so-called ally of much greater strength? And what would have happened if Stalin and Hitler had been even slightly competent strategists rather than clinically paranoid megalomaniacs?

It was not as if Stalin had not been warned about Germany's invasion. Commanders at the front had been warning him for months about the enormous German troop build-up along the borders, but the Germans told Stalin that this was a tactic to divert attention from its imminent invasion of Britain. He preferred to believe this red herring, "rewarding" reliable informants who tried to tell him otherwise with demotion, exile, torture, or death.

Hitler had the same propensity to "shoot the messenger" when given news he didn't like, or advice he didn't want. Throughout the Russian campaign, Hitler ignored almost every piece of strategic advice from his commanders, generally reacting in similar savage fashion to threats to his megalomaniac world view — which included the belief that he was a brilliant strategist, and that those who disagreed with him must be either weak or treacherous, and lacking his courage, vision, and will. The word "retreat" was not in his vocabulary. As the German forces advanced, the Red Army made a series of successful strategic withdrawals until the Germans were hopelessly mired in a morass of death by starvation, freezing, and lack of military (or any other) supplies. Meanwhile, Hitler positioned troops just behind the front line; their sole duty was to kill anyone who hesitated or retreated, a tactic also used by Stalin.

Since 1936, Stalin, in his paranoia, had been purging the communist party and the Red Army of all who might be a threat to him — effectively the cream of his leaders, many of whom had been loyal (or at least unthreatening) allies for decades. By 1941 more than 30 000 soldiers had been culled. After show "trials," where the typical charge was plotting against Stalin, most of the accused were executed and some were sent to concentration camps, where they soon died.

Stalin believed that all the talk of a German invasion was part of a plot by Winston Churchill to start a war between Germany and Russia. At 5.30 am on 22 June, when he received news of the German declaration of war (hours after the invasion had started), he said nothing to the populace, apparently too stunned at falling into a trap essentially of his own making. Finally, at noon the same day, Molotov's stuttering, hesitant voice emerged from the radio.

Citizens of the Soviet Union, the Soviet government and its head, Comrade Stalin, have authorized me to make the following statement:

Today at 4 o'clock am, without any claims having been presented to the Soviet Union, without a declaration of war, German troops attacked our country, attacked our borders at many points and bombed from their airplanes our cities; Zhitomir, Kiev, Sevastopol, Kaunas, and some others, killing and wounding over 200 persons. There were also enemy air raids and artillery shelling from Rumanian and Finnish territory.

This unheard of attack upon our country is perfidy unparalleled in the history of civilized nations. The attack on our country was perpetrated despite the fact that a treaty of non-aggression had been signed between the USSR and Germany and that the Soviet government most faithfully abided by all provisions of this treaty.

The attack upon our country was perpetrated despite the fact that during the entire period of operation of this treaty, the German government could not find grounds for a single complaint against the USSR as regards observance of this treaty.

Entire responsibility for this predatory attack upon the Soviet Union falls fully and completely upon the German Fascist rulers.

At 5.30 am — that is, after the attack had already been perpetrated, Von der Schulenburg, the German Ambassador in Moscow, on behalf of his government made the statement to me as People's Commissar of Foreign Affairs to the effect that the German government had decided to launch war against the USSR in connection with the concentration of Red Army units near the eastern German frontier.

In reply to this I stated on behalf of the Soviet government that, until the very last moment, the German government had not presented any claims to the Soviet government, that Germany attacked the USSR despite the peaceable position of the Soviet Union, and that for this reason Fascist Germany is the aggressor.

On instruction of the government of the Soviet Union I also stated that at no point had our troops or our air force committed a violation of the frontier and therefore the statement made this morning by the Rumanian radio to the effect that Soviet aircraft allegedly had fired on Rumanian aerodromes is a sheer lie and provocation.

Likewise a lie and provocation is the whole declaration made today by Hitler, who is trying belatedly to concoct accusations charging the Soviet Union with failure to observe the Soviet–German pact.

Now that the attack on the Soviet Union has already been committed, the Soviet government has ordered our troops to repulse the predatory assault and to drive German troops from the territory of our country.

This war has been forced upon us, not by the German people, not by German workers, peasants, and intellectuals, whose sufferings we well understand, but by the clique of bloodthirsty Fascist rulers of Germany who have enslaved Frenchmen, Czechs, Poles, Serbians, Norway, Belgium, Denmark, Holland, Greece, and other nations.

The government of the Soviet Union expresses its unshakable confidence that our valiant army and navy and brave falcons of the Soviet Air Force will acquit themselves with honor in performing their duty to the fatherland and to the Soviet people, and will inflict a crushing blow upon the aggressor.

This is not the first time that our people have had to deal with an attack of an arrogant foe. At the time of Napoleon's invasion of Russia our people's reply was war for the fatherland, and Napoleon suffered defeat and met his doom.

It will be the same with Hitler, who in his arrogance has proclaimed a new crusade against our country. The Red Army and our whole people will again wage victorious war for the fatherland, for our country, for honor, for liberty.

The government of the Soviet Union expresses the firm conviction that the whole population of our country, all workers, peasants, and intellectuals, men and women, will conscientiously perform their duties and do their work. Our entire people must now stand solid and united as never before.

Each one of us must demand of himself and of others discipline, organisation and self-denial worthy of real Soviet patriots, in order to provide for all the needs of the Red Army, Navy, and Air Force, to insure victory over the enemy.

The government calls upon you, citizens of the Soviet Union, to rally still more closely around our glorious Bolshevist party, around our Soviet government, around our great leader and comrade, Stalin. Ours is a righteous cause. The enemy shall be defeated. Victory will be ours.

FAMOUS LAST WORDS

"I feel here that this time they have succeeded."
Leon Trotsky, Russian revolutionary, pointing at his heart
after being assassinated by an ice pick blow to the head
in Mexico City, 1940

"*Es Lebe Die Freiheit!* Long live freedom!"
Hans Scholl, anti-Hitler resistance leader, before his execution
for high treason, 1943

"My dear Melinée, my beloved little orphan, in a few hours I will no
longer be of this world. We are going to be executed today at 3. This
is happening to me like an accident in my life; I don't believe it, but
I nevertheless know that I will never see you again."
Missak Manouchian, leader of the
Parisian section of a communist
Resistance movement, in a letter
to his daughter before being
executed by a German firing
squad, 1944

"I have a terrific headache."
Franklin Delano Roosevelt,
US president, as he was
dying of a cerebral
haemorrhage, 1945

"Shoot me in the chest!"
Benito Mussolini (pictured),
Italian dictator, before his execution
by communist Italian partisans, 1945.
Afterwards, as proof of his death,
his body was hung upside down in
a Milan petrol station.

German invasion of Russia
Winston Churchill, radio broadcast, 9 pm, 22 June 1941

Many of Churchill's advisors and colleagues believed that Russia would succumb quickly after the German invasion, but he believed otherwise. He said: "I will bet you a monkey to a mousetrap that the Russians are still fighting, and fighting victoriously, two years from now." "Monkey" and "mousetrap" are gambling terms; Churchill was, in effect, offering odds of 500 to 1 that the Russians would be fighting triumphantly two years' hence.

He turned out to be right, of course, and the following spring, he comically mocked Hitler in a radio broadcast: "..Thus he drove the youth and manhood of the German nation forward into Russia. Then Hitler made his second grand blunder. He forgot about the winter. There is a winter, you know, in Russia. For a good many months the temperature is apt to fall very low. There is snow, there is frost and all that. Hitler forgot about this Russian winter. He must have been very loosely educated. We all heard about it at school. But he forgot it. I have never made such a bad mistake as that."

The following speech shows Churchill at his rhetorical best, proving that Hitler did not hold a monopoly on florid insults. He uses a glorious array of language, from high-blown to earthy and — unlike most of Hitler's utterances — he is neither boring nor repetitive. He explains why his long-standing and oft-stated hatred of communism must now take a back seat in the face of an even greater threat.

…At 4 o'clock this morning Hitler attacked and invaded Russia. All his usual formalities of perfidy were observed with scrupulous technique. A non-aggression treaty had been solemnly signed and was in force between the two countries. No complaint had been made by Germany of its non-fulfilment. Under its cloak of false confidence the German armies drew up in immense strength along a line which stretched from the White Sea to the Black Sea and their air fleets and armored divisions slowly and methodically took up their stations.

Then, suddenly, without declaration of war, without even an ultimatum, the German bombs rained down from the sky upon the Russian cities; the German troops violated the Russian frontiers and an hour later the German Ambassador, who till the night before was lavishing his assurances of friendship, almost of alliance, upon the Russians, called upon the Russian Foreign Minister to tell him that a state of war existed between Germany and Russia.

Thus was repeated on a far larger scale the same kind of outrage against every form of signed compact and international faith which we have witnessed in Norway, in Denmark, in Holland, in Belgium and which Hitler's accomplice and jackal, Mussolini, so faithfully imitated in the case of Greece.

All this was no surprise to me. In fact I gave clear and precise warnings to Stalin of what was coming. I gave him warnings, as I have given warnings to others before. I can only hope that these warnings did not fall unheeded.

All we know at present is that the Russian people are defending their native soil and that their leaders have called upon them to resist to the utmost.

Hitler is a monster of wickedness, insatiable in his lust for blood and plunder. Not content with having all Europe under his heel or else terrorized into various forms of abject submission, he must now carry his work of butchery and desolation among the vast multitudes of Russia and of Asia. The terrible military machine which we and the rest of the civilized world so foolishly, so supinely, so insensately allowed the Nazi gangsters to build up year by year from almost nothing — this machine cannot stand idle, lest it rust or fall to pieces. It must be in continual motion, grinding up human lives and trampling down the homes and the rights of hundreds of millions of men.

Moreover, it must be fed not only with flesh but with oil. So now this bloodthirsty guttersnipe must launch his mechanized armies upon new fields of slaughter, pillage, and devastation. Poor as are the Russian peasants, workmen, and soldiers, he must steal from them their daily bread. He must devour their harvests. He must rob them of the oil which drives their ploughs and thus produce a famine without example in human history.

And even the carnage and ruin which his victory, should he gain it — though he's not gained it yet — will bring upon the Russian people, will itself be only a stepping stone to the attempt to plunge four or five hundred millions who live in China and the 350 million who live in India into that bottomless pit of human degradation over which the diabolic emblem of the swastika flaunts itself.

It is not too much to say here this pleasant summer evening that the lives and happiness of a thousand million additional human beings are now menaced with brutal Nazi violence. That is enough to make us hold our breath.

But presently I shall show you something else that lies behind and something that touches very nearly the life of Britain and of the United States.

The Nazi regime is indistinguishable from the worst features of communism. It is devoid of all theme and principle except appetite and racial domination. It excels in all forms of human wickedness, in the efficiency of its cruelty and ferocious aggression. No one has been a more consistent opponent of communism than I have for the last twenty-five years. I will unsay no words that I've spoken about it. But all this fades away before the spectacle which is now unfolding...

He wishes to destroy the Russian power because he hopes that if he succeeds in this he will be able to bring back the main strength of his army and air force from the East and hurl it upon this island, which he knows he must conquer or suffer the penalty of his crimes.

His invasion of Russia is no more than a prelude to an attempted invasion of the British Isles. He hopes, no doubt, that all this may be accomplished before the winter comes and that he can overwhelm Great Britain before the fleets and air power of the United States will intervene. He hopes that he may once again repeat upon a greater scale than ever before that process of destroying his enemies one by one, by which he has so long thrived and prospered, and that then the scene will be clear for the final act, without which all his conquests would be in vain, namely, the subjugation of the Western Hemisphere to his will and to his system.

The Russian danger is therefore our danger and the danger of the United States just as the cause of any Russian fighting for his hearth and home is the cause of free men and free peoples in every quarter of the globe.

Let us learn the lessons already taught by such cruel experience. Let us redouble our exertions and strike with united strength while life and power remain.

7 DECEMBER 1941
WAR IN THE PACIFIC

On 7 December 1941, the Japanese air force attacked the US naval base at Pearl Harbor, Hawaii, killing 2403 Americans and destroying eight battleships. The US command had ignored several intelligence reports that a fleet of Japanese aircraft carriers was heading towards the islands.

Japan was marching south through Indo-China, already occupying Burma, Cambodia, Vietnam, and parts of China. It planned to continue through Thailand, Malaya, Singapore, and across the South Pacific, on the way to invading North America.

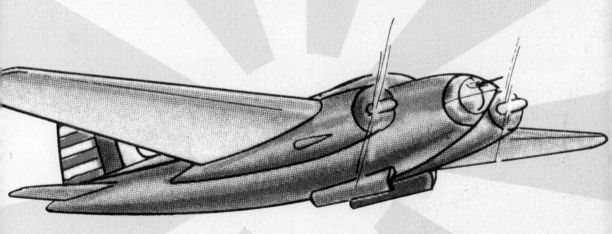

Declaration of war on Japan
Franklin D. Roosevelt, Address to Congress, 8 December 1941

President Roosevelt's speech to the US Congress, made the day after the attack on Pearl Harbor, was intended to evoke a stark emotional reaction, appealing to his people's fury over the Japanese attack and asking Congress to declare war on Japan. Roosevelt resolutely focused on the base ethical behavior and character of the Japanese government, and spoke of the "righteous might" of the American people. He avoided making an appeal to history (as Winston Churchill often did), preferring a shorter, punchier presentation.

The most famous line of the speech was originally "a date which will live in world history"; Roosevelt replaced "world history" with "infamy." This is quite a significant difference; it implies not just history, but the *judgment* of history in favor of America. It was intended as a statement on behalf of the entire American population in the face of their great communal distress. By expressing outrage at the "dastardly" nature of the Japanese strike, the speech was designed to focus the reaction of the nation into a collective response of determination and resolution to fight.

Roosevelt uses the passive voice in order to highlight America's "innocent victim" status: "...America was suddenly and deliberately attacked..." But he also uses the active voice, and repetition, to emphasize that he was reluctantly responding to a violent act that required a violent response. He also emphasizes his confidence in the strength of the American people, and reassures them that actions are being taken to guarantee their security.

Three days later, Germany and Italy declared war on the United States, and the European and South-East Asian wars blew up into a worldwide conflict, with the Axis — Japan, Germany, Italy, and others — facing the Allies — America, Russia, Australia, Britain, and others.

...Yesterday, December 7, 1941 — a date which will live in infamy — the United States of America was suddenly and deliberately attacked by naval and air forces of the Empire of Japan.

The United States was at peace with that nation, and, at the solicitation of Japan, was still in conversation with its government and its Emperor looking towards the maintenance of peace in the Pacific.

Indeed, one hour after Japanese air squadrons had commenced bombing in the American island of Oahu, the Japanese Ambassador to

The destroyer *Cassin* lies partly submerged, leaning against another destroyer, the *Downes*, after the surprise attack at Pearl Harbor.

the United States and his colleague delivered to our Secretary of State a formal reply to a recent American message. And, while this reply stated that it seemed useless to continue the existing diplomatic negotiations, it contained no threat or hint of war or of armed attack.

It will be recorded that the distance of Hawaii from Japan makes it obvious that the attack was deliberately planned many days or even weeks ago. During the intervening time the Japanese government has deliberately sought to deceive the United States by false statements and expressions of hope for continued peace.

The attack yesterday on the Hawaiian Islands has caused severe damage to American naval and military forces. I regret to tell you that very many American lives have been lost. In addition, American ships have been reported torpedoed on the high seas between San Francisco and Honolulu.

Yesterday the Japanese government also launched an attack against Malaya.

Last night Japanese forces attacked Hong Kong.

Last night Japanese forces attacked Guam.

Last night Japanese forces attacked the Philippine Islands.

Last night the Japanese attacked Wake Island.

And this morning the Japanese attacked Midway Island.

Japan has therefore undertaken a surprise offensive extending throughout the Pacific area. The facts of yesterday and today speak for themselves. The people of the United States have already formed their opinions and well understand the implications to the very life and safety of our nation.

As Commander-in-Chief of the Army and Navy I have directed that all measures be taken for our defence, that always will our whole nation remember the character of the onslaught against us.

No matter how long it may take us to overcome this premeditated invasion, the American people...will win through to absolute victory...

...our people, our territory, and our interests are in grave danger.

With confidence in our armed forces, with the unbounding determination of our people, we will gain the inevitable triumph. So help us God.

I ask that the Congress declare that since the unprovoked and dastardly attack by Japan on Sunday, December 7, 1941, a state of war has existed between the United States and the Japanese empire.

"The black of the night must pass"
John Curtin, radio speech to America, 14 March 1942, and radio speech to Britain, 17 April 1942

In October 1941, the Labor government, led by John Curtin, assumed office in Australia. It assessed Australia's home defences, and decided that they were close to non-existent. Most Australian troops were fighting the Germans and Italians in the Middle East, the Mediterranean and North Africa, or were scattered across the islands north of Australia. Its air force was mostly in England, serving alongside the Royal Air Force in the defence of Britain. Its navy was spread around the world, also serving British interests. The Australian government recognized the increasing danger of Japanese aggression and started to form volunteer militia contingents to defend the country.

The United States had joined the war the previous December, and by the time of these speeches, the Japanese occupied British Malaya (now Malaysia) and the Netherlands East Indies (Indonesia) and had their sights on Australia and the rest of the Pacific.

Obsessively committed to defeating Germany, to the exclusion of all other considerations, British prime minister Winston Churchill resisted the return of Australian troops from the Middle East to defend their country in the face of the rapid Japanese advance south. He had also made a secret pact with President Roosevelt to commit US forces to the defence of Britain, abandoning Asia and Australia to Japan (a plan which was later overturned on the advice of US military leaders).

On 26 December 1941, Curtin had said in a radio address: "...without any inhibitions of any kind, I make it quite clear that Australia looks to America, free of any pangs as to our traditional links or kinship with the United Kingdom." His comments caused an uproar; Churchill sent him an angry cable, while Roosevelt, believing that Australia was a British colony, considered the comments treacherous. (When it was later brought to his attention that Australia was actually an independent country, he came to respect Curtin's strong leadership.)

In a short-wave radio message, on 14 March 1942, Curtin addressed the people of the United States, urging them to unite with Australia against Japanese aggression. He reminded Americans of their own vulnerability, saying: "Australia is the last bastion between the west coast of America and the Japanese. If Australia goes, the Americas are wide open."

At the time, Australia's strongest economic and military links were still with Britain, rather than Asia and America. As such, Curtin's speech marks the beginning of a sea change in domestic foreign policy, initiating a closer relationship with the United States that continues to this day.

On 17 April he made a similar address to the British people. He asserts that Australia is still a staunch ally, beginning with "Fellow Britishers" and noting that: "Bone of your bone, the workers of Australia are kindred..."

14 MARCH 1942

Men and women of the United States:

I speak to you from Australia. I speak from a united people to a united people, and my speech is aimed to serve all the people of the nations united in the struggle to save mankind.

On the great waters of the Pacific Ocean war now breathes its bloody steam. From the skies of the Pacific pours down a deathly hail. In the countless islands of the Pacific the tide of war flows madly. For you in America; for us in Australia, it is flowing badly. Let me then address you as comrades in this war and tell you a little of Australia and Australians. I am not speaking to your government. We have long been admirers of Mr Roosevelt and have the greatest confidence that he understands fully the critical situation in the Pacific and that America will go right out to meet it. For all that America has done, both before and after entering the war, we have the greatest admiration and gratitude.

It is to the people of America I am now speaking; to you who are, or will be, fighting; to you who are sweating in factories and workshops to turn out the vital munitions of war; to all of you who are making sacrifices in one way or another to provide the enormous resources required for our great task. I speak to you at a time when the loss of Java and the splendid resistance of the gallant Dutch together give us a feeling of both sadness and pride. Japan has moved one step further in her speedy march south; but the fight of the Dutch and Indonese in Java has shown that a brave, freedom-loving people are more than a match for the yellow aggressor given even a shadow below equality in striking and fighting weapons.

But facts are stern things. We, the allied nations, were unready. Japan, behind her wall of secrecy, had prepared for war on a scale of which neither we nor you had knowledge. We have all made mistakes, we have all been too slow; we have all shown weakness — all the allied nations. This is not the time to wrangle about who has been most to blame. Now our eyes are open.

Widely admired as a strong wartime leader, Curtin died on 5 July 1945, only about six weeks before the Japanese surrender.

The Australian government has fought for its people. We never regarded the Pacific as a segment of the great struggle. We did not insist that it was the primary theater of war, but we did say, and events have so far, unhappily, proved us right, that the loss of the Pacific can be disastrous. Who among us, contemplating the future on that day in December last when Japan struck like an assassin at Pearl Harbor, at Manila, at Wake, and Guam, would have hazarded a guess that by March the enemy would be astride all the south-west Pacific except General MacArthur's gallant men, and Australia and New Zealand. But that is the case. And, realising very swiftly that it would be the case, the Australian government sought a full and proper recognition of the part the Pacific was playing in the general strategic disposition of the world's warring forces. It was, therefore, but natural that, within twenty days after Japan's first treacherous blow, I said on behalf of the Australian government that we looked to America as the paramount factor on the democracies' side of the Pacific.

There is no belittling of the Old Country in this outlook. Britain has fought and won in the air the tremendous Battle of Britain. Britain has fought, and with your strong help, has won, the equally vital battle of the Atlantic. She has a paramount obligation to supply all possible help to Russia. She cannot, at the same time, go all out in the Pacific. We Australians, with New Zealand, represent Great Britain here in the Pacific — we are her sons — and on us the responsibility falls. I pledge to you my word we will not fail. You, as I have said, must be our leader. We will pull knee to knee with you for every ounce of our weight...

We are, then, committed, heart and soul, to total warfare. How far, you may ask me, have we progressed along that road? I may answer you this way. Out of every ten men in Australia four are wholly engaged in war as members of the fighting forces or making the munitions and equipment to fight with. The other six, besides feeding and clothing the whole ten and their families, have to produce the food and wool and metals which Britain needs for her very existence. We are not, of course, stopping at four out of ten. We had over three when Japan challenged our life and liberty. The proportion is now growing every day. On the one hand we are ruthlessly cutting out unessential expenditure so as to free men and women for war work; and on the other, mobilising woman-power to the utmost to supplement the men. From four out of ten devoted to war, we shall pass to five and six out of ten. We have no limit...

I am not boasting to you. But were I to say less I would not be paying proper due to a band of men who have been tested in the crucible of world wars and hallmarked as pure metal. Our fighting forces and born attackers; we will hit the enemy wherever we can, as often as we can, and the extent of it will be measured only by the weapons in our hands...

We fight with what we have and what we have is our all. We fight for the same free institutions that you enjoy. We fight so that, in the words of Lincoln, "government of the people, for the people, by the people, shall not perish from the earth." Our legislature is elected the same as is yours; and we will fight for it, and for the right to have it, just as you will fight to keep the Capitol at Washington the meeting place of freely elected men and women representative of a free people.

But I give you this warning: Australia is the last bastion between the west coast of America and the Japanese. If Australia goes, the Americas are wide open. It is said that the Japanese will by-pass Australia and that they can be met and routed in India. I say to you that the saving of Australia is the saving of America's west coast. If you believe anything to the contrary then you delude yourselves.

Be assured of the calibre of our national character. This war may see the end of much that we have painfully and slowly built in our 150 years of existence. But even though all of it go, there will still be Australians fighting on Australian soil until the turning point be reached, and we will advance over blackened ruins, through blasted and fire-swept cities, across scorched plains, until we drive the enemy into the sea. I give you the pledge of my country. There will always be an Australian government and there will always be an Australian people. We are too strong in our hearts; our spirit is too high; the justice of our cause throbs too deeply in our being for that high purpose to be overcome.

I may be looking down a vista of weary months; of soul-shaking reverses; of grim struggle; of back-breaking work. But as surely as I sit here talking to you across the war-tossed Pacific Ocean I see our flag; I see Old Glory; I see the proud banner of the heroic Chinese; I see the standard of the valiant Dutch.

And I see them flying high in the wind of liberty over a Pacific from which aggression has been wiped out; over peoples restored to freedom; and flying triumphant as the glorified symbols of united nations strong in will and in power to achieve decency and dignity, unyielding to evil in any form.

Churchill (seated, center) with the leaders of Canada, South Africa, New Zealand, and Australia before the opening of the Empire Conference, 9 May 1944.

17 APRIL 1942

Fellow Britishers,

At this time of crisis and trial, with dark forebodings of things to come, I bring to you a message from Australia. A message not of mere words, but a factual statement of what we, in a Dominion of the British Commonwealth, are doing, and will do, so that your heroic struggle will be made easier and the ultimate victory so much swifter.

I will not dwell on what you have gone through in the past. That is a story of human gallantry, stoic courage, and grim determination unparalleled in history. It throbs our hearts with pride and gratitude. We say to you that we have taken a pattern from it. In Australia we have made up our minds that no sacrifice can be too great; no effort shall be beyond our ability; and no obstacle shall daunt us in ensuring that Australia's part in the Battle of Britain will be faithfully and inflexibly honored...

In this war, as you well know, the backbone of the nation is in the workshop and in the factory. The workers of Australia have made that backbone a very real thing and they have done so because they have a wholesale conviction of the justice of Britain's cause. They are with you in this struggle because they are assured that everything they regard as being worthwhile is at stake. Bone of your bone, the workers of Australia are kindred. They are of your stock. Their forebears came from England, and from Ireland, and from Scotland, and from Wales. They inherit the ties of blood and grace and tongue that have joined British people together for centuries. Australia is a British land of one race and one tongue. It is a land in which people came from the British Isles to carve out for themselves, in freedom and equality, an opportunity to make for themselves and their children a better and freer life. That opportunity and the opportunity to aspire to even better things are still here. We are not going to allow our hopes to be thrust aside by any doctrine of repression and any doctrine which abnegates human rights.

Australians feel that they are playing their part. Australians are modestly proud of what our soldiers and airmen in the Middle East have achieved. We are proud of what our navy has done and we are bringing the production of raw materials and manufactured materials very swiftly to a maximum so that Britain, as far as Australia is concerned, at least will not lack. We have our own problems and the working out of the tangled skein of ambitions and counter ambitions in the Pacific involves us very deeply.

Our position in the Pacific is shortly stated. We do not want war here. We believe that aggression should play no part in the policies of the peoples of the Pacific. Nevertheless, we will resist aggression and, just as you, our kinsmen in Britain, stand to arms in defence of those fair isles, so also do we stand ready to keep war out of Australia.

Be of good cheer. The black of the night must pass into the brightness of morning; a morning for a new world in which human freedoms will be the paramount factor. Australian labor sends a comradely message of united endeavor to British labor. Australia sends to Great Britain her unflinching devotion and her steadfastness in the belief that victory must come in the battle for all that is meant in the word freedom. Good luck to you all.

FIGHTING WORDS

"What difference does it make to the dead, the orphans, and the homeless, whether the mad destruction is wrought under the name of totalitarianism or the holy name of liberty and democracy?"
Mohandas ("Mahatma") Gandhi (1869–1948), *Time* magazine's Man of the Year in 1930, undertook a policy of non-violent resistance against the English in India.

"Never think that war, no matter how necessary, nor how justified, is not a crime."
Ernest Hemingway (1899–1961) was an American author and journalist who won the Nobel prize for literature in 1954.

"War is not an adventure. It is a disease. It is like typhus."
Antoine de Saint Exupery (1900–1944) was a French aviator and writer, best known for his novel *The Little Prince*. He disappeared on 31 July 1944 while collecting intelligence on German troop movements.

"Take the diplomacy out of the war and the thing would fall flat in a week."
"You can't say that civilisation don't advance, however, for in every war they kill you in a new way."
Will Rogers (1879–1935) was a famous Cherokee Indian comedian, satirist, social critic, journalist, and film star. He was listed in the *Guinness Book of World Records* for throwing three ropes simultaneously — one around the neck of a horse, another around its rider, and a third around the horse's four legs. One of his most famous lines — "I never yet met a man that I didn't like" — referred to Russian revolutionary Leon Trotsky.

"You can no more win a war than you can win an earthquake."
Jeannette Rankin (1880–1973) was a lifelong pacifist and the first woman elected to the US House of Representatives (1916), even though women did not yet have the right to vote.

"The object of war is not to die for your country but to make the other b****** die for his."
George S. Patton, one of the more colourful military figures of World War II, offers his men some sage advice.

"...War alone brings up to its highest tension all human energy and puts the stamp of notability upon the peoples who have courage to meet it...The foundation of Fascism is the conception of the State, its character, its duty, and its aim. Fascism conceives of the State as an absolute, in comparison with which all individuals or groups are relative, only to be conceived of in their relation to the State..."
Benito Mussolini (1883–1945) became prime minister of Italy in 1922, and Il Duce (duke; dictator) in 1925, and went on to lead Italy to a disastrous loss in World War II. This quote is from his definition of fascism in *The Italian Encyclopaedia* (1932).

"All men are brothers, like the seas throughout the world;
So why do winds and waves clash so fiercely everywhere?"
Emperor Hirohito (1901–1989) was emperor of Japan from 1926 until his death in 1989.

"When the rich wage war, it's the poor who die."
Jean-Paul Sartre (1905–1980) was a groundbreaking French existentialist philosopher, dramatist, novelist, and critic.

"We cannot accept the doctrine that war must be forever a part of man's destiny."
Franklin D. Roosevelt, on 2 November 1940, in his presidential campaign speech

"The children will not leave unless I do. I shall not leave unless their father does, and the King will not leave the country in any circumstances whatsoever."
Queen Elizabeth (pictured), the wife of King George VI, responds to concerned advice that she, her husband, and their children, including the future Queen Elizabeth II, should evacuate war-time London during the German bombing blitz of 1940. Shortly afterwards, after Buckingham Palace had been bombed several times, she said: "I'm glad we've been bombed. It makes me feel I can look the East End in the face."

Speech to the US Third Army
US General George S. Patton, England, May and June 1944

This inspirational speech is unusual in that it wasn't broadcast or recorded; it was a private pep talk to Allied troops, delivered to several different audiences in the weeks leading up to the successful Allied D-Day invasion of France on 6 June 1944. The language is very earthy at times; even so, we may assume that the grammar and language have been cleaned up.

In 1951 the *New American Mercury* magazine printed a version of the speech, which had originally appeared in the *New York Daily News* on 31 May 1945. After publication, the magazine received so many requests for reprints that the editors decided to make a gramophone recording of two versions of the speech, one more sanitized than the other. It was to be a nonprofit project and, despite there being no legal obligation to do so, they asked Patton's widow Beatrice for her blessing. However, as the *Mercury* editors said: "Mrs Patton considered the matter graciously and thoroughly, and gave us a disappointing decision. She took the position that this speech was made by the General only to the men who were going to fight and die with him; it was, therefore, not a speech for the public or for posterity. We think Mrs Patton is wrong; we think that what is great and worth preserving about General Patton was expressed in that invasion speech. The fact that he employed four-letter words was proper; four-letter words are the language of war; without them wars would be quite impossible."

The project was then abandoned, and the master recordings destroyed.

Patton's nephew and biographer Fred Ayer Jnr once asked him about his liberal use of profanity. Patton replied: "When I want my men to remember something important, to really make it stick, I give it to them double dirty. It may not sound nice to some bunch of little old ladies at an afternoon tea party, but it helps my soldiers to remember. You can't run an army without profanity; and it has to be eloquent profanity. An army without profanity couldn't fight its way out of a p***-soaked paper bag."

Ayer wrote that Patton "was a man who trained and disciplined his mind and body nearly every day of his life for the role he had always known he was to play...a man who believed in the aristocracy of achievement and in the sanctity of his country's course. He was conceited, sometimes ruthless, often inconsiderate, and outwardly very, very tough. He was often too much the impetuous showman and yet a deep and careful thinker. But he was also...deeply religious, soft-hearted, emotional, and easily moved to tears.

A 1943 portrait of General Patton.

Patton was born in California in 1885. A lifelong soldier, he joined the US Regular Army in 1909. He served in World War I, rising to the rank of Lieutenant Colonel in 1918, and in World War II, he commanded armies in Europe and North Africa, receiving numerous military awards. He wrote poems and prayers. His popular nickname was "Old Blood and Guts"; historians consider him a brilliant military leader whose record was flawed by disobedience and rash conduct. He died on 21 December 1945.

Be seated. Men, this stuff that some sources sling around about America wanting out of this war, not wanting to fight, is a crock of bull****. Americans love to fight, traditionally. All real Americans love the sting and clash of battle.

You are here today for three reasons. First, because you are here to defend your homes and your loved ones. Second, you are here for your own self-respect, because you would not want to be anywhere else. Third, you are here because you are real men and all real men like to fight. When you, here, every one of you, were kids, you all admired the champion marble player, the fastest runner, the toughest boxer, the big league ball players, and the All-American football players. Americans love a winner. Americans will not tolerate a loser. Americans despise cowards. Americans play to win all of the time. I wouldn't give a hoot in hell for a man who lost and laughed. That's why Americans have never lost nor will ever lose a war; for the very idea of losing is hateful to an American.

You are not all going to die. Only two percent of you right here today would die in a major battle. Death must not be feared. Death, in time, comes to all men. Yes, every man is scared in his first battle. If he says he's not, he's a liar. Some men are cowards but they fight the same as the brave men or they get the hell slammed out of them watching men fight who are just as scared as they are. The real hero is the man who fights even though he is scared. Some men get over their fright in a minute under fire. For some, it takes an hour. For some, it takes days. But a real man will never let his fear of death overpower his honor, his sense of duty to his country, and his innate manhood. Battle is the most magnificent competition in which a human being can indulge. It brings out all that is best and it removes all that is base. Americans pride themselves on being he-men and they ARE he-men.

Remember that the enemy is just as frightened as you are, and probably more so. They are not supermen. All through your army careers, you men have b****ed about what you call "chicken s*** drilling." That, like everything else in this army, has a definite purpose. That purpose is alertness. Alertness must be bred into every soldier. I don't give a f*** for a man who's not always on his toes.

You men are veterans or you wouldn't be here. You are ready for what's to come. A man must be alert at all times if he expects to stay alive. If you're not alert, sometime, a German son-of-an-a**hole-b**** is going to sneak up behind you and beat you to death with a sock full of s***! There are 400 neatly marked graves somewhere in Sicily, all because one man went to sleep on the job. But they are German graves, because we caught the b****** asleep before they did.

An army is a team. It lives, sleeps, eats and fights as a team. This individual heroic stuff is pure horses***. The bilious b******s who write that kind of stuff for the *Saturday Evening Post* don't know any more about real fighting under fire than they know about f***ing! We have the finest food, the finest equipment, the best spirit and the best men in the world. Why, by God, I actually pity those poor sons-of-b****es we're going up against. By God, I do. My men don't surrender, and I don't want to hear of any soldier under my command being captured unless he has been hit. Even if you are hit, you can still fight back. That's not just bulls*** either. The kind of man that I want in my command is just like the lieutenant in Libya, who, with a Luger against his chest, jerked off his helmet, swept the gun aside with one hand, and busted the hell out of the Kraut with his helmet. Then he jumped on the gun and went out and killed another German before they knew what the hell was coming off. And, all of that time, this man had a bullet through a lung. There was a real man!

All of the real heroes are not storybook combat fighters, either. Every single man in this army plays a vital role. Don't ever let up. Don't ever think that your job is unimportant. Every man has a job to do and he must do it. Every man is a vital link in the great chain. What if every truck driver suddenly decided that he didn't like the whine of those shells overhead, turned yellow, and jumped headlong into a ditch? The cowardly b****** could say, "Hell, they won't miss me, just one man in thousands." But, what if every man thought that way? Where in the hell would we be now? What would our country, our loved ones, our homes, even the world, be like? No, goddamn it, Americans don't think like that. Every man does his job. Every man serves the whole. Every department, every unit, is important in the vast scheme of this war. The ordnance men are needed to supply the guns and machinery of war to keep us rolling. The Quartermaster is

Patton inspects US troops on 22 April 1944, shortly after his arrival in Britain.

needed to bring up food and clothes because where we are going there isn't a hell of a lot to steal. Every last man on KP has a job to do, even the one who heats our water to keep us from getting the "GI S***s."

Each man must not think only of himself, but also of his buddy fighting beside him. We don't want yellow cowards in this army. They should be killed off like rats. If not, they will go home after this war and breed more cowards.

The brave men will breed more brave men. Kill off the goddamned cowards and we will have a nation of brave men. One of the bravest men that I ever saw was a fellow on top of a telegraph pole in the midst of a furious fire fight in Tunisia. I stopped and asked what the hell he was doing up there at a time like that. He answered, "Fixing the wire, sir." I asked, "Isn't that a little unhealthy right about now?" He answered, "Yes, sir, but the goddamned wire has to be fixed." I asked, "Don't those planes strafing the road bother you?" And he answered, "No, sir, but you sure as hell do!"

Now, there was a real man. A real soldier. There was a man who devoted all he had to his duty, no matter how seemingly insignificant his duty might appear at the time, no matter how great the odds. And you should have seen those trucks on the rode to Tunisia. Those drivers were magnificent. All day and all night they rolled over those son-of-a-b****ing roads, never stopping, never faltering from their course, with shells bursting all around them all of the time. We got through on good old American guts.

Many of those men drove for over 40 consecutive hours. These men weren't combat men, but they were soldiers with a job to do. They did it, and in one hell of a way they did it. They were part of a team. Without team effort, without them, the fight would have been lost. All of the links in the chain pulled together and the chain became unbreakable.

Don't forget, you men don't know that I'm here. No mention of that fact is to be made in any letters. The world is not supposed to know what the hell happened to me. I'm not supposed to be commanding this army. I'm not even supposed to be here in England. Let the first b******s to find out be the goddamned Germans. Someday I want to see them raise up on their p***-soaked hind legs and howl, "Jesus Christ, it's the goddamned Third Army again and that son-of-a-f***ing-b**** Patton. We want to get the hell over there." The quicker we clean up this goddamned mess, the quicker we can take a little jaunt against the purple p***ing Japs and clean out their nest, too. Before the goddamned Marines get all of the credit.

Sure, we want to go home. We want this war over with. The quickest way to get it over with is to go get the b******s who started it. The quicker they are whipped, the quicker we can go home. The shortest way home is through Berlin and Tokyo. And when we get to Berlin, I am personally going to shoot that paper-hanging son-of-a-b**** Hitler. Just like I'd shoot a snake!

When a man is lying in a shell hole, if he just stays there all day, a German will get to him eventually. The hell with that idea. The hell with taking it. My men don't dig foxholes. I don't want them to. Foxholes only slow up an offensive. Keep moving. And don't give the enemy time to dig one either. We'll win this war, but we'll win it only by fighting and by showing the Germans that we've got more guts than they have; or ever will have. We're not going to just shoot the sons-of-b****es, we're going to rip out their living goddamned guts and use them to grease the treads of our tanks. We're going to murder those lousy Hun c***suckers by the bushel-f***ing-basket.

War is a bloody, killing business. You've got to spill their blood, or they will spill yours. Rip them up the belly. Shoot them in the guts. When shells are hitting all around you and you wipe the dirt off your face and realize that instead of dirt it's the blood and guts of what once was your best friend beside you, you'll know what to do! I don't want to get any messages saying, "I am holding my position." We are not holding a goddamned thing. Let the Germans do that. We are advancing constantly and we are not interested in holding onto anything, except the enemy's balls. We are going to twist his balls and kick the living s*** out of him all of the time. Our basic plan of operation is to advance and to keep on advancing regardless of whether we have to go over, under, or through the enemy. We are going to go through him like crap through a goose; like s*** through a tin horn!

From time to time there will be some complaints that we are pushing our people too hard. I don't give a good goddamn about such complaints. I believe in the old and sound rule that an ounce of sweat will save a gallon of blood. The harder WE push, the more Germans we will kill. The more Germans we kill, the fewer of our men will be killed. Pushing means fewer casualties. I want you all to remember that.

There is one great thing that you men will all be able to say after this war is over and you are home once again. You may be thankful that twenty years from now when you are sitting by the fireplace with your grandson on your knee and he asks you what you did in the great World War II, you won't have to cough, shift him to the other knee and say, "Well, your Granddaddy shoveled s*** in Louisiana." No, sir, you can look him straight in the eye and say, "Son, your Granddaddy rode with the Great Third Army and a Son-of-a-Goddamned-B**** named Georgie Patton!" That is all.

The atom bomb
Harry S. Truman, diary entry, 25 July 1945

US president Truman (1884–1972) made this diary entry after the atom bomb had been tested in the New Mexico desert, but before it was used on Hiroshima and Nagasaki. Registering awe at its power, he states that it will be used on military targets only. (In fact it was dropped on heavily populated city areas of little military significance.) Debate long raged over whether its use had even been necessary; many argued that, had the Japanese been invited to observe the test in the desert, they would surely have surrendered.

In 1963 ex-president Dwight Eisenhower, who in 1945 was supreme commander of all Allied forces, told *Newsweek* magazine: "I voiced to him [Secretary of War Henry L. Stimson] my grave misgivings, first on the basis of my belief that Japan was already defeated and that dropping the bomb was completely unnecessary, and secondly because I thought that our country should avoid shocking world opinion by the use of a weapon whose employment was, I thought, no longer mandatory as a measure to save American lives. It was my belief that Japan was at that very moment seeking some way to surrender with a minimum of loss of 'face'...It wasn't necessary to hit them with that awful thing."

Fleet Admiral William D. Leahy, Chair of the Joint Chiefs of Staff during World War II, later said that, by using the bomb, the United States had "adopted an ethical standard common to the barbarians of the Dark Ages." But many believed that its use was justified on the grounds that it brought the war to an instant halt, avoiding the need to invade Japan.

We have discovered the most terrible bomb in the history of the world. It may be the fire destruction prophesied in the Euphrates Valley Era, after Noah and his fabulous Ark.

Anyway we "think" we have found the way to cause a disintegration of the atom. An experiment in the New Mexico desert was startling — to put it mildly. Thirteen pounds of the explosive caused the complete disintegration of a steel tower 60 feet high, created a crater 6 feet deep and 1200 feet in diameter, knocked over a steel tower half a mile away and knocked men down 10 000 yards away. The explosion was visible for more than 200 miles and audible for 40 miles and more.

This weapon is to be used against Japan between now and August 10th. I have told the Secretary of War, Mr Stimson, to use it so that military

The mushroom cloud rises more than 11 miles into the air over Nagasaki after the so-called "Fat Man" atomic bomb was dropped on 9 August 1945.

objectives and soldiers and sailors are the target and not women and children. Even if the Japs are savages, ruthless, merciless, and fanatic, we as the leader of the world for the common welfare cannot drop that terrible bomb on the old capital or the new.

He and I are in accord. The target will be a purely military one and we will issue a warning statement asking the Japs to surrender and save lives. I'm sure they will not do that, but we will have given them the chance. It is certainly a good thing for the world that Hitler's crowd or Stalin's did not discover this atomic bomb. It seems to be the most terrible thing ever discovered, but it can be made the most useful.

Surrender to the Allies
Emperor Hirohito, radio broadcast, 14 August 1945

Hirohito (1901–1989), emperor of Japan, delivered this radio message to his subjects after US atomic bombs, dropped by the US B-29 bomber *Enola Gay*, obliterated the cities of Hiroshima and Nagasaki. This speech signified the end of World War II and also the end of the emperor's status as a deity.

Hirohito delivers his speech — designed to be as obscure as possible, presumably to mask the humiliation of the surrender to the Allies — in the very formal vernacular of the Imperial Court, which many Japanese could not understand. He does not use the term "surrender"; instead he refers to "the provisions of the joint declaration," the terms of which were unknown to the majority of his audience. He paints Japan as the innocent victim of US aggression, conveniently ignoring the Japanese attack on the US naval base at Pearl Harbor, which had drawn the previously neutral US into the war.

...After pondering deeply the general trends of the world and the actual conditions obtaining in our empire today, we have decided to effect a settlement of the present situation by resorting to an extraordinary measure.

We have ordered our government to communicate to the governments of the United States, Great Britain, China, and the Soviet Union that our empire accepts the provisions of their joint declaration.

To strive for the common prosperity and happiness of all nations as well as the security and wellbeing of our subjects is the solemn obligation which has been handed down by our imperial ancestors and which we lay close to the heart.

Indeed, we declared war on America and Britain out of our sincere desire to ensure Japan's self-preservation and the stabilization of East Asia, it being far from our thought either to infringe upon the sovereignty of other nations or to embark upon territorial aggrandizement.

But now the war has lasted for nearly four years. Despite the best that has been done by everyone — the gallant fighting of our military and naval forces, the diligence of our servants of State, and the devoted service of our 100 million — the war situation has developed not necessarily to Japan's advantage, while the general trends of the world have all turned against her interest.

Moreover, the enemy has begun to employ a new and most cruel bomb, the power of which to do damage is, indeed, incalculable, taking

the toll of many innocent lives. Should we continue to fight, it would not only result in an ultimate collapse and obliteration of the Japanese nation, but also it would lead to the total extinction of human civilisation.

Such being the case, how are we to save the millions of our subjects, nor to atone ourselves before the hallowed spirits of our imperial ancestors? This is the reason why we have ordered the acceptance of the provisions of the joint declaration of the powers.

We cannot but express the deepest sense of regret to our allied nations of East Asia, who have consistently cooperated with the Empire towards the emancipation of East Asia.

The thought of those officers and men as well as others who have fallen in the fields of battle, those who died at their posts of duty, and all their bereaved families, pains our heart night and day.

The welfare of the wounded and the war sufferers and of those who lost their homes and livelihood is the object of our profound solicitude. The hardships and sufferings to which our nation is to be subjected hereafter will be certainly great.

We are keenly aware of the inmost feelings of all of you, our subjects. However, it is according to the dictates of time and fate that we have resolved to pave the way for a grand peace for all the generations to come by enduring the unavoidable and suffering what is unsufferable. Having been able to save and maintain the structure of the Imperial State, we are always with you, our good and loyal subjects, relying upon your sincerity and integrity.

Beware most strictly of any outbursts of emotion that may engender needless complications, of any fraternal contention and strife that may create confusion, lead you astray and cause you to lose the confidence of the world.

Let the entire nation continue as one family from generation to generation, ever firm in its faith of the imperishableness of its divine land, and mindful of its heavy burden of responsibilities, and the long road before it. Unite your total strength to be devoted to the construction for the future. Cultivate the ways of rectitude, nobility of spirit, and work with resolution so that you may enhance the innate glory of the Imperial State and keep pace with the progress of the world.

On the USS *Missouri* in Tokyo Bay, on 4 September 1945, General Douglas MacArthur reaches into his pocket for one of the five pens he used to sign the documents bringing the Pacific War with Japan to an end.

"It is always a simple matter to drag the people along"
Hermann Goering, Nuremberg, Germany, 18 April 1946

A World War I pilot and war hero, Hermann Goering (1893–1946) had been Hitler's loyal deputy since joining the fledgling Nazi party in 1922, in search of adventure and an outlet for his deep-seated lust for power. Hitler appointed him head of the Luftwaffe (air force), but he proved himself spectacularly incompetent, leading the Germans to massive defeats from dominant positions in the Battle of Britain, and then on the Russian front. His costliest tactical error was to launch bombing attacks on British cities (rather than military targets) after losing the Battle of Britain, when, unknown to him, the British air force had been almost eliminated.

Hitler never forgave him for these failures, but it is perhaps a measure of his respect for Goering that he did not have him murdered — the usual fate for anyone who failed (or even disagreed with) him. However, Hitler blamed him for most of the Germans' subsequent defeats and, humiliated, Goering sunk into depression and drug abuse. His last masterpiece of poor timing and tactics was to attempt to take control of the Reich after Hitler announced he would remain in his Berlin bunker until the end. Hitler had him dismissed from all his positions of power, expelled from the party, and arrested. He was captured by forces of the American Seventh Army on 9 May 1945, a week after Hitler committed suicide.

The following comments were made privately to Gustave Gilbert, a German-speaking spy and psychologist who was granted free access by the Allies to prisoners held in Nuremberg jail during the war crimes trials that followed World War II. Hence the interview does not appear in trial transcripts. The two men spoke in Goering's cell during a break in proceedings. Goering's last comment was used by peace activists in the 1960s, and has recently been revived because of its applicability to the war in Iraq.

Goering was tried for war crimes and crimes against humanity, and sentenced to death by hanging. But on 15 October 1946, before the sentence could be carried out, he committed suicide, ingesting potassium cyanide in his prison cell.

Goering: "Why, of course, the people don't want war. Why would some poor slob on a farm want to risk his life in a war when the best that he can get out of it is to come back to his farm in one piece? Naturally, the

Hermann Goering on trial in Nuremberg, 1946.

common people don't want war; neither in Russia, nor in England, nor in America, nor for that matter in Germany. That is understood. But, after all, it is the leaders of the country who determine the policy and it is always a simple matter to drag the people along, whether it is a democracy, or a fascist dictatorship, or a parliament, or a communist dictatorship."

Gilbert: "There is one difference. In a democracy the people have some say in the matter through their elected representatives, and in the United States only Congress can declare wars."

Goering: "Oh, that is all well and good, but, voice or no voice, the people can always be brought to the bidding of the leaders. That is easy. All you have to do is tell them they are being attacked, and denounce the pacifists for lack of patriotism and exposing the country to danger. It works the same in any country."

PROPAGANDA

The Latin word "propaganda" was coined in 1422 when Pope Gregory V established the Congregatio de Propaganda Fide or "Congregation for Spreading the Faith." This section of the papal administration was charged with publicising and spreading Catholicism, and regulating religious affairs. Of course, propaganda as a concept has existed for much longer. Ever since people decided they wanted to persuade others to their own political or religious opinions, they have used persuasive techniques, whether honest or deceptive.

Propaganda may be defined as a concentrated series of messages aimed at altering the opinions or behavior of a large group of people. Rather than providing impartial information, propaganda presents a biased, partisan view. It is often truthful, but is more often partly, or completely, dishonest. It may deceive by omission, presenting facts selectively, or give a manipulative message to produce an emotional rather than rational response in the recipient.

Wars, of course, have always provided governments with a good reason to persuade populaces of the justice of their cause, hide their failures or misinform the enemy. Misinformation and disinformation are widely used to distract people from the truth and create new realities. Propaganda is used to create hatred towards the enemy by creating a false image. This is often done by using derogatory or racist terms; for example, the German Nazis referred to Slavs and Russians as *Untermenschen*. Propaganda may be aimed at the military or the civilian population, to convince them that the enemy has inflicted an injustice, whether factual or otherwise.

Propaganda that presents selected facts can be seen as the corollary of censorship, which deliberately conceals information.

In 1521, in an early example of religious propaganda, German university professor and church reformer Martin Luther commissioned a print by Lucas Cranach with the caption "The Pope is Antichrist."

In 1792 German author and dramatist Johann Wolfgang von Goethe described some of the methods used by France to export its revolution to neighboring countries:

> They did not attack us with their sabres, or with their handguns or with their cannons, they used much more dangerous weapons. They disseminated

big packages of small printed paper which described the fundamentals of freedom and equality in a language easily understood by the common man. Handbills containing messages were hidden in bread or pasted to wine bottles handed surreptitiously to enemy outposts...

In World War I both (or more correctly, all) sides accused each other of non-existent atrocities. On 6 September 1918, a few weeks before the defeat of Germany, Field Marshal Hindenburg said of Allied propaganda:

...If numerical superiority alone guaranteed victory, Germany would long since have lain shattered on the ground. The enemy knows, however, that Germany and her allies cannot be conquered by arms alone. The enemy knows that the spirit which dwells within our troops and our people makes us unconquerable. Therefore, together with the struggle against German arms, he has undertaken a struggle against the German spirit; he seeks to poison our spirit and believes that German arms will also become blunted if the German spirit is eaten away.

In 1933 Adolf Hitler, realising the value of propaganda, appointed Joseph Goebbels as a highly effective Minister for Propaganda.

Three years later, Boston merchant Edward Filene established the Institute for Propaganda Analysis, designed to educate Americans in how to to recognize propaganda techniques. The Institute produced a list of seven separate propaganda categories:

- **Name-calling** Denigrate, demonize, or dehumanize opponents.
- **Bandwagon** Attempt to persuade the audience to join in and do what everyone else is doing.
- **Card-stacking** Construct a biased case to support your own position.
- **Glittering generalities** Use powerful words to evoke strong emotions.
- **Plain folks** Appeal to the people by making the leader seem ordinary, credible, and humane.
- **Testimonial** Use an apparently impartial expert to inspire trust.
- **Transfer** Associate the leader with others who are trusted.

Another common technique is to continually state and re-state a lie until it eventually acquires some sort of warped credibility through sheer repetition, as exemplified in the Nazis' success in convincing large numbers of people that Jews are inferior, and responsible for most of the world's ills.

The following article appeared in England's *Daily Telegraph* newspaper on 9 September 1939, six days after the start of World War II. It may itself be considered propaganda, designed to reassure the British population that the RAF was at least capable of flying (and more importantly, returning from) missions over Germany. The text of the leaflet was in German; an English translation follows the *Daily Telegraph* article.

AIR RAID FOR PROPAGANDA
13 TONS OF PAPER DROPPED

By Our Diplomatic Correspondent.

The fact that the Royal Air Force planes, which carried out raids over north and western Germany during Sunday–Monday night, were not engaged either by German fighters or anti-aircraft guns would seem to throw an important light on the efficiency of German air raid precautions.

During their visit they scattered 6,000,000 leaflets telling the German people something of the circumstances in which they had been plunged into a world war by Hitler.

It can readily be judged that a large number of British bombers must have taken part in this operation since the bulk of paper carried and dropped over German territory would approximate in weight to about 13 tons. It should not be assumed however, that the statement that the British raiders were "not engaged" means that no effort was made to intercept them.

On the contrary. It is probable that German fighters were up with a view to intercepting the machines, but failed to find them.

BERLIN'S ADMISSION

The Berlin wireless admits that British planes succeeded in dropping leaflets over Germany. It alleges that the machines flew over the Netherlands, and that they were driven back by German anti-aircraft guns after having dropped leaflets.

The German wireless adds that according to a statement from The Hague the planes flew so high that it was impossible to recognise to which Air Force they belonged.

WARNING! ENGLAND TO THE GERMAN PEOPLE

The Nazi regime has, in spite of the endeavours of the leading great Powers, plunged the world into war.

This war is a crime. The German people must quite clearly distinguish between the pretexts employed by its government so as to unleash war and the principles which have forced England and France to defend Poland.

From the very beginning the English government has made it clear that the Polish question is not one which can justify a European war with all its tragic consequences.

Five months after the Munich Agreement the independence of Czecho-Slovakia was brutally trodden underfoot. So that Poland shall not also suffer the same fate, we must insist that peaceful methods of negotiation shall not be rendered impossible through threats of force, and that in the negotiations which are requisite the Poles' right to live must be guaranteed and honourably kept. We cannot accept or admit a Diktat.

If Herr Hitler believes that the English government, out of fear of war, will allow the Poles to be left in the lurch, then he has been deceiving himself. In the first place England will not break her pledged word. Furthermore, it is high time that the brutal force with which the Nazi regime strives to dominate the World should be halted.

Through this war the German Chancellor places himself against the unbending resolution of the English government, a resolution which has behind it not only the resources and means of the whole English Commonwealth, but also a union of other great Powers. It is a question of the salvation of human freedom and the right of peoples to live free.

Up to the very last moment the Pope, the President of the United States and the King of the Belgians, in the name of Belgium, Holland, Luxembourg, Denmark, Sweden, Norway, and Finland, made fruitless appeals to your Nazi government, urgently requesting that negotiations should be chosen in the place of war.

Now a catastrophe has broken out upon you in that the Reich finds itself isolated from the community of civilised peoples, without any support save that of Communist Russia.

You cannot win this war. Against you are arrayed resources and materials far greater than your own.

For years you have been subjected to the most stringent censorship, and by means of an incredible system of secret police and informers the truth has been withheld from you.

Against you stands the united strength of the free peoples, who with open eyes will fight for freedom to the last.

This war is as repulsive to us as it is to you, but do not forget that England, once forced into war, will wage it unwaveringly to the end. England's nerves are strong, her resources inexhaustible. We will not relent.

Pass on this leaflet.

The British did not persevere with such complicated, logical propaganda, soon opting (like everyone else) for simpler, more subliminal messages that were easier to absorb, harder to ignore, and less boring.

Sex propaganda

In both world wars, both sides printed pornographic propaganda leaflets in an attempt to dishearten enemy soldiers. They usually featured a scantily clad or naked woman, often in the arms of a handsome civilian or soldier. The most common themes were the fate of the girl the soldier left behind (being raped or seduced, for example) and the seductive pleasures awaiting the enemy troops if they should surrender.

The Germans often used "divide and conquer" themes, attempting to drive a wedge between American and British troops, French and British troops, soldiers and cowardly civilian "idlers" at home, and Christians and Jews.

One problem with supplying explicit images was that the recipients, far from becoming lonely and too demoralized to fight, received the pictures gratefully, often using them as "pin-ups" in their vehicles and elsewhere. Some became highly prized collectors' items, and were often traded like sport cards, while others were used as toilet paper (always in short supply). They were delivered by artillery and aircraft, and were received far more enthusiastically than the anticipated bombs. The use of sexual propaganda largely disappeared after World War II; similar productions in the Korea and Vietnam wars are generally far less lascivious.

One German image dropped over Britain and France during the early stages of the war — designed to exploit and inflame supposed latent anti-Semitic sentiments among the Allies — shows a pretty, shapely blonde holding a copy of *The Times* newspaper and looking into a full-length mirror. She is clad only in a British Army helmet and high heels. But her image in the mirror is that of a dumpy, dark-haired woman with a menacing leer on her face. *Times* is reversed and now reads "Semit."

The Germans also produced a few see-through leaflets, which revealed an extra picture when held up to the light. One example, used in Poland to foment anti-Soviet sentiment, shows a beautiful, happy Polish woman, lying in a field with a flower in her mouth. The text says "Carefree youth — or cruel fate?" When held up to the light an ape-like Russian soldier appears, defiling the now naked girl. (One doubts its efficacy as propaganda, considering the violence and murder being inflicted on Poland by Germany at the time.)

Other examples portrayed American soldiers (or unscrupulous British civilian opportunists) raping or seducing the wives of British soldiers, with messages such as "While you face death."

A series produced for American troops featured the misadventures of "the girl you left behind," showing her in ever-increasing states of undress at the hands of an unscrupulous, rich (of course) Jew.

One leaflet, dropped by the Luftwaffe over The Hague, and elsewhere in Holland, as Germany invaded in May 1940, is much more concise and accessible than the British example quoted on pages 264–5, if less honest. It reads, in part: "The German army protects the life and property of every peace-loving citizen."

Late in the war, the British government authorized the manufacture of a few pornographic leaflets, but their use was not widespread — probably because the British command did not think they would be effective enough, given the expense and effort involved in creating and delivering them, and perhaps, according to some reports, due to moral qualms.

Although the use of sexually explicit propaganda leaflets was always against official US policy — and always denied by US government and intelligence authorities — some examples started surfacing for auction in the 1970s. Some were the personal property of former US OSS (Office of Strategic Services) agents; others had been lost or thrown away when US forces left Italy after the war.

Propaganda in the twenty-first century

In the modern world, advertising and public relations use many of the same manipulative techniques as propaganda, while governments of all persuasions use facts selectively, telling their constituencies (and their opponents) only what they think they need to know.

Propaganda continues unabated; it was practiced on a large scale by all parties in recent wars in the Balkans, Afghanistan, and Iraq, and will undoubtedly be used in future conflicts.

Part 7

THE POST-WAR WORLD

"

The Second Half of the Twentieth Century

"Enemies from within"
Joseph R. McCarthy, Wheeling, West Virginia, 9 February 1950

Anti-communist Wisconsin Republican Joseph R. McCarthy (1908–1957) was elected to the US Senate in 1946. On 9 February 1950, Abraham Lincoln's birthday, he made this speech to the Senate, claiming that there were large numbers of communists and Soviet spies in the government, civil service, army, and many other fields. He waved a piece of paper that allegedly held the names of 205 "traitors" — he later reduced this to 57 — but never made the list public, or backed up his claims with any plausible evidence.

His sensational accusations, which attracted a considerable amount of support at first, made him temporarily famous for the first and last time in his undistinguished political career. The Truman government asked the standing House Un-American Activities Committee — established in 1938, primarily to investigate Nazism and the white supremacist Ku Klux Klan organisation — to investigate McCarthy's claims. This led to a 1954 "witch hunt," in which numerous suspects were forced to attend public, televised hearings to deny or confess their guilt. Denials were generally ignored, however, and many defendants were "blacklisted" (made unemployable). Many, including iconic actor Charlie Chaplin, went overseas to find work.

McCarthy was formally condemned by the Senate on 2 December 1954; he then returned to political obscurity, dying of alcoholism in 1957. "McCarthyism" has since become a synonym for mindless nationalistic fervor, baseless mudslinging, slander, and character assassination.

Ladies and gentlemen, tonight as we celebrate the 141st birthday of one of the greatest men in American history, I would like to be able to talk about what a glorious day today is in the history of the world. As we celebrate the birth of this man who with his whole heart and soul hated war, I would like to be able to speak of peace in our time — of war being outlawed — and of worldwide disarmament. These would be truly appropriate things to be able to mention as we celebrate the birthday of Abraham Lincoln.

Five years after a world war has been won, men's hearts should anticipate a long peace — and men's minds should be free from the heavy weight that comes with war. But this is not such a period — for this is not a period of peace. This is a time of "the cold war." This is a time when all

the world is split into two vast, increasingly hostile armed camps — a time of a great armament race.

Today we can almost physically hear the mutterings and rumblings of an invigorated god of war. You can see it, feel it, and hear it all the way from the Indochina hills, from the shores of Formosa, right over into the very heart of Europe itself.

The one encouraging thing is that the "mad moment" has not yet arrived for the firing of the gun or the exploding of the bomb which will set civilisation about the final task of destroying itself. There is still a hope for peace if we finally decide that no longer can we safely blind our eyes and close our ears to those facts which are shaping up more and more clearly…and that is that we are now engaged in a show-down fight…not the usual war between nations for land areas or other material gains, but a war between two diametrically opposed ideologies.

The great difference between our western Christian world and the atheistic communist world is not political, gentlemen, it is moral. For instance, the Marxian idea of confiscating the land and factories and running the entire economy as a single enterprise is momentous. Likewise, Lenin's invention of the one-party police state as a way to make Marx's idea work is hardly less momentous.

Stalin's resolute putting across of these two ideas, of course, did much to divide the world. With only these differences, however, the East and the West could most certainly still live in peace.

The real, basic difference, however, lies in the religion of immoralism… invented by Marx, preached feverishly by Lenin, and carried to unimaginable extremes by Stalin. This religion of immoralism, if the Red half of the world triumphs — and well it may, gentlemen — this religion of immoralism will more deeply wound and damage mankind than any conceivable economic or political system.

Karl Marx dismissed God as a hoax, and Lenin and Stalin have added in clear-cut, unmistakable language their resolve that no nation, no people who believe in a god, can exist side by side with their communistic state.

Karl Marx, for example, expelled people from his Communist Party for mentioning such things as love, justice, humanity, or morality. He called this "soulful ravings" and "sloppy sentimentality"…

Today we are engaged in a final, all-out battle between communistic atheism and Christianity. The modern champions of communism have selected this as the time, and ladies and gentlemen, the chips are down…

McCarthy at a hearing of a Senate Subcommittee in March 1950.

Lest there be any doubt that the time has been chosen, let us go directly to the leader of communism today — Joseph Stalin. Here is what he said — not back in 1928, not before the war, not during the war — but two years after the last war was ended: "To think that the communist revolution can be carried out peacefully, within the framework of a Christian democracy, means one has either gone out of one's mind and lost all normal understanding, or has grossly and openly repudiated the communist revolution."...

Ladies and gentlemen, can there be anyone tonight who is so blind as to say that the war is not on? Can there be anyone who fails to realize that the communist world has said the time is now?...that this is the time for the showdown between the democratic Christian world and the communistic atheistic world? Unless we face this fact, we shall pay the price that must be paid by those who wait too long.

Six years ago...there was within the Soviet orbit, 180 million people. Lined up on the anti-totalitarian side there were in the world at that time, roughly 1625 million people. Today, only six years later, there are 800 million people under the absolute domination of Soviet Russia — an increase of over 400 percent. On our side, the figure has shrunk to around 500 million. In other words, in less than six years, the odds have changed from 9 to 1 in our favor to 8 to 5 against us.

This indicates the swiftness of the tempo of communist victories and American defeats in the Cold War. As one of our outstanding historical figures once said, "When a great democracy is destroyed, it will not be from enemies from without, but rather because of enemies from within."...

The reason why we find ourselves in a position of impotency is not because our only powerful potential enemy has sent men to invade our shores...but rather because of the traitorous actions of those who have been treated so well by this nation. It has not been the less fortunate, or members of minority groups who have been traitorous to this nation, but rather those who have had all the benefits that the wealthiest nation on earth has had to offer...the finest homes, the finest college education, and the finest jobs in government we can give.

This is glaringly true in the State Department. There the bright young men who are born with silver spoons in their mouths are the ones who have been most traitorous...

I have here in my hand a list of 205...a list of names that were made known to the Secretary of State as being members of the Communist

The journalist Edward R. Murrow on Senator Joseph McCarthy, in 1954: "The line between investigating and persecuting is a very fine one and the junior senator from Wisconsin has stepped over it repeatedly."

Party and who nevertheless are still working and shaping policy in the State Department...

As you know, very recently the Secretary of State proclaimed his loyalty to a man guilty of what has always been considered as the most abominable of all crimes — being a traitor to the people who gave him a position of great trust — high treason...

He has lighted the spark which is resulting in a moral uprising and will end only when the whole sorry mess of twisted, warped thinkers are swept from the national scene so that we may have a new birth of honesty and decency in government.

FIGHTING WORDS

"All men are created equal. They are endowed by their creator with certain inalienable rights; among these are life, liberty, and the pursuit of happiness...The whole Vietnamese people, animated by a common purpose, are determined to fight to the bitter end against any attempt by the French colonialists to reconquer their country."
On 2 September 1945, Ho Chi Minh (1890–1969), a Vietnamese revolutionary who served as both prime minister (1946–55) and president (1955–69), announced the Vietnamese Declaration of Independence, based on the American Declaration of Independence (1776). Until his death, Ho led the North Vietnamese in the Vietnam War, which ultimately ended in a North Vietnamese victory. Note the similarities to Abraham Lincoln's Gettysburg address (see page 122).

"That since wars begin in the minds of men, it is in the minds of men that the defences of peace must be constructed."
From the UNESCO (United Nations Educational, Scientific, and Cultural Organization) Constitution, 16 November 1945

"War may sometimes be a necessary evil. But no matter how necessary, it is always an evil, never a good. We will not learn how to live together in peace by killing each other's children."
Jimmy Carter was president of the United States between 1977 and 1981.

"War is Peace," "Freedom is Slavery" and "Ignorance is Strength"
These aphorisms, from George Orwell's novel *Nineteen Eighty-Four* (1949), are examples of "doublespeak," used by the ruling powers to confuse and subjugate the populace. The novel was seen by anti-fascists as anti-fascist, and by anti-communists as anti-communist. Orwell was non-committal; to him a totalitarian was a totalitarian, whatever the brand.

"...we today have concluded an agreement to...bring peace with honor in Vietnam and South-East Asia."
US president Richard Nixon announces the end of the Vietnam War in January 1973.

"I know not with what weapons World War III will be fought, but World War IV will be fought with sticks and stones."
German physicist Albert Einstein (1879–1955), pictured, is best known for his theory of relativity, represented by $E = mc^2$.

"Let us not be deceived — we are today in the midst of a cold war. Our enemies are to be found abroad and at home. Let us never forget this: our unrest is the heart of their success. The peace of the world is the hope and the goal of our political system; it is the despair and defeat of those who stand against us."
The term "cold war" was coined by Herbert Bayard Swope, who wrote speeches for Bernard Mannes Baruch (1870–1965). This is part of an address Baruch gave at the unveiling of his portrait in the South Carolina legislature, Columbia, South Carolina, on 16 April 1947.

Farewell speech
Douglas MacArthur, United States Military Academy at West Point, 12 May 1962

Douglas MacArthur (1880–1964) was a US soldier who fought in both world wars and the Korean War. One of only five men to rise to the rank of General of the Army, he is credited with these military aphorisms: "In war, there is no substitute for victory" and "The soldier, above all other people, prays for peace, for he must suffer and bear the deepest wounds and scars of war."

In 1941 he was appointed Commander of the US Armed Forces in the Far East, and in 1942 promoted to Supreme Commander of Allied Forces in the Southwest Pacific Area. On 2 September 1945, he accepted the Japanese surrender on the battleship USS *Missouri*, signaling the end of World War II. He is remembered as a brilliant tactician and leader, who was nonetheless sometimes led astray by megalomania and insubordination. His active military service ended unceremoniously in April 1951, when President Harry S. Truman sacked him for publicly disagreeing with his Korean War policy.

MacArthur was 82 years old when he gave this poetic speech for 34 minutes without notes to more than 2000 cadets at the United States Military Academy at West Point, New York. He was accepting the Sylvanus Thayer Award for outstanding service to the nation. He speaks as a representative of long-gone wars, conveying timeless wisdom to those who will carry the military load in a new, ever-changing world. He makes an incorrect reference to Plato, who did not say: "Only the dead have seen the end of war" — although philosopher George Santayana did, in his *Later Soliloquies* (1922).

...No human being could fail to be deeply moved by such a tribute as this, coming from a profession I have served so long and a people I have loved so well. It fills me with an emotion I cannot express. But this award is not intended primarily for a personality, but to symbolize a great moral code — the code of conduct and chivalry of those who guard this beloved land of culture and ancient descent. That is the meaning of this medallion. For all eyes and for all time, it is an expression of the ethics of the American soldier. That I should be integrated in this way with so noble an ideal arouses a sense of pride and yet of humility which will be with me always.

"Duty," "Honor," "Country" — those three hallowed words reverently dictate what you want to be, what you can be, what you will be. They

Douglas MacArthur habitually smoked a corncob pipe.

are your rallying point to build courage when courage seems to fail, to regain faith when there seems to be little cause for faith, to create hope when hope becomes forlorn. Unhappily, I possess neither that eloquence of diction, that poetry of imagination, nor that brilliance of metaphor to tell you all that they mean...

They teach you to be proud and unbending in honest failure, but humble and gentle in success; not to substitute words for action; not to seek the path of comfort, but to face the stress and spur of difficulty and challenge; to learn to stand up in the storm, but to have compassion on those who fall; to master yourself before you seek to master others; to have a heart that is clean, a goal that is high; to learn to laugh, yet never forget how to weep; to reach into the future, yet never neglect the past; to be serious, yet never take yourself too seriously; to be modest so that you will remember the simplicity of true greatness; the open mind of true wisdom, the meekness of true strength.

They give you a temperate will, a quality of imagination, a vigor of the emotions, a freshness of the deep springs of life, a temperamental predominance of courage over timidity, an appetite for adventure over love of ease. They create in your heart the sense of wonder, the unfailing hope of what next, and the joy and inspiration of life. They teach you in this way to be an officer and a gentleman...

From one end of the world to the other, [the American man-at-arms] has drained deep the chalice of courage. As I listened to those songs of the glee club, in memory's eye I could see those staggering columns of the First World War, bending under soggy packs on many a weary march, from dripping dusk to drizzling dawn, slogging ankle deep through the mire of shell-pocked roads; to form grimly for the attack, blue-lipped, covered with sludge and mud, chilled by the wind and rain, driving home to their objective, and for many, to the judgment seat of God...

And twenty years after, on the other side of the globe, against the filth of dirty foxholes, the stench of ghostly trenches, the slime of dripping dugouts, those boiling suns of the relentless heat, those torrential rains of devastating storms, the loneliness and utter desolation of jungle trails, the bitterness of long separation from those they loved and cherished, the deadly pestilence of tropic disease, the horror of stricken areas of war.

Their resolute and determined defence, their swift and sure attack, their indomitable purpose, their complete and decisive victory — always victory, always through the bloody haze of their last reverberating shot, the vision of gaunt, ghastly men, reverently following your password of Duty, Honor, Country...

You now face a new world, a world of change...

And through all this welter of change and development your mission remains fixed, determined, inviolable. It is to win our wars. Everything else in your professional career is but corollary to this vital dedication. All other public purpose, all other public projects, all other public needs, great or small, will find others for their accomplishments; but you are the ones who are trained to fight...

Others will debate the controversial issues, national and international, which divide men's minds. But serene, calm, aloof, you stand as the Nation's war guardians, as its lifeguards from the raging tides of international conflict, as its gladiators in the arena of battle. For a century and a half you have defended, guarded, and protected its hallowed traditions of liberty and freedom, of right and justice...

You are the leaven which binds together the entire fabric of our national system of defence. From your ranks come the great captains who hold the nation's destiny in their hands the moment the war tocsin sounds.

The long gray line has never failed us. Were you to do so, a million ghosts in olive drab, in brown khaki, in blue and gray, would rise from their white crosses, thundering those magic words: Duty, Honor, Country.

This does not mean that you are warmongers. On the contrary, the soldier above all other people prays for peace, for he must suffer and bear the deepest wounds and scars of war. But always in our ears ring the ominous words of Plato, that wisest of all philosophers: "Only the dead have seen the end of war."

The shadows are lengthening for me. The twilight is here...

In my dreams I hear again the crash of guns, the rattle of musketry, the strange, mournful mutter of the battlefield. But in the evening of my memory I come back to West Point. Always there echoes and re-echoes: Duty, Honor, Country.

Today marks my final roll call with you. But I want you to know that when I cross the river, my last conscious thoughts will be of the Corps, and the Corps, and the Corps.

I bid you farewell.

Cuban missile crisis
John F. Kennedy, Washington, DC, 22 October 1962

At 7 pm on 22 October 1962, US president John F. Kennedy made this televised speech to inform Americans of a recent Soviet military build-up in Cuba that included the installation of nuclear missiles.

He had learnt of the build-up one week earlier, after seeing aerial photos taken by an American U-2 spy plane over Cuba, just 90 miles off the Florida coast. On 18 October, the Soviet Minister of Foreign Affairs, Andrei Gromyko, told Kennedy that the weapons were for purely defensive purposes. Kennedy then discussed military options with his brother Robert, the US Attorney-General, and his top military aides. Of the two options under consideration, they chose to set up a trade embargo supported by a naval blockade of Cuba, rather than order an air strike against the Soviet bases.

In the address, Kennedy outlined the threat, announced the blockade, and stated that the United States would consider any missile launched from Cuba — regardless of its destination — as a Soviet attack on the United States.

On 28 October, USSR president Khrushchev announced on Radio Moscow that he would remove the missiles from Cuba; in exchange, Kennedy secretly agreed to remove all US missiles from the Soviet border in Turkey. However, the trade embargo is still in place; even though the United States is Cuba's seventh largest importer, US companies are forbidden from exporting more than $700 million worth of goods to Cuba per year.

The "Cuba crisis" is generally agreed to be the moment in which the so-called "Cold War" between the USSR and the United States came closest to escalating into a nuclear war. It led to the creation of the "hotline" between Moscow and Washington, a direct telephone link by which the leaders of the two countries could communicate directly to better solve a similar crisis. Communism went on to flourish in Cuba, freed as it now was from the threat of US invasion — which may well have been the Soviet intention all along.

Good evening my fellow citizens:

This Government, as promised, has maintained the closest surveillance of the Soviet military build-up on the island of Cuba. Within the past week, unmistakable evidence has established the fact that a series of offensive missile sites is now in preparation on that imprisoned island. The purpose of these bases can be none other than to provide a nuclear strike capability against the Western Hemisphere...

This urgent transformation of Cuba into an important strategic base — by the presence of these large, long-range, and clearly offensive weapons of sudden mass destruction — constitutes an explicit threat to the peace and security of all the Americas, in flagrant and deliberate defiance of the Rio Pact of 1947, the traditions of this nation and hemisphere, the joint resolution of the 87th Congress, the Charter of the United Nations, and my own public warnings to the Soviets on 4 and 13 September. This action also contradicts the repeated assurances of Soviet spokesmen, both

John F. Kennedy talks to the nation about the Cuban missile crisis.

publicly and privately delivered, that the arms build-up in Cuba would retain its original defensive character, and that the Soviet Union had no need or desire to station strategic missiles on the territory of any other nation.

The size of this undertaking makes clear that it has been planned for some months...

Neither the United States of America nor the world community of nations can tolerate deliberate deception and offensive threats on the part of any nation, large or small. We no longer live in a world where only the actual firing of weapons represents a sufficient challenge to a nation's security to constitute maximum peril. Nuclear weapons are so destructive and ballistic missiles are so swift, that any substantially increased possibility of their use or any sudden change in their deployment may well be regarded as a definite threat to peace.

For many years both the Soviet Union and the United States, recognising this fact, have deployed strategic nuclear weapons with great care, never upsetting the precarious status quo which insured that these weapons would not be used in the absence of some vital challenge. Our own strategic missiles have never been transferred to the territory of any other nation under a cloak of secrecy and deception; and our history — unlike that of the Soviets since the end of World War II — demonstrates that we have no desire to dominate or conquer any other nation or impose our system upon its people. Nevertheless, American citizens have become adjusted to living daily on the bull's-eye of Soviet missiles located inside the USSR or in submarines.

In that sense, missiles in Cuba add to an already clear and present danger — although it should be noted the nations of Latin America have never previously been subjected to a potential nuclear threat...

Our policy has been one of patience and restraint, as befits a peaceful and powerful nation, which leads a worldwide alliance. We have been determined not to be diverted from our central concerns by mere irritants and fanatics. But now further action is required — and it is under way; and these actions may only be the beginning. We will not prematurely or unnecessarily risk the costs of worldwide nuclear war in which even the fruits of victory would be ashes in our mouth — but neither will we shrink from that risk at any time it must be faced.

Acting, therefore, in the defence of our own security and of the entire Western Hemisphere, and under the authority entrusted to me by the Constitution as endorsed by the resolution of the Congress, I have directed that the following initial steps be taken immediately:

JOHN F. KENNEDY

"The Chinese use two brush strokes to write the word 'crisis.' One brush stroke stands for danger; the other for opportunity. In a crisis, be aware of the danger — but recognise the opportunity."
In a speech in Indianapolis, Indiana, on 12 April 1959

"And so, my fellow Americans: ask not what your country can do for you — ask what you can do for your country. My fellow citizens of the world: ask not what America will do for you, but what together we can do for the freedom of man."
In his Inaugural Address, 21 January 1961, Washington, DC

"This Nation was founded by men of many nations and backgrounds. It was founded on the principle that all men are created equal, and that the rights of every man are diminished when the rights of one man are threatened."
On 11 June 1963, Kennedy gave a speech on radio and television on civil rights after two Black American students, escorted by 100 National Guardsmen, were at first denied access to the University of Alabama by the governor, George Wallace.

"Two thousand years ago the proudest boast was *'Civis Romanus sumi'* ['I am a Roman']. Today, in the world of freedom, the proudest boast is *'Ich bin ein Berliner'* ['I am a Berliner']. All free men, wherever they may live, are citizens of Berlin, and, therefore, as a free man, I take pride in the words *'Ich bin ein Berliner.'* "
On 26 June 1963, President Kennedy spoke to the crowd in Berlin, West Germany, stressing American support for democratic West Germany after the erection of the Berlin Wall by Soviet-supported East Germany.

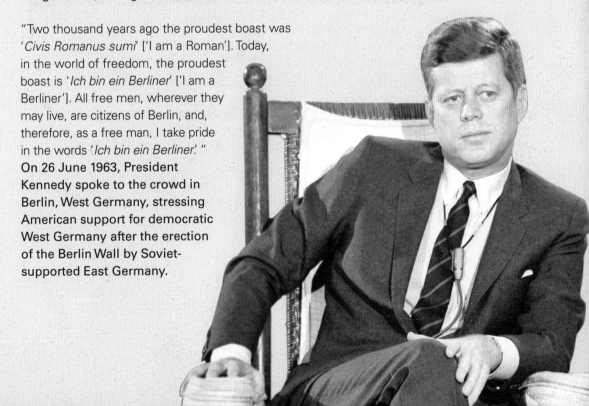

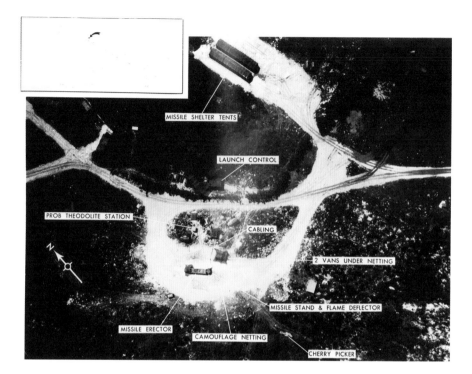

An aerial view of a Soviet Medium Range Ballistic Missile site in Cuba, one of the photographs that precipitated the Cuban missile crisis in October 1962.

First: To halt this offensive build-up, a strict quarantine on all offensive military equipment under shipment to Cuba is being initiated. All ships of any kind bound for Cuba from whatever nation or port will, if found to contain cargoes of offensive weapons, be turned back. This quarantine will be extended, if needed, to other types of cargo and carriers. We are not at this time, however, denying the necessities of life as the Soviets attempted to do in their Berlin blockade of 1948.

Second: I have directed the continued and increased close surveillance of Cuba and its military build-up. The foreign ministers of the OAS [Organization of American States], in their communiqué of October 6, rejected secrecy in such matters in this hemisphere. Should these offensive military preparations continue, thus increasing the threat to the hemisphere, further action will be justified. I have directed the armed forces to prepare for any eventualities; and I trust that in the interest of both the Cuban people and the Soviet technicians at the sites, the hazards to all concerned in continuing this threat will be recognized.

Third: It shall be the policy of this nation to regard any nuclear missile launched from Cuba against any nation in the Western Hemisphere as an attack by the Soviet Union on the United States, requiring a full retaliatory response upon the Soviet Union.

Fourth: As a necessary military precaution, I have reinforced our base at Guantanamo, evacuated today the dependents of our personnel there, and ordered additional military units to be on a standby alert basis.

Fifth: We are calling tonight for an immediate meeting of the Organ of Consultation under the Organization of American States, to consider this threat to hemispheric security and to invoke articles 6 and 8 of the Rio Treaty in support of all necessary action. The United Nations Charter allows for regional security arrangements — and the nations of this hemisphere decided long ago against the military presence of outside powers. Our other allies around the world have also been alerted.

Sixth: Under the Charter of the United Nations, we are asking tonight that an emergency meeting of the Security Council be convoked without delay to take action against this latest Soviet threat to world peace. Our resolution will call for the prompt dismantling and withdrawal of all offensive weapons in Cuba, under the supervision of UN observers, before the quarantine can be lifted.

Seventh and finally: I call upon Chairman Khrushchev to halt and eliminate this clandestine, reckless, and provocative threat to world peace and to stable relations between our two nations. I call upon him further to abandon this course of world domination, and to join in an historic effort to end the perilous arms race and to transform the history of man...

My fellow citizens: let no one doubt that this is a difficult and dangerous effort on which we have set out. No one can see precisely what course it will take or what costs or casualties will be incurred. Many months of sacrifice and self-discipline lie ahead — months in which our patience and our will will be tested — months in which many threats and denunciations will keep us aware of our dangers. But the greatest danger of all would be to do nothing...

Our goal is not the victory of might, but the vindication of right — not peace at the expense of freedom, but both peace and freedom, here in this hemisphere, and, we hope, around the world. God willing, that goal will be achieved.

Thank you and good night.

"I have a dream..."

Martin Luther King, Lincoln Memorial, Washington, DC, 28 August 1963

Baptist minister and civil rights activist King (1929–1963) made this iconic address during the "March on Washington for Jobs and Freedom" demonstration. It is regarded as one of the greatest speeches ever made, and a watershed moment in the American civil rights movement.

It portrays King's vision of a United States where all, regardless of race, may live in equality and harmony. There is an echo of Abraham Lincoln's Gettysburg Address in the opening "Five score years ago...," indicating that King was aware of the portentousness of his words. King also invokes such respected sources as the Bible, the US Constitution, and the Declaration of Independence. His rhetorical flourishes include several uses of epanaphora, the repetition of a phrase at the beginning of a sentence for emphasis.

King was honored with *Time* magazine's "Man of the Year" award in 1963, and the following year became the youngest recipient of the Nobel Peace Prize. He continued to agitate for peace and equal rights until his assassination on 30 March 1968 in Memphis, Tennessee.

...Five score years ago, a great American, in whose symbolic shadow we stand today, signed the Emancipation Proclamation. This momentous decree came as a great beacon light of hope to millions of Negro slaves who had been seared in the flames of withering injustice. It came as a joyous daybreak to end the long night of their captivity.

But one hundred years later, the Negro still is not free. One hundred years later, the life of the Negro is still sadly crippled by the manacles of segregation and the chains of discrimination. One hundred years later, the Negro lives on a lonely island of poverty in the midst of a vast ocean of material prosperity. One hundred years later, the Negro is still languishing in the corners of American society and finds himself an exile in his own land. So we have come here today to dramatize a shameful condition.

In a sense we have come to our nation's capital to cash a check. When the architects of our republic wrote the magnificent words of the Constitution and the Declaration of Independence, they were signing a promissory note to which every American was to fall heir. This note was a promise that all men, yes, black men as well as white men, would be guaranteed the unalienable rights of life, liberty, and the pursuit of happiness.

Martin Luther King addresses the crowd at the Lincoln Memorial in Washington, DC.

It is obvious today that America has defaulted on this promissory note insofar as her citizens of color are concerned. Instead of honoring this sacred obligation, America has given the Negro people a bad check, a check which has come back marked "insufficient funds." But we refuse to believe that the bank of justice is bankrupt. We refuse to believe that there are insufficient funds in the great vaults of opportunity of this nation. So we have come to cash this check — a check that will give us upon demand the riches of freedom and the security of justice. We have also come to this hallowed spot to remind America of the fierce urgency of now. This is no time to engage in the luxury of cooling off or to take the tranquilizing drug of gradualism. Now is the time to make real the promises of democracy. Now is the time to rise from the dark and desolate valley of segregation to the sunlit path of racial justice. Now is the time to lift our nation from the quicksands of racial injustice to the solid rock of brotherhood. Now is the time to make justice a reality for all of God's children.

It would be fatal for the nation to overlook the urgency of the moment. This sweltering summer of the Negro's legitimate discontent will not pass until there is an invigorating autumn of freedom and equality. Nineteen sixty-three is not an end, but a beginning. Those who hope that the Negro needed to blow off steam and will now be content will have a rude awakening if the nation returns to business as usual. There will be neither rest nor tranquillity in America until the Negro is granted his citizenship rights. The whirlwinds of revolt will continue to shake the foundations of our nation until the bright day of justice emerges.

But there is something that I must say to my people who stand on the warm threshold which leads into the palace of justice. In the process of gaining our rightful place we must not be guilty of wrongful deeds. Let us not seek to satisfy our thirst for freedom by drinking from the cup of bitterness and hatred.

We must forever conduct our struggle on the high plane of dignity and discipline. We must not allow our creative protest to degenerate into physical violence. Again and again we must rise to the majestic heights of meeting physical force with soul force. The marvellous new militancy which has engulfed the Negro community must not lead us to a distrust of all white people, for many of our white brothers, as evidenced by their presence here today, have come to realize that their destiny is tied up with our destiny. They have come to realize that their freedom is inextricably bound to our freedom. We cannot walk alone.

As we walk, we must make the pledge that we shall always march ahead. We cannot turn back. There are those who are asking the devotees of civil rights, "When will you be satisfied?" We can never be satisfied as long as the Negro is the victim of the unspeakable horrors of police brutality. We can never be satisfied, as long as our bodies, heavy with the fatigue of travel, cannot gain lodging in the motels of the highways and the hotels of the cities. We cannot be satisfied as long as the Negro's basic mobility is from a smaller ghetto to a larger one. We can never be satisfied as long as our children are stripped of their selfhood and robbed of their dignity by signs stating "For Whites Only." We cannot be satisfied as long as a Negro in Mississippi cannot vote and a Negro in New York believes he has nothing for which to vote. No, no, we are not satisfied, and we will not be satisfied until justice rolls down like waters and righteousness like a mighty stream.

I am not unmindful that some of you have come here out of great trials and tribulations. Some of you have come fresh from narrow jail cells. Some of you have come from areas where your quest for freedom left you battered by the storms of persecution and staggered by the winds of police brutality. You have been the veterans of creative suffering. Continue to work with the faith that unearned suffering is redemptive.

Go back to Mississippi, go back to Alabama, go back to South Carolina, go back to Georgia, go back to Louisiana, go back to the slums and ghettos of our northern cities, knowing that somehow this situation can and will be changed. Let us not wallow in the valley of despair.

I say to you today, my friends, so even though we face the difficulties of today and tomorrow, I still have a dream. It is a dream deeply rooted in the American dream.

I have a dream that one day this nation will rise up and live out the true meaning of its creed: "We hold these truths to be self-evident: that all men are created equal."

I have a dream that one day on the red hills of Georgia the sons of former slaves and the sons of former slave owners will be able to sit down together at the table of brotherhood.

I have a dream that one day even the state of Mississippi, a state sweltering with the heat of injustice, sweltering with the heat of oppression, will be transformed into an oasis of freedom and justice.

I have a dream that my four little children will one day live in a nation where they will not be judged by the color of their skin but by the content of their character.

King's speech, delivered in the style of a Baptist sermon, established his reputation as one of the greatest orators in US history.

I have a dream today.

I have a dream that one day, down in Alabama, with its vicious racists, with its governor having his lips dripping with the words of interposition and nullification; one day right there in Alabama, little black boys and black girls will be able to join hands with little white boys and white girls as sisters and brothers.

I have a dream today.

I have a dream that one day every valley shall be exalted, every hill and mountain shall be made low, the rough places will be made plain, and the crooked places will be made straight, and the glory of the Lord shall be revealed, and all flesh shall see it together.

This is our hope. This is the faith that I go back to the South with. With this faith we will be able to hew out of the mountain of despair a stone of hope. With this faith we will be able to transform the jangling discords of our nation into a beautiful symphony of brotherhood. With this faith we will be able to work together, to pray together, to struggle together, to go to jail together, to stand up for freedom together, knowing that we will be free one day.

This will be the day when all of God's children will be able to sing with a new meaning, "My country, 'tis of thee, sweet land of liberty, of thee I sing. Land where my fathers died, land of the pilgrim's pride, from every mountainside, let freedom ring."

And if America is to be a great nation this must become true. So let freedom ring from the prodigious hilltops of New Hampshire. Let freedom ring from the mighty mountains of New York. Let freedom ring from the heightening Alleghenies of Pennsylvania!

Let freedom ring from the snowcapped Rockies of Colorado!

Let freedom ring from the curvaceous slopes of California!

But not only that; let freedom ring from Stone Mountain of Georgia!

Let freedom ring from Lookout Mountain of Tennessee!

Let freedom ring from every hill and molehill of Mississippi. From every mountainside, let freedom ring.

And when this happens, when we allow freedom to ring, when we let it ring from every village and every hamlet, from every state and every city, we will be able to speed up that day when all of God's children, black men and white men, Jews and Gentiles, Protestants and Catholics, will be able to join hands and sing in the words of the old Negro spiritual, "Free at last! Free at last! Thank God Almighty, we are free at last!"

"I am prepared to die"
Nelson Mandela, Johannesburg Court, South Africa, 20 April 1964

Born in 1918 at Qunu, South Africa, Nelson Mandela chose a political and legal career, joining the African National Congress (ANC) in 1944. In 1962 he was arrested for opposing the anti-black apartheid ("separateness") policy of the white government, and two years later he was found guilty on four charges of sabotage and sentenced to life imprisonment.

On 11 February 1990, following a worldwide campaign, Mandela was released. He was greeted by the world with great joy, and the threads of apartheid began to unravel. In 1993 he and the South African president, F. W. de Klerk, shared the Nobel Peace Prize. The following year, with black and colored South Africans granted the vote for the first time, Mandela was elected president of South Africa.

His crowning, magnificent achievement was to negotiate the handover of power by the white minority and unite the country while avoiding a bloodbath — a result that, until his inspirational intervention, seemed highly unlikely.

This is an excerpt from Mandela's brilliant (and very long — more than 11 000-word) statement from the dock at the opening of his defence.

I am the First Accused.

At the outset, I want to say that the suggestion made by the State in its opening that the struggle in South Africa is under the influence of foreigners or communists is wholly incorrect. I have done whatever I did, both as an individual and as a leader of my people, because of my experience in South Africa and my own proudly felt African background, and not because of what any outsider might have said.

...Having said this, I must deal immediately and at some length with the question of violence. Some of the things so far told to the court are true and some are untrue. I do not, however, deny that I planned sabotage. I did not plan it in a spirit of recklessness, nor because I have any love of violence. I planned it as a result of a calm and sober assessment of the political situation that had arisen after many years of tyranny, exploitation, and oppression of my people by the whites.

...The ideological creed of the ANC is, and always has been, the creed of African Nationalism. It is not the concept of African Nationalism expressed in the cry, "Drive the white man into the sea." The African

Nelson Mandela spent twenty-five years in prison, mostly on Robben Island, 7½ miles off the coast of Cape Town, South Africa.

Nationalism for which the ANC stands is the concept of freedom and fulfilment for the African people in their own land. The most important political document ever adopted by the ANC is the "Freedom Charter." It is by no means a blueprint for a socialist state. It calls for redistribution, but not nationalisation, of land; it provides for nationalisation of mines, banks, and monopoly industry, because big monopolies are owned by one race only, and without such nationalisation racial domination would be perpetuated despite the spread of political power.

...The government often answers its critics by saying that Africans in South Africa are economically better off than the inhabitants of the other countries in Africa. I do not know whether this statement is true and doubt whether any comparison can be made without having regard to the cost-of-living index in such countries. But even if it is true, as far as the African people are concerned it is irrelevant. Our complaint is not that we are poor by comparison with people in other countries, but that we are poor by comparison with the white people in our own country, and that we are prevented by legislation from altering this imbalance.

The lack of human dignity experienced by Africans is the direct result of the policy of white supremacy. White supremacy implies black inferiority. Legislation designed to preserve white supremacy entrenches this notion. Menial tasks in South Africa are invariably performed by Africans. When anything has to be carried or cleaned the white man will look around for an African to do it for him, whether the African is employed by him or not. Because of this sort of attitude, whites tend to regard Africans as a separate breed. They do not look upon them as people with families of their own; they do not realize that they have emotions — that they fall in love like white people do; that they want to be with their wives and children like white people want to be with theirs; that they want to earn enough money to support their families properly, to feed and clothe them and send them to school. And what "house-boy" or "garden-boy" or laborer can ever hope to do this?

Pass laws, which to the Africans are among the most hated bits of legislation in South Africa, render any African liable to police surveillance at any time. I doubt whether there is a single African male in South Africa who has not at some stage had a brush with the police over his pass. Hundreds and thousands of Africans are thrown into jail each year under pass laws. Even worse than this is the fact that pass laws keep husband and wife apart and lead to the breakdown of family life.

...Africans want to be paid a living wage. Africans want to perform work which they are capable of doing, and not work which the government declares them to be capable of. Africans want to be allowed to live where they obtain work, and not be endorsed out of an area because they were not born there. Africans want to be allowed to own land in places where they work, and not to be obliged to live in rented houses which they can never call their own. Africans want to be part of the general population, and not confined to living in their own ghettoes. African men want to have their wives and children to live with them where they work, and not be forced into an unnatural existence in men's hostels. African women want to be with their menfolk and not be left permanently widowed in the Reserves. Africans want to be allowed out after 11 o'clock at night and not to be confined to their rooms like little children. Africans want to be allowed to travel in their own country and to seek work where they want to and not where the Labor Bureau tells them to. Africans want a just share in the whole of South Africa; they want security and a stake in society.

Above all, we want equal political rights, because without them our disabilities will be permanent. I know this sounds revolutionary to the whites in this country, because the majority of voters will be Africans. This makes the white man fear democracy.

But this fear cannot be allowed to stand in the way of the only solution which will guarantee racial harmony and freedom for all. It is not true that the enfranchisement of all will result in racial domination. Political division, based on color, is entirely artificial and, when it disappears, so will the domination of one color group by another. The ANC has spent half a century fighting against racialism. When it triumphs it will not change that policy.

This then is what the ANC is fighting. Their struggle is a truly national one. It is a struggle of the African people, inspired by their own suffering and their own experience. It is a struggle for the right to live.

During my lifetime I have dedicated myself to this struggle of the African people. I have fought against white domination, and I have fought against black domination. I have cherished the ideal of a democratic and free society in which all persons live together in harmony and with equal opportunities. It is an ideal which I hope to live for and to achieve. But if needs be, it is an ideal for which I am prepared to die.

"I am not for peace at any price"

Eugene J. McCarthy, press conference, Washington, DC, 30 November 1967

Eugene J. McCarthy (1916–2005) was a US politician who served in the House of Representatives from 1949 to 1959, and in the Senate from 1959 to 1971. He unsuccessfully sought the presidency five times, usually on a nuclear disarmament/anti-war platform. When he died in December 2005, former president Bill Clinton delivered his funeral eulogy.

This speech was made at the media conference where McCarthy announces that he will, for the first time, seek the Democratic Party nomination for the 1968 presidential election, standing against incumbent Democrat president Lyndon Johnson. He outlines the reasons for his opposition to US involvement in the Vietnam War.

…My decision to challenge the President's position and the Administration's position has been strengthened by recent announcements out of the Administration, the evident intention to escalate and to intensify the war in Vietnam and, on the other hand, the absence of any positive indications or suggestions for a compromise or for a negotiated political settlement. I am concerned that the Administration seems to have set no limit to the price which it is willing to pay for a military victory.

Let me summarize the cost of the war up to this point:

- the physical destruction of much of a small and weak nation by military operations of the most powerful nation in the world;
- 100 000 to 150 000 civilian casualties in South Vietnam alone, to say nothing of the destruction of life and property in North Vietnam;
- the uprooting and the fracturing of the structure of the society of South Vietnam, where one-fourth to one-third of the population are now reported to be refugees;
- for the United States, as of yesterday, over 15 000 combat dead and nearly 95 000 wounded through November;
- a monthly expenditure in pursuit of the war running somewhere between $2 and $3 billion.

I am also concerned about the bearing of the war on other areas of United States responsibility, both at home and abroad:

- the failure to appropriate adequate funds for the poverty program here, for housing, for education, and to meet other national needs, and

Senator Eugene J. McCarthy with his supporters during the 1968 campaign for the Democratic Party presidential nomination.

the prospect of additional cuts as a condition to a possible passage of the surtax tax bill;

- the drastic reduction of our foreign aid program in other parts of the world;
- a dangerous rise in inflation; and one of the indirect and serious consequences of our involvement in Vietnam — the devaluation of the British pound, which in many respects is more important east of Suez today than the British Navy.

In addition, there's a growing evidence of the deepening moral crisis in America: discontent and frustration, and a disposition to take extra-legal, if not illegal, actions to manifest protest.

I am hopeful that this challenge which I am making, which I hope will be supported by other members of the Senate and other politicians, may alleviate at least in some degree of this sense of political helplessness and restore to many people a belief in the processes of American politics and of American government; that on the college campuses especially and also among adult, thoughtful Americans, it may come to the growing sense of alienation from politics which I think is currently reflected in a tendency to withdraw from political action, to talk of non-participation, to become cynical and to make threats of support for third parties or fourth parties or other irregular political movements.

...Let me say that — as I am sure I shall be charged — I am not for peace at any price, but for an honorable, rational, and political solution to this war; a solution which I believe will enhance our world position, encourage the respect of our allies and our potential adversaries, which will permit us to get the necessary attention to other commitments — both at home and abroad, militarily and not militarily — and leave us with resources and moral energy to deal effectively with the pressing domestic problems of the United States itself. In this total effort, I believe we can restore to this nation a clear sense of purpose and of dedication to the achievement of our traditional purposes as a great nation in the twentieth century...

Bobby Kennedy campaigned against McCarthy for the Democratic presidential nomination, but was assassinated in June 1968 after winning the California primary.

Discrimination speech
Shirley Chisholm, US Congress, Washington, DC, 21 May 1969

Shirley Chisholm (1924–2005) was an educator, administrator, and activist for minority rights. In 1968 she became the first African-American woman elected to the House of Representatives, and hired an all-female staff. In 1972 she became the first African-American candidate to nominate for US president. She was active in the National Association for the Advancement of Colored People (NAACP) and co-founder of the National Organization for Women (NOW). She published two books: *Unbought and Unbowed* (1970) and *The Good Fight* (1973).

Here she points out many of the subtle (and not so subtle) methods used by society to discriminate against women. She also observes that sexism has become more socially acceptable than racism in the United States.

...Mr Speaker, when a young woman graduates from college and starts looking for a job, she is likely to have a frustrating and even demeaning experience ahead of her. If she walks into an office for an interview, the first question she will be asked is "Do you type?"

There is a calculated system of prejudice that lies unspoken behind that question. Why is it acceptable for women to be secretaries, librarians, and teachers, but totally unacceptable for them to be managers, administrators, doctors, lawyers, and members of Congress?

The unspoken assumption is that women are different. They do not have executive ability, orderly minds, stability, leadership skills, and they are too emotional.

It has been observed before that society, for a long time, discriminated against another minority, the blacks, on the same basis — that they were different and inferior. The happy little homemaker and the contented "old darkey" on the plantation were both produced by prejudice.

As a black person, I am no stranger to race prejudice. But the truth is that in the political world I have been far oftener discriminated against because I am a woman than because I am black.

Prejudice against blacks is becoming unacceptable although it will take years to eliminate it. But it is doomed because, slowly, white America is beginning to admit that it exists. Prejudice against women is still acceptable. There is very little understanding yet of the immorality involved

Shirley Chisholm announces her run for the Democratic Party presidential nomination in January 1972.

in double pay scales and the classification of most of the better jobs as "for men only."

More than half of the population of the United States is female. But women occupy only 2 percent of the managerial positions. They have not even reached the level of tokenism yet. No women sit on the AFL-CIO council or Supreme Court. There have been only two women who have held Cabinet rank, and at present there are none. Only two women now hold ambassadorial rank in the diplomatic corps. In Congress, we are down to one senator and ten representatives.

Considering that there are about three and a half million more women in the United States than men, this situation is outrageous.

...part of the problem has been that women have not been aggressive in demanding their rights. This was also true of the black population for many years. They submitted to oppression and even cooperated with it. Women have done the same thing. But now there is an awareness of this situation particularly among the younger segment of the population.

As in the field of equal rights for blacks, Spanish-Americans, the Indians, and other groups, laws will not change such deep-seated problems overnight. But they can be used to provide protection for those who are most abused, and to begin the process of evolutionary change by compelling the insensitive majority to re-examine its unconscious attitudes.

It is for this reason that I wish to introduce today a proposal that has been before every Congress for the last forty years and that sooner or later must become part of the basic law of the land — the Equal Rights Amendment.

Let me note and try to refute two of the commonest arguments that are offered against this amendment. One is that women are already protected under the law and do not need legislation. Existing laws are not adequate to secure equal rights for women. Sufficient proof of this is the concentration of women in lower paying, menial, unrewarding jobs, and their incredible scarcity in the upper level jobs. If women are already equal, why is it such an event whenever one happens to be elected to Congress?

It is obvious that discrimination exists. Women do not have the opportunities that men do. And women that do not conform to the system, who try to break with the accepted patterns, are stigmatized as "odd" and "unfeminine." The fact is that a woman who aspires to be chairman of the board, or a Member of the House, does so for exactly the same reasons as any man. Basically, these are that she thinks she can do the job and she wants to try.

...As for the marriage laws, they are due for a sweeping reform, and an excellent beginning would be to wipe the existing ones off the books. Regarding special protection for working women, I cannot understand why it should be needed. Women need no protection that men do not need. What we need are laws to protect working people, to guarantee them fair pay, safe working conditions, protection against sickness and layoffs, and provision for dignified, comfortable retirement. Men and women need these things equally. That one sex needs protection more than the other is a male supremacist myth as ridiculous and unworthy of respect as the white supremacist myths that society is trying to cure itself of at this time.

Response to "Zionism is Racism" resolution
Chaim Herzog, UN General Assembly, New York, 10 November 1975

Chaim Herzog (1918–1997) was born in Ireland, attained a law degree in London, and served with distinction in the British Army in World War II. He participated in the liberation of several concentration camps, and identified a captured German soldier as Gestapo head Heinrich Himmler. In 1947 he left the British Army with the rank of major, then served in the newly formed Israeli Army until 1962, attaining the rank of major-general.

Herzog served as Israeli ambassador to the United Nations from 1975 to 1978. Early in his term the UN carried an infamous resolution that equated Zionism with racism. As he made this speech, Herzog condemned the resolution and symbolically tore up a copy of it. (The resolution was eventually revoked in 1991.) In 1983 Herzog was elected President of Israel, serving two terms before his retirement from politics in 1993. He was also a noted military historian.

...It is symbolic that this debate, which may well prove to be a turning point in the fortunes of the United Nations and a decisive factor in the possible continued existence of this organisation, should take place on November 10. Tonight, thirty-seven years ago, has gone down in history as *Kristallnacht*, the Night of the Crystals. This was the night in 1938 when Hitler's Nazi storm troopers launched a coordinated attack on the Jewish community in Germany, burned the synagogues in all its cities and made bonfires in the streets of the Holy Books and the Scrolls of the Holy Law and Bible. It was the night when Jewish homes were attacked and heads of families taken away, many of them never to return. It was the night when the windows of all Jewish businesses and stores were smashed, covering the streets in the cities of Germany with a film of broken glass which dissolved into the millions of crystals which gave that night its name. It was the night which led eventually to the crematoria and the gas chambers, Auschwitz, Birkenau, Dachau, Buchenwald, Theresienstadt, and others. It was the night which led to the most terrifying holocaust in the history of man.

It is indeed befitting Mr President, that this debate, conceived in the desire to deflect the Middle East from its moves towards peace and born of a deep pervading feeling of anti-Semitism, should take place on the anniversary of this day. It is indeed befitting, Mr President, that the United

Chaim Herzog wrote several historical works, including *The Arab-Israeli Wars* and *War of Atonement: The Inside Story of the Yom Kippur War.*

Nations, which began its life as an anti-Nazi alliance, should thirty years later find itself on its way to becoming the world center of anti-Semitism. Hitler would have felt at home on a number of occasions during the past year, listening to the proceedings in this forum, and above all to the proceedings during the debate on Zionism.

...I do not come to this rostrum to defend the moral and historical values of the Jewish people. They do not need to be defended. They speak for themselves. They have given to mankind much of what is great and eternal. They have done for the spirit of man more than can readily be appreciated by a forum such as this one.

I come here to denounce the two great evils which menace society in general and a society of nations in particular. These two evils are hatred and ignorance. These two evils are the motivating force behind the proponents of this resolution and their supporters. These two evils characterize those who would drag this world organisation, the ideals of which were first conceived by the prophets of Israel, to the depths to which it has been dragged today.

...Zionism is the name of the national movement of the Jewish people and is the modern expression of the ancient Jewish heritage. The Zionist ideal, as set out in the Bible, has been, and is, an integral part of the Jewish religion.

Zionism is to the Jewish people what the liberation movements of Africa and Asia have been to their own people.

Zionism is one of the most dynamic and vibrant national movements in human history. Historically it is based on a unique and unbroken connection, extending some four thousand years, between the People of the Book and the Land of the Bible.

In modern times, in the late nineteenth century, spurred by the twin forces of anti-Semitic persecution and of nationalism, the Jewish people organized the Zionist movement in order to transform their dream into reality. Zionism as a political movement was the revolt of an oppressed nation against the depredation and wicked discrimination and oppression of the countries in which anti-Semitism flourished. It is no coincidence that the co-sponsors and supporters of this resolution include countries who are guilty of the horrible crimes of anti-Semitism and discrimination to this very day.

Support for the aim of Zionism was written into the League of Nations Mandate for Palestine and was again endorsed by the United Nations in 1947, when the General Assembly voted by overwhelming majority for the restoration of Jewish independence in our ancient land.

...This malicious resolution, designed to divert us from its true purpose, is part of a dangerous anti-Semitic idiom which is being insinuated into every public debate by those who have sworn to block the current move towards accommodation and ultimately towards peace in the Middle East. This, together with similar moves, is designed to sabotage the efforts of the Geneva Conference for peace in the Middle East and to deflect those who are moving along the road towards peace from their purpose. But they will not succeed, for I can but reiterate my government's policy to make every move in the direction towards peace, based on compromise.

...On the issue before us, the world has divided itself into good and bad, decent and evil, human and debased. We, the Jewish people, will recall in history our gratitude to those nations who stood up and were counted and who refused to support this wicked proposition. I know that this episode will have strengthened the forces of freedom and decency in this world and will have fortified the free world in their resolve to strengthen the ideals they so cherish. I know that this episode will have strengthened Zionism as it has weakened the United Nations.

As I stand on this rostrum...I see the oppressors of our people over the ages as they pass one another in evil procession into oblivion. I stand here before you as the representative of a strong and flourishing people which has survived them all and which will survive this shameful exhibition and the proponents of this resolution.

...I stand here not as a supplicant. Vote as your moral conscience dictates to you. For the issue is neither Israel nor Zionism. The issue is the continued existence of this organisation, which has been dragged to its lowest point of discredit by a coalition of despots and racists.

The vote of each delegation will record in history its country's stand on anti-Semitic racism and anti-Judaism. You yourselves bear the responsibility for your stand before history, for as such will you be viewed in history. We, the Jewish people, will not forget.

...We put our trust in our Providence, in our faith and beliefs, in our time-hallowed tradition, in our striving for social advance and human values, and in our people wherever they may be. For us, the Jewish people, this resolution based on hatred, falsehood, and arrogance, is devoid of any moral or legal value.

Falklands War

Margaret Thatcher, Speech to the Conservative Women's Conference, London, 26 May 1982

Margaret Thatcher, prime minister of Britain from 1979 to 1990, delivered this speech during the (undeclared) 1982 war between Argentina and Britain over Argentina's occupation of the Falkland, South Georgia and Sandwich islands. The war was triggered by England's naval and military response to the occupation of South Georgia by Argentina on 19 March, followed by its occupation of the Falklands. It ended after a series of land and sea battles when Argentina surrendered on 14 June. Both countries claimed (and still claim) sovereignty over the region.

Argentina did not expect Britain to respond with military force, as the remote islands are of little strategic use. The war resulted in the death of 649 Argentines and 258 Britons. The defeat discredited the Argentine military government and led to the restoration of civilian rule in 1983. On the other hand, Thatcher, whose government had been suffering from dwindling public support before the war, was returned to power with an increased parliamentary majority.

Madam Chairman.

Our conference takes place at a time when great and grave issues face our country. Our hearts and minds are focused on the South Atlantic. You have been debating defence policy at a time when our fighting men are engaged in one of the most remarkable military operations in modern times.

We have sent an immensely powerful task force, more than one hundred ships, and 27 000 sailors, marines, soldiers, and airmen, some 8000 miles away in the South Atlantic.

In a series of measured and progressive steps, over the past weeks, our forces have tightened their grip of the Falkland Islands. They have re-taken South Georgia. Gradually they have denied fresh supplies to the Argentine garrison.

Finally, by the successful landing at San Carlos Bay in the early hours of Friday morning, they have placed themselves in a position to re-take the islands and reverse the illegal invasion by Argentina.

By the skill of our pilots, our sailors, and those manning the Rapier missile on shore they have inflicted heavy losses on the Argentine Air Force — over fifty aircraft have been destroyed...

Margaret Thatcher, also known as the "Iron Lady," was one of the longest serving prime ministers in British history.

We in Britain know the reality of war. We know its hazards and its dangers. We know the task that faces our fighting men.

They are now established on the Falkland Islands with all the necessary supplies. Although they still face formidable problems in difficult terrain with a hostile climate, their morale is high...

Madam Chairman, the theme of this conference is "Living with our Neighbors" and it may seem inappropriate to be debating such a thing when there was open conflict between Britain and Argentina, and the lives of young men on both sides are being lost. But the whole basis of our foreign and defence policy, and indeed of the international political order depends on the friendship of neighbors, cooperating with them, and abiding by the rule of law.

These are the very things which the illegal invasion of the Falkland Islands, had it gone unchallenged, would have subverted and destroyed. The Falkland Islands are British. The Falkland Islanders are British. They don't want to be ruled by Argentina, as those pictures of the welcome given to British marines and soldiers showed more clearly than a thousand words...

...there were those who said we should have accepted the Argentine invasion as a *fait accompli*. But Madam Chairman, whenever the rule of force rather than the rule of law is seen to succeed, the world moves a step closer to anarchy.

The older generation in our country, and generations before them, have made sacrifices so that we could be a free society and belong to a community of nations which seeks to resolve disputes by civilized means.

Today it falls to us to bear the same responsibility, we shall not shirk it. What has happened since that day, eight weeks ago, is a matter of history — the history of a nation which rose instinctively to the needs of the occasion.

For decades, the peoples of the Falkland Islands had enjoyed peace — with freedom — peace with justice, peace with democracy. They are our people and let no one doubt our profound longing for peace. But that peace was shattered by a wanton act of armed aggression by Argentina in blatant violation of international law. And everything that has happened since has stemmed from the invasion by the military dictatorship of Argentina. And sometimes I feel people need reminding of that fact more often. We want peace restored. But we want it with the same freedom, justice, and democracy that the Islanders previously enjoyed...

We are the victims; they are the aggressors...

FAMOUS LAST WORDS

"No, you certainly can't."
John F. Kennedy, US president, replying to Nellie Connally, wife of Texas governor John Connally, when she said to him: "You certainly can't say that the people of Dallas haven't given you a nice welcome, Mr President." Seconds later Kennedy was fatally shot, 1963.

"Is it my birthday or am I dying?"
Nancy Astor, British politician, after waking to find her bed surrounded by well-wishers, 1964. Her son Jakie responded, "A bit of both, Mom."

"Oh, I am so bored with it all."
Winston Churchill, British statesman, just before lapsing into a coma and dying nine days later, 1965

"Let's cool it brothers…"
Malcolm X (pictured), African-American leader, to his three assassins, 1966

"I know you are here to kill me. Shoot, coward, you are only going to kill a man."
Che Guevara, Argentine Marxist revolutionary and Cuban guerrilla leader, 1967

"I failed!"
Jean-Paul Sartre, French existentialist philosopher, and writer, 1980

"Don't worry, relax!"
Rajiv Gandhi, Indian prime minister, to security staff moments before being killed by a female suicide bomber, 1991

We came to military action reluctantly. But when territory which has been British for almost 150 years is seized and occupied; when not only British land, but British citizens, are in the power of an aggressor; then we have to restore our rights and the rights of the Falkland Islanders...

When their land was invaded and their homes were overrun, they naturally turned to us for help, and we, their fellow citizens, 8000 miles away in our own much larger island, could not and did not beg to be excused...

Surely we, of all people, have learned the lesson of history: that to appease an aggressor is to invite aggression elsewhere, and on an ever-increasing scale.

Other voices — again only a few — have accused us of clinging to colonialism or even imperialism. Let us remind those who advance that argument that we British have a record second to none of leading colony after colony to freedom and independence. We cling not to colonialism but to self-determination of peoples everywhere.

Still others — again only a few — say we must not put at risk our investments and interests in Latin America; that trade and commerce are too important to us to put in jeopardy some of the valuable markets of the world.

What would the Islanders, under the heel of the invader, say to that?

What kind of people would we be if, enjoying the birthright of freedom ourselves, we were to abandon British citizens for the sake of commercial gain? We would never do it. Now we are present in strength on the Falkland Islands. Our purpose is to re-possess them and we shall persevere until that purpose is accomplished.

Madam Chairman, our cause is just...

It is the cause of freedom and the rule of law.

It is the cause of support for the weak against aggression by the strong.

Let us then draw together in the name, not of jingoism, but of justice.

Finally, let our nation, as it has so often in the past, remind itself — and the world: "Nought shall make us rue, If England to herself do rest but true." [William Shakespeare, *King John*, Act V, Scene 7]

Attack on Iraq
George Bush Snr, Washington, DC, 16 January 1991

This televised speech was made two hours after the US and Allied forces launched a major attack, dubbed "Desert Storm," against Baghdad, in Iraq. The raid was broadcast live around the world by television correspondents perched on a rooftop.

In August 1990, Iraqi forces had invaded oil-rich Kuwait, forcing the government to flee to Saudi Arabia. Kuwait asked for US assistance as Iraqi troops massed along the Saudi border, so US troops were sent to protect Saudi oil fields. This action was called "Desert Shield."

The UN Security Council instigated a trade and financial embargo against Iraq, and authorized naval forces in the Persian Gulf to use force to prevent violations of the sanctions. On 29 November the Security Council authorized the use of "all necessary means" to oust Iraqi troops from Kuwait if they had not retreated by 15 January 1991.

But the Iraqi command, in a disastrous miscalculation, ignored the deadline. It did not believe that the US, its recent ally in a war against neighboring Iran, would use military force. By now there were 539 000 US troops and 270 000 Allied troops from more than two dozen nations in the region. One wonders what Saddam Hussein and his commanders thought they were doing there.

The Allied attack started the day after the deadline expired. Iraq was expelled from Kuwait but Saddam retained power in Iraq until March 2003, when a US-led coalition launched another invasion, resulting in Saddam's capture, trial, and execution. At the time of writing, the second Iraq War was still raging.

Bush's approval ratings skyrocketed temporarily after the battle, but he was nonetheless defeated by Democrat candidate Bill Clinton in the 1992 presidential election.

Just two hours ago, Allied air forces began an attack on military targets in Iraq and Kuwait. These attacks continue as I speak. Ground forces are not engaged. This conflict started August 2, when the dictator of Iraq invaded a small and helpless neighbor. Kuwait, a member of the Arab League and a member of the United Nations, was crushed, its people brutalized. Five months ago, Saddam Hussein started this cruel war against Kuwait; tonight, the battle has been joined.

This military action, taken in accord with United Nations resolutions and with the consent of the United States Congress, follows months of constant and virtually endless diplomatic activity on the part of the United Nations, the United States and many, many other countries.

Arab leaders sought what became known as an Arab solution, only to conclude that Saddam Hussein was unwilling to leave Kuwait. Others traveled to Baghdad in a variety of efforts to restore peace and justice. Our Secretary of State, James Baker, held an historic meeting in Geneva, only to be totally rebuffed.

This past weekend, in a last ditch effort, the Secretary General of the United Nations went to the Middle East with peace in his heart — his second such mission. And he came back from Baghdad with no progress at all in getting Saddam Hussein to withdraw from Kuwait.

Now, the twenty-eight countries with forces in the Gulf area have exhausted all reasonable efforts to reach a peaceful resolution, and have no choice but to drive Saddam from Kuwait by force. We will not fail.

As I report to you, air attacks are under way against military targets in Iraq. We are determined to knock out Saddam Hussein's nuclear bomb potential. We will also destroy his chemical weapons facilities. Much of Saddam's artillery and tanks will be destroyed. Our operations are designed to best protect the lives of all the Coalition forces by targeting Saddam's vast military arsenal.

...Our objectives are clear: Saddam Hussein's forces will leave Kuwait. The legitimate government of Kuwait will be restored to its rightful place, and Kuwait will once again be free.

Iraq will eventually comply with all relevant United Nations resolutions, and then, when peace is restored, it is our hope that Iraq will live as a peaceful and cooperative member of the family of nations, thus enhancing the security and stability of the Gulf.

Some may ask, why act now? Why not wait? The answer is clear. The world could wait no longer. Sanctions, though having some effect, showed no signs of accomplishing their objective. Sanctions were tried for well over five months, and we and our allies concluded that sanctions alone would not force Saddam from Kuwait.

While the world waited, Saddam Hussein systematically raped, pillaged, and plundered a tiny nation no threat to his own. He subjected the people of Kuwait to unspeakable atrocities, and among those, maimed and murdered innocent children.

Two significant political events occurred during Bush's presidency — the fall of the Berlin Wall in 1989, and the dissolution of the Soviet Union two years later.

MIKHAIL GORBACHEV

Mikhail Gorbachev was president of the USSR from 1985 to 1991 and a winner of the 1991 Nobel Prize for Peace. His reforms helped to end the Cold War and dissolve the Soviet Union.

"...certain people in the United States are driving nails into this structure of our relationship, then cutting off the heads. So the Soviets must use their teeth to pull them out."
In an interview published in *Time* magazine, 9 September 1985, Gorbachev refers to the US's reluctance to limit its strategic programs.

"The idea of democratising the entire world order has become a powerful socio-political force. At the same time, the scientific and technological revolution has turned many economic, food, energy, environmental, information, and population problems, which only recently we treated as national or regional ones, into global problems."
On 7 December 1988, Gorbachev gives a speech to the UN General Assembly in New York.

"Tolerance is the alpha and omega of a new world order."
Gorbachev, quoted in *The New York Times* while on a tour of the United States in June 1990

"...all members of the world community should resolutely discard old stereotypes and motivations nurtured by the Cold War, and give up the habit of seeking each other's weak spots and exploiting them in their own interests...Has not the political thinking in the world changed substantially? Does not most of the world community already regard weapons of mass destruction as unacceptable for achieving political objectives?"
Gorbachev accepts the Nobel Peace Prize in June 1991.

While the world waited, Saddam sought to add to the chemical weapons arsenal and he now possesses an infinitely more dangerous weapon of mass destruction — a nuclear weapon. And while the world waited, while the world talked peace and withdrawal, Saddam Hussein dug in and moved massive forces into Kuwait.

While the world waited, while Saddam stalled, more damage was being done to the fragile economies of the Third World, emerging democracies of Eastern Europe, to the entire world, including to our own economy.

The United States, together with the United Nations, exhausted every means at our disposal to bring this crisis to a peaceful end. However, Saddam clearly felt that by stalling and threatening and defying the United Nations, he could weaken the forces arrayed against him.

While the world waited, Saddam Hussein met every overture of peace with open contempt.

While the world prayed for peace, Saddam prepared for war.

I had hoped that when the United States Congress, in historic debate, took its resolute action, Saddam would realize he could not prevail, and would move out of Kuwait in accord with the United Nations resolutions. He did not do that. Instead, he remained intransigent, certain that time was on his side.

Saddam was warned over and over again to comply with the will of the United Nations: leave Kuwait or be driven out. Saddam has arrogantly rejected all warnings. Instead, he tried to make this a dispute between Iraq and the United States of America.

Well, he failed. Tonight twenty-eight nations — countries from five continents, Europe and Asia, Africa and the Arab League — have forces in the Gulf area standing shoulder-to-shoulder against Saddam Hussein. These countries had hoped the use of force could be avoided. Regrettably, we now believe that only force will make him leave.

Prior to ordering our forces into battle, I instructed our military commanders to take every necessary step to prevail, as quickly as possible, and with the greatest degree of protection possible for American and Allied servicemen and -women.

I've told the American people before that this will not be another Vietnam, and I repeat this here tonight. Our troops will have the best possible support in the entire world, and they will not be asked to fight with one hand tied behind their back. I'm hopeful that this fighting will not go on for long, and that casualties will be held to an absolute minimum.

US paramedics escort a wounded soldier to a waiting helicopter in the Gulf War, 1991.

This is an historic moment. We have in this past year made great progress in ending the long era of conflict and cold war. We have before us the opportunity to forge for ourselves and for future generations a new world order, a world where the rule of law, not the law of the jungle, governs the conduct of nations.

When we are successful, and we will be, we have a real chance at this new world order, an order in which a credible United Nations can use its peace-keeping role to fulfil the promise and vision of the UN's founders.

We have no argument with the people of Iraq. Indeed, for the innocents caught in this conflict, I pray for their safety.

Our goal is not the conquest of Iraq. It is the liberation of Kuwait. It is my hope that somehow the Iraqi people can, even now, convince their dictator that he must lay down his arms, leave Kuwait, and let Iraq itself rejoin the family of peace-loving nations.

Thomas Paine wrote many years ago: "These are the times that try men's souls." Those well known words are so very true today. But even as planes of the multinational forces attack Iraq, I prefer to think of peace, not war. I am convinced not only that we will prevail, but that out of the horror of combat will come the recognition that no nation can stand against a world united. No nation will be permitted to brutally assault its neighbor.

No president can easily commit our sons and daughters to war. They are the nation's finest. Ours is an all-volunteer force, magnificently trained, highly motivated. The troops know why they're there. And listen to what they say, because they've said it better than any president or prime minister ever could.

Listen to "Hollywood" Huddleston, Marine lance corporal. He says: "Let's free these people so we can go home and be free again."

And he's right. The terrible crimes and tortures committed by Saddam's henchmen against the innocent people of Kuwait are an affront to mankind and a challenge to the freedom of all.

Listen to one of our great officers out there, Marine Lieutenant-General Walter Boomer: "There are things worth fighting for. A world in which brutality and lawlessness are allowed to go unchecked isn't the kind of world we're going to want to live in."

Listen to Master Sergeant J. P. Kendall of the 82nd Airborne: "We're here for more than just the price of a gallon of gas. What we're doing is going to chart the future of the world for the next hundred years. It's better to deal with this guy now than five years from now."

And finally, we should all sit up and listen to Jackie Jones, an army lieutenant, when she says: "If we let him get away with this, who knows what's going to be next."

I've called upon Hollywood and Walter and J. P. and Jackie, and all their courageous comrades-in-arms, to do what must be done. Tonight, America and the world are deeply grateful to them and to their families.

And let me say to everyone listening or watching tonight: when the troops we've sent in finish their work, I'm determined to bring them home as soon as possible. Tonight, as our forces fight, they and their families are in our prayers.

May God bless each and every one of them, and the coalition forces at our side in the Gulf, and may He continue to bless our nation, the United States of America.

Speech for the Unknown Soldier
Don Watson for Paul Keating, Canberra, 11 November 1993

Armistice Day, 11 November, celebrated by the Allied countries that fought in World War I, was the day chosen for the entombment of the Australian Unknown Soldier in a shrine at the Australian War Memorial in Canberra.

The speech has some points of comparison with Abraham Lincoln's famous Gettysburg Address. Both commemorate the war dead, and are relatively brief, using short, sharp sentences for emphasis. Each uses the sacrifice of the dead to shed light on larger issues: democracy and freedom for Lincoln, courage and ingenuity and the bonds of mateship for Keating. Both make references to the audience, with frequent use of the pronoun "we."

This speech was written by author and wordsmith Don Watson and delivered by Australian prime minister Paul Keating (b. 1944). Watson went on to publish a biography of Keating, called *Recollections of a Bleeding Heart* (2002), in which he offers some pertinent questions for any aspiring writer or speaker: "How to take in words that would move people — as sometimes they visibly did? How to describe complex, subtle, near-invisible meanings in words that could be understood on first hearing them? How to interpret the country without offending other interpretations? How to avoid cliché, pedantry, sentimentality and yet never venture too far from the familiar? How to advance the argument, pull the audience beyond what they knew to what they didn't know?"

Keating was famous for the quality of his invective, referring to opposition leader John Howard as "brain-damaged" and an "intellectual rust-bucket" and "mangy maggot." He served as prime minister of Australia until his defeat by Howard's Liberal/National Party coalition in the 1996 federal election.

We do not know this Australian's name and we never will. We do not know his rank or his battalion. We do not know where he was born, or precisely how and when he died. We do not know where in Australia he had made his home or when he left it for the battlefields of Europe. We do not know his age or his circumstances: whether he was from the city or the bush; what occupation he left to become a soldier; what religion, if he had a religion; if he was married or single. We do not know who loved him or whom he loved. If he had children, we do not know who they are. His family is lost to us as he was lost to them. We will never know who this Australian was.

Former Australian prime minister Paul Keating speaking at the University of New South Wales, Sydney, in 1996.

Yet he has always been among those we have honored. We know that he was one of the 45 000 Australians who died on the Western Front. One of the 416 000 Australians who volunteered for service in the First World War. One of the 324 000 Australians who served overseas in that war, and one of the 60 000 Australians who died on foreign soil. One of the 100 000 Australians who have died in wars this century.

He is all of them. And he is one of us.

This Australia and the Australia he knew are like foreign countries. The tide of events since he died has been so dramatic, so vast and all-consuming, a world has been created beyond the reach of his imagination. He may have been one of those who believed the Great War would be an adventure too grand to miss. He may have felt that he would never live down the shame of not going. But the chances are that he went for no other reason than that he believed it was his duty — the duty he owed his country and his king.

Because the Great War was a mad, brutal, awful struggle, distinguished more often than not by military and political incompetence: because the waste of human life was so terrible that some said victory was scarcely discernible from defeat; and because the war which was supposed to end all wars in fact sowed the seeds of a second, even more terrible, war, we might think that this Unknown Soldier died in vain.

Keating lays a wreath on the tomb of the Unknown Soldier.

But in honoring our war dead as we always have, we declare that this is not true. For out of the war came a lesson which transcended the horror and tragedy and the inexcusable folly. It was a lesson about ordinary people — and the lesson was that they were not ordinary. On all sides they were the heroes of that war; not the generals and the politicians, but the soldiers and sailors and nurses — those who taught us to endure hardship, show courage, to be bold as well as resilient, to believe in ourselves, to stick together. The Unknown Australian Soldier we inter today was one of those who by his deeds proved that real nobility and grandeur belong not to empires and nations, but to the people on whom they, in the last resort, always depend.

That is surely at the heart of the Anzac story, the Australian legend which emerged from the war. It is a legend not of sweeping military victories so much as triumphs against the odds, of courage and ingenuity in adversity. It is a legend of free and independent spirits whose discipline derived less from military formalities and customs than from the bonds of mateship and the demands of necessity. It is a democratic tradition, the tradition in which Australians have gone to war ever since.

This unknown Australian is not interred here to glorify war over peace; or to assert a soldier's character above a civilian's; or one race or one nation or one religion above another; or men above women; or the war in which he fought and died above any other war; or one generation above any that has or will come later.

The Unknown Soldier honors the memory of all those men and women who laid down their lives for Australia. His tomb is a reminder of what we have lost in war and what we have gained. We have lost more than 100 000 lives, and with them all their love of this country, and all their hope and energy. We have gained a legend: a story of bravery and sacrifice, and with it a deeper faith in ourselves and our democracy, and a deeper understanding of what it means to be Australian.

It is not too much to hope, therefore, that this Unknown Australian Soldier might continue to serve his country. He might enshrine a nation's love of peace and remind us that, in the sacrifice of the men and women whose names are recorded here, there is faith enough for all of us.

The Perils of Indifference
Elie Wiesel, White House, Washington, DC, 12 April 1999

Transylvanian-born teacher and humanist Elie Wiesel (b. 1928) survived the Nazi Holocaust to become a writer who is famous for his determination to keep its horrors alive in our minds lest such a travesty recur. Among many other decorations, he was awarded the Nobel Peace Prize in 1986.

The topic of this speech — part of the Millennium Lectures series, given to an invited audience at the White House — is the evil of indifference, and the obligation to intervene when others' lives are in peril. He points out that, when humans react with indifference to the suffering of others, it is a descent into inhumanity. After the speech, President Bill Clinton said to Wiesel: "You have taught us never to forget. You have made sure that we always listen to the victims of indifference, hatred, and evil."

In October 1986 Wiesel had said:

"The opposite of love is not hate, it's indifference.

"The opposite of art is not ugliness, it's indifference.

"The opposite of faith is not heresy, it's indifference.

"And the opposite of life is not death, it's indifference."

...Fifty-four years ago to the day, a young Jewish boy from a small town in the Carpathian Mountains woke up, not far from Goethe's beloved Weimar, in a place of eternal infamy called Buchenwald. He was finally free, but there was no joy in his heart. He thought there never would be again.

Liberated a day earlier by American soldiers, he remembers their rage at what they saw. And even if he lives to be a very old man, he will always be grateful to them for that rage, and also for their compassion. Though he did not understand their language, their eyes told him what he needed to know — that they, too, would remember, and bear witness.

And now, I stand before you, Mr President — Commander-in-Chief of the army that freed me, and tens of thousands of others — and I am filled with a profound and abiding gratitude to the American people...

We are on the threshold of a new century, a new millennium. What will the legacy of this vanishing century be? How will it be remembered in the new millennium? Surely it will be judged, and judged severely, in both moral and metaphysical terms. These failures have cast a dark shadow over humanity: two world wars, countless civil wars, the senseless chain of assassinations — Gandhi, the Kennedys, Martin Luther King, Sadat,

Elie Wiesel is the founding chair of the United States Holocaust Memorial and, since 1976, has been Andrew Mellon Professor in the Humanities at Boston University.

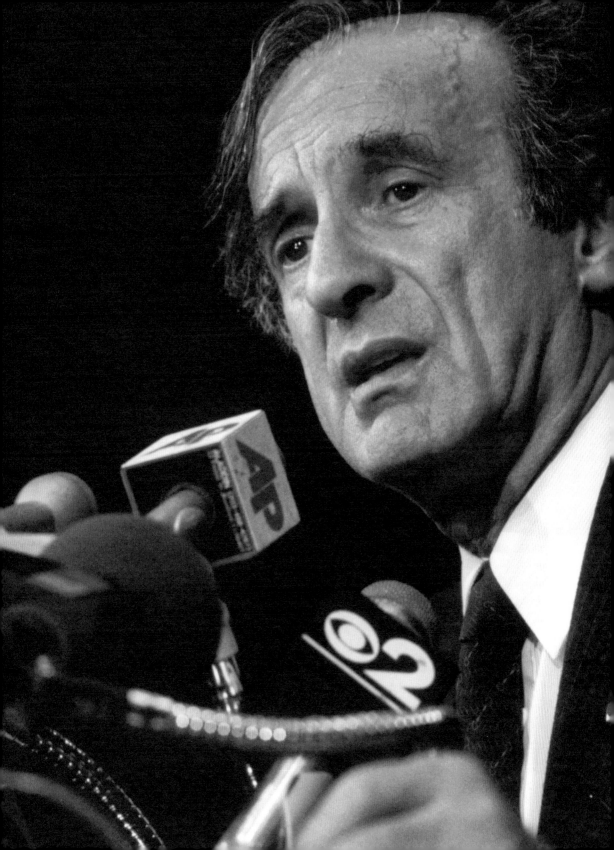

Rabin — bloodbaths in Cambodia and Nigeria, India and Pakistan, Ireland and Rwanda, Eritrea and Ethiopia, Sarajevo and Kosovo; the inhumanity in the gulag and the tragedy of Hiroshima. And, on a different level, of course, Auschwitz and Treblinka. So much violence, so much indifference.

What is indifference? Etymologically, the word means "no difference." A strange and unnatural state in which the lines blur between light and darkness, dusk and dawn, crime and punishment, cruelty and compassion, good and evil.

What are its courses and inescapable consequences? Is it a philosophy? Is there a philosophy of indifference conceivable? Can one possibly view indifference as a virtue? Is it necessary at times to practice it simply to keep one's sanity, live normally, enjoy a fine meal and a glass of wine, as the world around us experiences harrowing upheavals?

Of course, indifference can be tempting — more than that, seductive. It is so much easier to look away from victims. It is so much easier to avoid such rude interruptions to our work, our dreams, our hopes. It is, after all, awkward, troublesome, to be involved in another person's pain and despair. Yet, for the person who is indifferent, his or her neighbors are of no consequence. And, therefore, their lives are meaningless. Their hidden or even visible anguish is of no interest. Indifference reduces the other to an abstraction.

Over there, behind the black gates of Auschwitz, the most tragic of all prisoners were the "*Muselmänner*" [literally, Muslim], as they were called. Wrapped in their torn blankets, they would sit or lie on the ground, staring vacantly into space, unaware of who or where they were, strangers to their surroundings. They no longer felt pain, hunger, thirst. They feared nothing. They felt nothing. They were dead and did not know it.

Rooted in our tradition, some of us felt that to be abandoned by humanity then was not the ultimate. We felt that to be abandoned by God was worse than to be punished by Him. Better an unjust God than an indifferent one. For us to be ignored by God was a harsher punishment than to be a victim of His anger. Man can live far from God — not outside God. God is wherever we are. Even in suffering? Even in suffering.

In a way, to be indifferent to that suffering is what makes the human being inhuman. Indifference, after all, is more dangerous than anger and hatred. Anger can at times be creative. One writes a great poem, a great symphony, one does something special for the sake of humanity because one is angry at the injustice that one witnesses. But indifference is never creative. Even hatred at times may elicit a response. You fight it. You denounce it. You disarm it. Indifference elicits no response. Indifference is not a response.

Indifference is not a beginning, it is an end. And, therefore, indifference is always the friend of the enemy, for it benefits the aggressor — never his victim, whose pain is magnified when he or she feels forgotten. The political prisoner in his cell, the hungry children, the homeless refugees — not to respond to their plight, not to relieve their solitude by offering them a spark of hope is to exile them from human memory. And in denying their humanity we betray our own.

Indifference, then, is not only a sin, it is a punishment. And this is one of the most important lessons of this outgoing century's wide-ranging experiments in good and evil.

In the place that I come from, society was composed of three simple categories: the killers, the victims, and the bystanders. During the darkest of times, inside the ghettoes and death camps — and I'm glad that Mrs Clinton mentioned that we are now commemorating that event, that period, that we are now in the Days of Remembrance — but then, we felt abandoned, forgotten. All of us did.

And our only miserable consolation was that we believed that Auschwitz and Treblinka were closely guarded secrets; that the leaders of the free world did not know what was going on behind those black gates and barbed wire; that they had no knowledge of the war against the Jews that Hitler's armies and their accomplices waged as part of the war against the Allies.

If they knew, we thought, surely those leaders would have moved heaven and earth to intervene. They would have spoken out with great outrage and conviction. They would have bombed the railways leading to Birkenau, just the railways, just once.

And now we knew, we learned, we discovered that the Pentagon knew, the State Department knew. And the illustrious occupant of the White House then, who was a great leader — and I say it with some anguish and pain, because today is exactly 54 years marking his death — Franklin Delano Roosevelt died on April the 12th, 1945, so he is very much present to me and to us.

No doubt, he was a great leader. He mobilized the American people and the world, going into battle, bringing hundreds and thousands of valiant and brave soldiers in America to fight fascism, to fight dictatorship, to fight

In 1985, Elie Wiesel appealed to President Reagan to cancel his visit to Bitburg military cemetery in West Germany where the German SS are buried.

Hitler. And so many of the young people fell in battle. And, nevertheless, his image in Jewish history...is flawed.

The depressing tale of the *St. Louis* is a case in point. Sixty years ago, its human cargo — maybe 1000 Jews — was turned back to Nazi Germany. And that happened after the *Kristallnacht*, after the first state-sponsored pogrom, with hundreds of Jewish shops destroyed, synagogues burned, thousands of people put in concentration camps. And that ship, which was already on the shores of the United States, was sent back.

I don't understand. Roosevelt was a good man, with a heart. He understood those who needed help. Why didn't he allow these refugees to disembark? A thousand people — in America, a great country, the greatest democracy, the most generous of all new nations in modern history. What happened? I don't understand. Why the indifference, on the highest level, to the suffering of the victims?

But then, there were human beings who were sensitive to our tragedy. Those non-Jews, those Christians, that we called the "Righteous Gentiles," whose selfless acts of heroism saved the honor of their faith. Why were they so few? Why was there a greater effort to save SS murderers after the war than to save their victims during the war?

Why did some of America's largest corporations continue to do business with Hitler's Germany until 1942? It has been suggested, and it was documented, that the Wehrmacht could not have conducted its invasion of France without oil obtained from American sources. How is one to explain their indifference?

And yet, my friends, good things have also happened in this traumatic century: the defeat of Nazism, the collapse of communism, the rebirth of Israel on its ancestral soil, the demise of apartheid, Israel's peace treaty with Egypt, the peace accord in Ireland. And let us remember the meeting, filled with drama and emotion, between Rabin and Arafat that you, Mr President, convened in this very place. I was here and I will never forget it.

And then, of course, the joint decision of the United States and NATO to intervene in Kosovo and save those victims, those refugees, those who were uprooted by a man whom I believe that because of his crimes, should be charged with crimes against humanity. But this time, the world was not silent. This time, we do respond. This time, we intervene.

Does it mean that we have learned from the past? Does it mean that society has changed? Has the human being become less indifferent and more human? Have we really learned from our experiences? Are we less insensitive to the plight of victims of ethnic cleansing and other forms of injustices in places near and far? Is today's justified intervention in Kosovo, led by you, Mr President, a lasting warning that never again will the deportation, the terrorisation of children and their parents be allowed anywhere in the world? Will it discourage other dictators in other lands to do the same?

What about the children? Oh, we see them on television, we read about them in the papers, and we do so with a broken heart. Their fate is always the most tragic, inevitably. When adults wage war, children perish. We see their faces, their eyes. Do we hear their pleas? Do we feel their pain, their agony? Every minute one of them dies of disease, violence, famine. Some of them — so many of them — could be saved.

And so, once again, I think of the young Jewish boy from the Carpathian Mountains. He has accompanied the old man I have become throughout these years of quest and struggle. And together we walk towards the new millennium, carried by profound fear and extraordinary hope.

FIGHTING WORDS

"Mankind must put an end to war before war puts an end to mankind."
John F. Kennedy (1917–1963) was US president from 1961 until his assassination in Dallas, Texas, on 22 November 1963.

"If it's natural to kill, how come men have to go into training to learn how?"
Joan Baez (b. 1941) is an American singer and songwriter. Her songs are generally concerned with human rights and non-violence.

"Fighting for peace is like f***ing for chastity"
Protest placard slogan, Australia and elsewhere, from 1965

MURPHY'S LAWS OF COMBAT
Anything you do can get you killed, including doing nothing.
Incoming fire has the right of way.
If it's stupid and it works, it isn't stupid.
If the enemy is in range, so are you.
Don't look conspicuous, it draws fire.
When in doubt, empty your magazine.
Military intelligence is an oxymoron.
Try to look unimportant, they may be low on ammunition.
Teamwork is essential, it gives them someone else to shoot at.
Never draw fire, it annoys everyone around you.
Never share a weapons pit with anyone braver than you.
A sucking chest wound is nature's way of telling you to slow down.
If your attack is going well, it's an ambush.
The easy way is always mined.
Never forget that your weapon was made by the lowest bidder.
Professional soldiers are predictable; the world is full of dangerous amateurs.
When you have secured the area, make sure the enemy knows it too.
There is no such thing as an atheist in a foxhole.
Mines are equal opportunity weapons.
These "laws" were created by Vietnam War (1959–75) troops (probably Australian), and are typical of the black humor to which soldiers resort in times of war. The last law refers to the fact that, in Vietnam, one was just as likely to be killed by a "friendly" landmine as one positioned by the enemy.

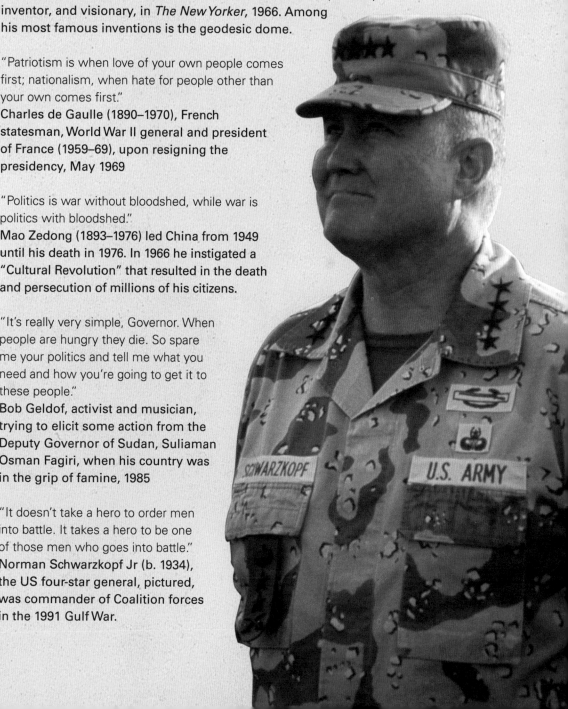

"Either war is obsolete or men are."
R. Buckminster Fuller (1895–1983), an American architect, author, inventor, and visionary, in *The New Yorker*, 1966. Among his most famous inventions is the geodesic dome.

"Patriotism is when love of your own people comes first; nationalism, when hate for people other than your own comes first."
Charles de Gaulle (1890–1970), French statesman, World War II general and president of France (1959–69), upon resigning the presidency, May 1969

"Politics is war without bloodshed, while war is politics with bloodshed."
Mao Zedong (1893–1976) led China from 1949 until his death in 1976. In 1966 he instigated a "Cultural Revolution" that resulted in the death and persecution of millions of his citizens.

"It's really very simple, Governor. When people are hungry they die. So spare me your politics and tell me what you need and how you're going to get it to these people."
Bob Geldof, activist and musician, trying to elicit some action from the Deputy Governor of Sudan, Suliaman Osman Fagiri, when his country was in the grip of famine, 1985

"It doesn't take a hero to order men into battle. It takes a hero to be one of those men who goes into battle."
Norman Schwarzkopf Jr (b. 1934), the US four-star general, pictured, was commander of Coalition forces in the 1991 Gulf War.

Part 8

TIMES OF TERROR

The Twenty-First Century

11 SEPTEMBER 2001
WAR ON TERROR

On 11 September 2001, nineteen Middle Eastern Islamic terrorists hijacked four US commercial airliners. Two of the planes were flown into the twin towers of New York City's World Trade Center. Soon afterwards, witnessed by millions around the world on "live" television, the buildings collapsed in spectacular fashion, killing thousands. Not since the American Civil War (1861–65) had so many perished on US soil in one day.

A third plane crashed into the Pentagon, the US military headquarters in Arlington, Virginia, but caused little serious damage. The fourth plane was apparently heading for a target in Washington, DC, but some passengers realized what was happening and heroically foiled the plot. They accosted the hijackers and caused the plane to crash in a field in Pennsylvania, in the full knowledge that they would all be killed.

The hijackers were members of the radical anti-US Islamic group al'Qaeda, led by Osama bin Laden, who has both denied involvement in — and taken credit for — the attacks.

On 26 October 2001, in response to the attacks, the US Congress rushed through the *USA Patriot Act*, an acronym for "Uniting and Strengthening America by Providing Appropriate Tools Required to Intercept and Obstruct Terrorism." It widens the power of US agencies to fight terrorism both in the US and overseas, and increases the ability of law enforcement agencies to monitor telephone and email communications as well as private medical, financial, and other records. It also loosens restrictions on foreign intelligence gathering within the United States, and provides increased powers in various areas of immigration and financial law. The Act was passed by a large majority in both houses of Congress, and was supported by both the Democratic and Republican parties.

Another indirect repercussion of the September 11 attacks was the invasion of Iraq on 19 March 2003 by the "coalition of the willing," comprising the United Kingdom, Australia, Denmark, and Poland. The US stated its belief that Iraqi dictator Saddam Hussein was involved in September 11, but this was later debunked. The coalition also justified the invasion on the grounds that Hussein possessed "weapons of mass destruction," which he may provide to terrorists, or use in attacks on the US or its allies. This also turned out to be incorrect.

The following three speeches were made in the period between the September 11 attacks and the invasion of Iraq by the "coalition of the willing" on 19 March 2003. The fourth speech is a call to arms by Lieutenant Colonel Tim Collins, one of the coalition commanders involved in the Iraq War.

"Freedom from fear"
Rudy Giuliani, Opening Remarks to the United Nations General Assembly, New York, 1 October 2001

Lawyer and politician Rudy Giuliani was Republican mayor of New York at the time of the September 11 attacks. His mayoral approval rating had been dismal, but it skyrocketed as he displayed what was seen as strong leadership in the aftermath of the tragedy. *Time* magazine honored him as its 2001 "Person of the Year," while the British government awarded him an honorary knighthood in February 2002.

Originally a Democrat who supported both John F. Kennedy (1961) and George McGovern (1972) in their presidential campaigns, Giuliani joined the Republican Party in 1980 and was elected mayor of New York in 1993.

Since leaving office at the end of 2001 — as with US presidents, New York mayors are not permitted to serve more than two terms — Giuliani has been in constant demand on the speakers' circuit. He ran for the Republican Party presidential nomination in 2008, but withdrew in the face of poor ratings and caucus results. He endorsed John McCain, who went on to win the nomination.

...On September 11th 2001, New York City — the most diverse city in the world — was viciously attacked in an unprovoked act of war. More than 5000 innocent men, women, and children of every race, religion, and ethnicity are lost. Among these were people from 80 different nations. To their representatives here today, I offer my condolences to you as well as on behalf of all New Yorkers who share this loss with you. This was the deadliest terrorist attack in history. It claimed more lives than Pearl Harbor or D-Day.

This was not just an attack on the city of New York or on the United States of America. It was an attack on the very idea of a free, inclusive, and civil society.

It was a direct assault on the founding principles of the United Nations itself. The Preamble to the UN Charter states that this organisation exists "to reaffirm faith in fundamental human rights, in the dignity and worth of the human person...to practice tolerance and live together in peace as good neighbors [and] to unite our strength to maintain international peace and security."

Indeed, this vicious attack places in jeopardy the whole purpose of the United Nations.

Terrorism is based on the persistent and deliberate violation of fundamental human rights. With bullets and bombs — and now with hijacked airplanes — terrorists deny the dignity of human life. Terrorism preys particularly on cultures and communities that practice openness and tolerance. Their targeting of innocent civilians mocks the efforts of those who seek to live together in peace as neighbors. It defies the very notion of being a neighbor.

This massive attack was intended to break our spirit. It has not done that. It has made us stronger, more determined, and more resolved.

The bravery of our firefighters, our police officers, our emergency workers, and civilians we may never learn of, in saving over 25 000 lives that day — carrying out the most effective rescue operation in our history — inspires all of us…

The strength of America's response, please understand, flows from the principles upon which we stand.

Americans are not a single ethnic group.

Americans are not of one race or one religion.

Americans emerge from all your nations.

We are defined as Americans by our beliefs — not by our ethnic origins, our race, or our religion. Our beliefs in religious freedom, political freedom, and economic freedom — that's what makes an American. Our belief in democracy, the rule of law, and respect for human life — that's how you become an American. It is these very principles — and the opportunities these principles give to so many to create a better life for themselves and their families — that make America, and New York, a "shining city on a hill"…

It is tragic and perverse that it is because of these very principles — particularly our religious, political, and economic freedoms — that we find ourselves under attack by terrorists.

Our freedom threatens them, because they know that if our ideas of freedom gain a foothold among their people it will destroy their power. So they strike out against us to keep those ideas from reaching their people…

The terrorists have no ideas or ideals with which to combat freedom and democracy. So their only defence is to strike out against innocent civilians, destroying human life in massive numbers and hoping to deter all of us from our pursuit and expansion of freedom.

But the long-term deterrent of spreading our ideals throughout the world is just not enough, and may never be realized, if we do not act — and act together — to remove the clear and present danger posed by terrorism and terrorists.

New York mayor Rudy Giuliani addresses the United Nations after the September 11 attacks on his city.

The United Nations must hold accountable any country that supports or condones terrorism, otherwise you will fail in your primary mission as peacekeeper.

It must ostracize any nation that supports terrorism.

It must isolate any nation that remains neutral in the fight against terrorism.

Now is the time, in the words of the UN Charter, "to unite our strength to maintain international peace and security." This is not a time for further study or vague directives. The evidence of terrorism's brutality and inhumanity — of its contempt for life and the concept of peace — is lying beneath the rubble of the World Trade Center...

Look at that destruction, that massive, senseless, cruel loss of human life and then I ask you to look in your hearts and recognize that there is no room for neutrality on the issue of terrorism. You're either with civilization or with terrorists.

New Yorkers start to react after the first plane hits one of the twin towers.

On one side is democracy, the rule of law and respect for human life; on the other is tyranny, arbitrary executions, and mass murder.

We're right and they're wrong. It's as simple as that.

And by that I mean that America and its allies are right about democracy, about religious, political, and economic freedom.

The terrorists are wrong, and in fact evil, in their mass destruction of human life in the name of addressing alleged injustices…

On this issue — terrorism — the United Nations must draw a line. The era of moral relativism between those who practice or condone terrorism, and those nations who stand up against it, must end. Moral relativism does not have a place in this discussion and debate…

…from the first day of this attack, an attack on New York and America, and I believe an attack on the basic principles that underlie this organisation, I have told the people of New York that we should not allow this to divide us, because then we would really lose what this city is all about. We have very strong and vibrant Arab and Muslim communities in New York City. They are an equally important part of the life of our City. We respect their religious beliefs. We respect everybody's religious beliefs — that's what America's about, that's what New York City is about. I have urged New Yorkers not to engage in any form of group blame or group hatred. This is exactly the evil that we are confronting with these terrorists. And if we are going to prevail over terror, our ideals, principles, and values must transcend all forms of prejudice. This is a very important part of the struggle against terrorism…

Freedom from fear is a basic human right. We need to reassert our right to live free from fear with greater confidence and determination than ever before, here in New York City, across America, and around the world. With one clear voice, unanimously, we need to say that we will not give in to terrorism.

Surrounded by our friends of every faith, we know that this is not a clash of civilisations; it is a conflict between murderers and humanity.

This is not a question of retaliation or revenge. It is a matter of justice leading to peace. The only acceptable result is the complete and total eradication of terrorism.

New Yorkers are strong and resilient. We are unified. And we will not yield to terror. We do not let fear make our decisions for us.

We choose to live in freedom.

"A turning point in history"
Tony Blair, address to Labour Party Conference, 2 October 2001

This powerful speech is British prime minister Tony Blair's response to the September 11 attacks. In 54 emotional minutes he sets out a persuasive case for military action against Afghanistan's Taliban government, which supported al'Qaeda and its policy of attacking the United States and its allies. Blair (b. 1953) argues that inaction would be much more dangerous than action, and that terrorism must be fought worldwide at all military and governmental levels. He rebuts many of his critics' arguments and concludes with a call for a new, more vigorous approach to the world's problems.

In retrospect, the Millennium marked only a moment in time. It was the events of September 11 that marked a turning point in history, where we confront the dangers of the future and assess the choices facing humankind. It was a tragedy. An act of evil. From this nation, goes our deepest sympathy and prayers for the victims and our profound solidarity with the American people. We were with you at the first. We will stay with you to the last.

Just two weeks ago, in New York, after the church service I met some of the families of the British victims. It was in many ways a very British occasion. Tea and biscuits. It was raining outside. Around the edge of the room, strangers making small talk, trying to be normal people in an abnormal situation. And as you crossed the room, you felt the longing and sadness; hands clutching photos of sons and daughters, wives and husbands; imploring you to believe them when they said there was still an outside chance of their loved ones being found alive, when you knew in truth that all hope was gone.

And then a middle-aged mother looks you in the eyes and tells you her only son has died, and asks you: why? I tell you: you do not feel like the most powerful person in the country at times like that. Because there is no answer. There is no justification for their pain. Their son did nothing wrong. The woman, seven months pregnant, whose child will never know its father, did nothing wrong. They don't want revenge. They want something better in memory of their loved ones.

I believe their memorial can and should be greater than simply the punishment of the guilty. It is that out of the shadow of this evil, should emerge lasting good: destruction of the machinery of terrorism wherever

"We...here in Britain stand shoulder to shoulder with our American friends in this hour of tragedy, and we, like them, will not rest until this evil is driven from our world."

342

FIGHTING WORDS

"In today's wars, there are no morals. We believe the worst thieves in the world today and the worst terrorists are the Americans. We do not have to differentiate between military or civilian. As far as we are concerned, they are all targets."
Osama bin Laden (pictured), militant Islamist, believed to be founder of the Jihad (holy war) organisation al'Qaeda, 1998

"Terrorist attacks can shake the foundations of our biggest buildings, but they cannot touch the foundation of America. These acts shatter steel, but they cannot dent the steel of American resolve."
George W. Bush, President of the United States (2001–2009), addressing the nation after the September 11 terrorist attacks on the US, 2001

"I think the real issue is the danger that these chemical or biological or radiological, or even nuclear weapons could fall into the hands of terrorists. And I think they are weapons of mass terror. That is what concerns us, that we are trying in every way we know how to deal with the Iraqi issue peacefully..."
Paul Wolfowitz, US Deputy Secretary of Defense, in an interview with South-East Asian journalists, January 2003

"September 11 was, and remains, above all an immense human tragedy... The target of the terrorists was not only New York and Washington but the very values of freedom, tolerance, and decency which underpin our way of life."
Tony Blair, British prime minister from 1997 to 2007

it is found; hope amongst all nations of a new beginning where we seek to resolve differences in a calm and ordered way; greater understanding between nations and between faiths; and above all justice and prosperity for the poor and dispossessed, so that people everywhere can see the chance of a better future through the hard work and creative power of the free citizen, not the violence and savagery of the fanatic...

What happened on 11 September was without parallel in the bloody history of terrorism. Within a few hours, up to 7000 people were annihilated, the commercial center of New York was reduced to rubble and in Washington and Pennsylvania further death and horror on an unimaginable scale. Let no one say this was a blow for Islam when the blood of innocent Muslims was shed along with those of the Christian, Jewish, and other faiths around the world.

We know those responsible. In Afghanistan are scores of training camps for the export of terror. Chief amongst the sponsors and organizers is Osama bin Laden. He is supported, shielded, and given succor by the Taliban regime. Two days before the 11 September attacks, Masood, the leader of the opposition Northern Alliance, was assassinated by two suicide bombers. Both were linked to bin Laden. Some may call that coincidence. I call it payment — payment in the currency these people deal in: blood. Be in no doubt: bin Laden and his people organized this atrocity. The Taliban aid and abet him. He will not desist from further acts of terror. They will not stop helping him. Whatever the dangers of the action we take, the dangers of inaction are far, far greater.

Look for a moment at the Taliban regime. It is undemocratic. That goes without saying. There is no sport allowed, or television, or photography. No art or culture is permitted. All other faiths, all other interpretations of Islam are ruthlessly suppressed. Those who practice their faith are imprisoned. Women are treated in a way almost too revolting to be credible. First driven out of university; girls not allowed to go to school; no legal rights; unable to go out of doors without a man. Those that disobey are stoned. There is now no contact permitted with Western agencies, even those delivering food. The people live in abject poverty. It is a regime founded on fear and funded on the drugs trade. The biggest drugs hoard in the world is in Afghanistan, controlled by the Taliban. Ninety percent of the heroin on British streets originates in Afghanistan. The arms the Taliban are buying today are paid for with the lives of young British people buying their drugs on British streets. That is another part of their regime that we should seek to destroy.

So what do we do? Don't overreact some say. We aren't. We haven't lashed out. No missiles on the first night just for effect. Don't kill innocent people. We are not the ones who waged war on the innocent. We seek the guilty. Look for a diplomatic solution. There is no diplomacy with bin Laden or the Taliban regime. State an ultimatum and get their response. We stated the ultimatum; they haven't responded. Understand the causes of terror. Yes, we should try, but let there be no moral ambiguity about this: nothing could ever justify the events of 11 September, and it is to turn justice on its head to pretend it could. The action we take will be proportionate; targeted; we will do all we humanly can to avoid civilian casualties.

But understand what we are dealing with. Listen to the calls of those passengers on the planes. Think of the children on them, told they were going to die. Think of the cruelty beyond our comprehension as amongst the screams and the anguish of the innocent, those hijackers drove at full throttle planes laden with fuel into buildings where tens of thousands worked. They have no moral inhibition on the slaughter of the innocent. If they could have murdered not 7000 but 70 000 does anyone doubt they would have done so and rejoiced in it? There is no compromise possible with such people, no meeting of minds, no point of understanding with such terror. Just a choice: defeat it or be defeated by it. And defeat it we must. Any action taken will be against the terrorist network of bin Laden...

Here in this country and in other nations round the world, laws will be changed, not to deny basic liberties but to prevent their abuse and protect the most basic liberty of all: freedom from terror. New extradition laws will be introduced; new rules to ensure asylum is not a front for terrorist entry. This country is proud of its tradition in giving asylum to those fleeing tyranny. We will always do so. But we have a duty to protect the system from abuse. It must be overhauled radically so that from now on, those who abide by the rules get help and those that don't, can no longer play the system to gain unfair advantage over others...

In all of this, at home and abroad, the same beliefs throughout: that we are a community of people, whose self-interest and mutual interest at crucial points merge, and that it is through a sense of justice that community is born and nurtured. And what does this concept of justice consist of? Fairness, people all of equal worth, of course. But also reason and tolerance. Justice has no favorites; not amongst nations, peoples or faiths. When we act to bring to account those that committed the atrocity of September 11, we do so, not out of bloodlust.

We do so because it is just. We do not act against Islam. The true followers of Islam are our brothers and sisters in this struggle. Bin Laden is no more obedient to the proper teaching of the Koran than those Crusaders of the twelfth century who pillaged and murdered, represented the teaching of the Gospel. It is time the west confronted its ignorance of Islam. Jews, Muslims, and Christians are all children of Abraham. This is the moment to bring the faiths closer together in understanding of our common values and heritage, a source of unity and strength. It is time also for parts of Islam to confront prejudice against America and not only Islam but parts of western societies too...

So I believe this is a fight for freedom. And I want to make it a fight for justice too. Justice not only to punish the guilty. But justice to bring those same values of democracy and freedom to people round the world. And I mean: freedom, not only in the narrow sense of personal liberty but in the broader sense of each individual having the economic and social freedom to develop their potential to the full. That is what community means, founded on the equal worth of all. The starving, the wretched, the dispossessed, the ignorant, those living in want and squalor from the deserts of Northern Africa to the slums of Gaza, to the mountain ranges of Afghanistan: they too are our cause.

This is a moment to seize. The kaleidoscope has been shaken. The pieces are in flux. Soon they will settle again. Before they do, let us reorder this world around us. Today, humankind has the science and technology to destroy itself or to provide prosperity to all. Yet science can't make that choice for us. Only the moral power of a world, acting as a community, can. "By the strength of our common endeavor we achieve more together than we can alone." For those people who lost their lives on September 11 and those that mourn them: now is the time for the strength to build that community. Let that be their memorial.

"Axis of Evil"
George W. Bush, State of the Union address, Washington, DC, 29 January 2002

In this annual State of the Union speech, George W. Bush declares that an "axis of evil" comprising North Korea, Iraq, and Iran is jeopardising "the peace of the world." He sets out what would become known as "the Bush doctrine" — that the "war on terror" justifies a preventative invasion where a threat to the US is perceived. The speech was roundly criticized by friend and foe alike. No one with any knowledge of international politics actually believed that the three named countries were part of an "axis" — that is, an alliance of states with a common aim.

North Korean state television dubbed Bush a "nuclear maniac"; Iranian president Khatami said Bush was "warmongering" and "insulting"; and Iraqi vice president Taha Yassin Ramadan called Bush's comments "stupid" and "inappropriate." None of this is surprising, but British foreign secretary Jack Straw stated that Bush's remarks were designed to increase his domestic standing before looming congressional elections, rather than identify a plausible danger. On 6 February, French foreign minister Hubert Védrine labeled Bush's approach "simplistic," and on 9 February, Chris Patten, head of the European Union's foreign policy, called the speech "unhelpful" and "more rhetoric than substance."

Shortly after this speech, Bush began claiming — wrongly, as it turned out — that Iraq was involved in the September 11 attacks, an inaccuracy that was eventually used to help justify the 2003 Iraq invasion.

As the original reasons for the Iraq War were discredited, and US (and other) casualties grew, Bush achieved both the highest and lowest Gallup poll approval rating of any US president, sinking from about 90 percent after the September 11 attacks to 28 percent in April 2008.

...As we gather tonight, our nation is at war, our economy is in recession, and the civilized world faces unprecedented dangers. Yet the state of our Union has never been stronger.

We last met in an hour of shock and suffering. In four short months, our nation has comforted the victims, begun to rebuild New York and the Pentagon, rallied a great coalition, captured, arrested, and rid the world of thousands of terrorists, destroyed Afghanistan's terrorist training camps, saved a people from starvation, and freed a country from brutal oppression.

On 16 September 2001, President George W. Bush predicted: "This crusade, this war on terrorism, is going to take a while."

349

The American flag flies again over our embassy in Kabul. Terrorists who once occupied Afghanistan now occupy cells at Guantanamo Bay. And terrorist leaders who urged followers to sacrifice their lives are running for their own.

America and Afghanistan are now allies against terror. We'll be partners in rebuilding that country...

The last time we met in this chamber, the mothers and daughters of Afghanistan were captives in their own homes, forbidden from working or going to school. Today women are free, and are part of Afghanistan's new government. And we welcome the new Minister of Women's Affairs, Doctor Sima Samar.

Our progress is a tribute to the spirit of the Afghan people, to the resolve of our coalition, and to the might of the United States military. When I called our troops into action, I did so with complete confidence in their courage and skill. And tonight, thanks to them, we are winning the war on terror. The men and women of our Armed Forces have delivered a message now clear to every enemy of the United States: even 7000 miles away, across oceans and continents, on mountaintops and in caves — you will not escape the justice of this nation...

What we have found in Afghanistan confirms that, far from ending there, our war against terror is only beginning. Most of the 19 men who hijacked planes on September the 11th were trained in Afghanistan's camps, and so were tens of thousands of others. Thousands of dangerous killers, schooled in the methods of murder, often supported by outlaw regimes, are now spread throughout the world like ticking time bombs, set to go off without warning.

Thanks to the work of our law enforcement officials and coalition partners, hundreds of terrorists have been arrested. Yet, tens of thousands of trained terrorists are still at large. These enemies view the entire world as a battlefield, and we must pursue them wherever they are. So long as training camps operate, so long as nations harbor terrorists, freedom is at risk. And America and our allies must not, and will not, allow it.

Our nation will continue to be steadfast and patient and persistent in the pursuit of two great objectives. First, we will shut down terrorist camps, disrupt terrorist plans, and bring terrorists to justice. And, second, we must prevent the terrorists and regimes who seek chemical, biological, or nuclear weapons from threatening the United States and the world...

FIGHTING TALK IN THE 21ST CENTURY

Fighting talk of all kinds continues to be created in the 21st century. As political and military alliances chop and change according to the expediency of the moment, we invent neologisms to explain why last week's "terrorist" is this week's "freedom fighter."

"Spin doctors" (liars, especially professional ones) have brought us such vile euphemisms as "collateral damage" (death of innocent non-combatants), "friendly fire" (our weapons that kill our forces), "rendition" (torture), "targets" (people we want to kill), "ethnic cleansing" (mass murder), "waterboarding" (drowning someone to within an inch of their life); and dysphemisms such as "terrorist" (anyone who disagrees with us and uses force).

"Weapons of mass destruction" has been further euphemized into "WMD," much as Kentucky Fried Chicken disappeared in favour of "KFC," and for a similar reason — people are more likely to buy it.

Fighting talk has even invaded other spheres.

In medicine we "fight off" a cold with a "shot" of medicine or perhaps a "magic bullet." If that doesn't work, we may have "invasive" surgery to prevent a heart "attack." Obituaries routinely refer to someone dying after a long "battle" with (insert disease).

In commerce we "fight" for market share, engage in a "price war" or "launch" a corporate "raid" on another company. In desperate times we may seek a "white knight" to forestall a "hostile takeover."

And in information technology we may be confronted with the "blue screen of death" as we "rip" and "burn" CDs. If someone "hacks" into our computer, we may be "attacked" by a virus, possibly a "Trojan Horse," which may cause our computer to "crash."

My hope is that all nations will heed our call, and eliminate the terrorist parasites who threaten their countries and our own. Many nations are acting forcefully. Pakistan is now cracking down on terror, and I admire the strong leadership of President Musharraf.

But some governments will be timid in the face of terror. And make no mistake about it: if they do not act, America will.

Our second goal is to prevent regimes that sponsor terror from threatening America or our friends and allies with weapons of mass destruction. Some of these regimes have been pretty quiet since September 11. But we know their true nature. North Korea is a regime arming with missiles and weapons of mass destruction, while starving its citizens.

Iran aggressively pursues these weapons and exports terror, while an unelected few repress the Iranian people's hope for freedom.

Iraq continues to flaunt its hostility toward America and to support terror. The Iraqi regime has plotted to develop anthrax, and nerve gas, and nuclear weapons for over a decade. This is a regime that has already used poison gas to murder thousands of its own citizens — leaving the bodies of mothers huddled over their dead children. This is a regime that agreed to international inspections — then kicked out the inspectors. This is a regime that has something to hide from the civilized world.

States like these, and their terrorist allies, constitute an axis of evil, arming to threaten the peace of the world. By seeking weapons of mass destruction, these regimes pose a grave and growing danger. They could provide these arms to terrorists, giving them the means to match their hatred. They could attack our allies or attempt to blackmail the United States. In any of these cases, the price of indifference would be catastrophic.

We will work closely with our coalition to deny terrorists and their state sponsors the materials, technology, and expertise to make and deliver weapons of mass destruction. We will develop and deploy effective missile defences to protect America and our allies from sudden attack...America will do what is necessary to ensure our nation's security.

We'll be deliberate, yet time is not on our side. I will not wait on events, while dangers gather. I will not stand by, as peril draws closer and closer. The United States of America will not permit the world's most dangerous regimes to threaten us with the world's most destructive weapons.

Our war on terror is well begun, but it is only begun. This campaign may not be finished on our watch — yet it must be and it will be waged on our watch.

We can't stop short. If we stop now — leaving terror camps intact and terror states unchecked — our sense of security would be false and temporary. History has called America and our allies to action, and it is both our responsibility and our privilege to fight freedom's fight...

The last time I spoke here, I expressed the hope that life would return to normal. In some ways, it has. In others, it never will. Those of us who have lived through these challenging times have been changed by them. We've come to know truths that we will never question: evil is real, and it must be opposed. Beyond all differences of race or creed, we are one country, mourning together and facing danger together. Deep in the American character, there is honor, and it is stronger than cynicism. And many have discovered again that even in tragedy — especially in tragedy — God is near.

In a single instant, we realized that this will be a decisive decade in the history of liberty, that we've been called to a unique role in human events. Rarely has the world faced a choice more clear or consequential.

Our enemies send other people's children on missions of suicide and murder. They embrace tyranny and death as a cause and a creed. We stand for a different choice, made long ago, on the day of our founding. We affirm it again today. We choose freedom and the dignity of every life.

Steadfast in our purpose, we now press on. We have known freedom's price. We have shown freedom's power. And in this great conflict, my fellow Americans, we will see freedom's victory.

Thank you all. May God bless.

KOFI ANNAN

Ghanaian diplomat and 2001 Nobel Peace Laureate Kofi Annan (b. 1938) was secretary-general of the United Nations from 1997 to 2007. He cautioned against the 2003 invasion of Iraq by the US-led coalition, primarily on the grounds that UN inspectors had found no trace of weapons of mass destruction (a key justification for the strike), but also because the attack was illegal under the UN charter.

"You can do a lot with diplomacy, but with diplomacy backed up by force you can get a lot more done."
Annan comments on the use of force to gain compliance from Iraqi dictator Saddam Hussein in 1998. UK and US military forces were making sporadic attacks on Iraq in an attempt to make Hussein comply with United Nations Security Council resolutions.

"More than ever before in human history, we share a common destiny. We can master it only if we face it together. And that, my friends, is why we have the United Nations."
The UN Secretary-General gives his official message for the new millennium on 31 December 1999.

"Today's real borders are not between nations, but between powerful and powerless, free and fettered, privileged and humiliated. Today, no walls can separate humanitarian or human rights crises in one part of the world from national security crises in another…We have entered the third millennium through a gate of fire. If today, after the horror of 11 September, we see better, and we see further — we will realize that humanity is indivisible."
Annan accepts the Nobel Peace Prize in December 2001.

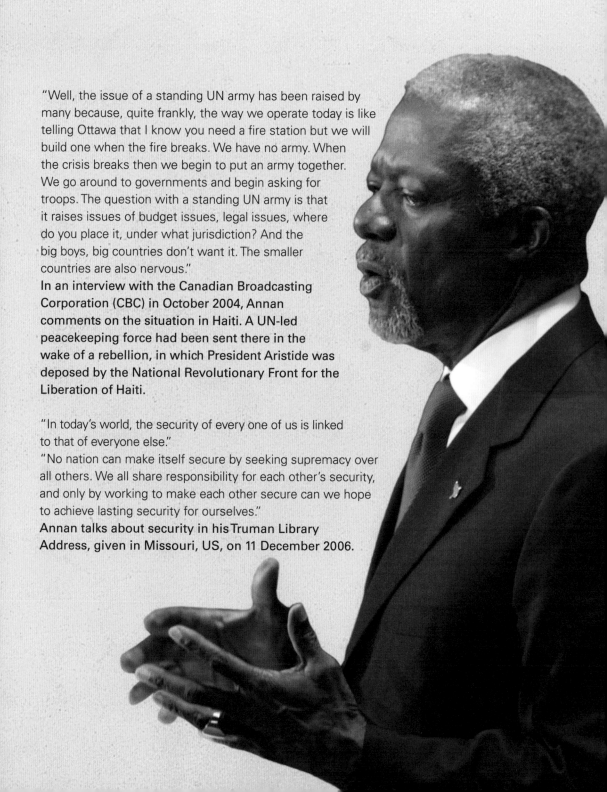

"Well, the issue of a standing UN army has been raised by many because, quite frankly, the way we operate today is like telling Ottawa that I know you need a fire station but we will build one when the fire breaks. We have no army. When the crisis breaks then we begin to put an army together. We go around to governments and begin asking for troops. The question with a standing UN army is that it raises issues of budget issues, legal issues, where do you place it, under what jurisdiction? And the big boys, big countries don't want it. The smaller countries are also nervous."

In an interview with the Canadian Broadcasting Corporation (CBC) in October 2004, Annan comments on the situation in Haiti. A UN-led peacekeeping force had been sent there in the wake of a rebellion, in which President Aristide was deposed by the National Revolutionary Front for the Liberation of Haiti.

"In today's world, the security of every one of us is linked to that of everyone else."

"No nation can make itself secure by seeking supremacy over all others. We all share responsibility for each other's security, and only by working to make each other secure can we hope to achieve lasting security for ourselves."

Annan talks about security in his Truman Library Address, given in Missouri, US, on 11 December 2006.

"We go to liberate, not to conquer"
Tim Collins, Kuwait, 22 March 2003

Lieutenant Colonel Tim Collins (known as "Nails," as in "tough as") was commander of the 1st Battalion of the Royal Irish Regiment, part of a US-led coalition of forces that had launched an attack on Iraq two days earlier. Their stated aim was to "disarm Iraq of weapons of mass destruction (WMD), end Saddam's support of terrorism, and free the Iraqi people." The UN, whose inspectors had found no evidence of WMD in Iraq despite exhaustive attempts, had refused to support the action. However, Britain, along with small contingents from Australia, Poland, and Denmark joined in, while countries such as France and Germany were vehemently opposed.

In this humane and stirring address to about 800 of his men at Fort Blair Mayne camp in the Kuwaiti desert, just before they went into battle, Collins sets out their purpose and demands respect for the foe. He spoke without notes.

His first sentence echoes the words of Sir Mark Sykes of the British Foreign Office in 1917, before Britain invaded Iraq: "Our armies do not come into your cities and lands as conquerors or enemies, but as liberators." The British did not achieve their aim that time; it remains to be seen whether they do better this time.

We go to liberate, not to conquer. We will not fly our flags in their country. We are entering Iraq to free a people and the only flag which will be flown in that ancient land is their own. Show respect for them.

There are some who are alive at this moment who will not be alive shortly. Those who do not wish to go on that journey, we will not send. As for the others I expect you to rock their world. Wipe them out if that is what they choose. But if you are ferocious in battle remember to be magnanimous in victory.

Iraq is steeped in history. It is the site of the Garden of Eden, of the Great Flood, and the birthplace of Abraham. Tread lightly there. You will see things that no man could pay to see and you will have to go a long way to find a more decent, generous, and upright people than the Iraqis. You will be embarrassed by their hospitality even though they have nothing. Don't treat them as refugees for they are in their own country. Their children will be poor, in years to come they will know that the light of liberation in their lives was brought by you.

Lieutenant Colonel Tim Collins speaks off the cuff to his men, who stand at ease around him.

If there are casualties of war then remember that when they woke up and got dressed in the morning they did not plan to die this day. Allow them dignity in death. Bury them properly and mark their graves.

It is my foremost intention to bring every single one of you out alive but there may be people among us who will not see the end of this campaign. We will put them in their sleeping bags and send them back. There will be no time for sorrow.

The enemy should be in no doubt that we are his nemesis and that we are bringing about his rightful destruction. There are many regional commanders who have stains on their souls and they are stoking the fires of hell for Saddam. He and his forces will be destroyed by this coalition for what they have done. As they die they will know their deeds have brought them to this place. Show them no pity.

It is a big step to take another human life. It is not to be done lightly. I know of men who have taken life needlessly in other conflicts, I can assure you they live with the mark of Cain upon them. If someone surrenders to you then remember they have that right in international law and ensure that one day they go home to their family.

The ones who wish to fight, well, we aim to please.

If you harm the regiment or its history by over-enthusiasm in killing or in cowardice, know it is your family who will suffer. You will be shunned unless your conduct is of the highest for your deeds will follow you down through history. We will bring shame on neither our uniform or our nation.

[Regarding WMD] It is not a question of if, it's a question of when. We know he has already devolved the decision to lower commanders, and that means he has already taken the decision himself. If we survive the first strike we will survive the attack.

As for ourselves, let's bring everyone home and leave Iraq a better place for us having been there. Our business now is north.

FAMOUS LAST WORDS

"Let's roll!"
Todd Beamer, passenger on hijacked United Airlines flight 93, at the end
of a cell phone call on 11 September 2001, just before he and other
passengers overpowered the hijackers, causing the plane to crash.
"Let's roll!" became the war cry for troops fighting
al'Qaeda in Afghanistan.

"The b******s got me but they won't
get everybody."
Alexander Litvinenko, former KGB
agent and critic of Russian President
Putin, before he died of poisoning
from radioactive polonium, 2006

"There is no God but Allah and
Muhammad is God's messenger."
Saddam Hussein, before his
execution by hanging, at Camp
Justice in Baghdad, 2006

"I put my life in danger and came here
because I feel this country is in danger.
People are worried. We will bring the
country out of this crisis."
Benazir Buttho, former Pakistan
premier (pictured), shortly before
she was assassinated while
campaigning in Rawalpindi, in
Pakistan, 2007. Her actual last
words were "Long live Buttho."

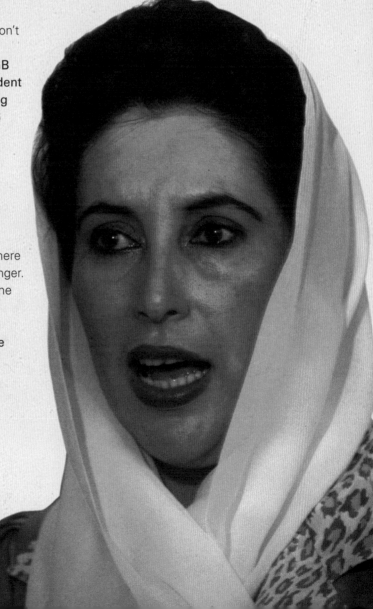

- maz - ing grace! how
'Twas grace that taught
Thro' man - y dan-
When we've been there
4.

FIGHTING SONG
Amazing Grace

Amazing Grace, how sweet the sound,
That saved a wretch like me!
I once was lost but now am found,
Was blind, but now, I see.

"Twas Grace that taught my heart to fear,
And Grace, my fears relieved.
How precious did that Grace appear
The hour I first believed.

Through many dangers, toils and snares
We have already come.
"Twas Grace that brought us safe thus far
And Grace will lead us home.

The Lord has promised good to me,
His word my hope secures.
He will my shield and portion be
As long as life endures.

When we've been here ten thousand years,
Bright shining as the sun,
We've no less days to sing God's praise
Than when we first begun.

Amazing Grace, how sweet the sound,
That saved a wretch like me!
I once was lost but now am found,
Was blind, but now, I see.

This well known and much loved Christian hymn, originally named "Faith's Review and Expectation," was written in 1772 by English priest and reformed slave-trafficker John Newton. The lyrics, which sum up the concept of divine grace, are based on 1 Chronicles 17:16–17. Newton had become a Christian following his apparently miraculous escape from a tempest at sea, during the course of which he decided that only the grace of God could save him.

    The song has attained a notoriety beyond its Christian origin. It was used by both sides in the American Civil War (as "Lili Marlene" was used by both sides in World War II), and has been an anthem for various civil rights and peace movements around the world. It is also routinely performed and sung at many of the annual events held around America to commemorate the anniversary of the September 11 terrorist attacks on New York's World Trade Center. It is the very antithesis of fighting talk.

BIBLIOGRAPHY

Author unknown (translated by Garmonsway, G. N.) (1953). *The Anglo-Saxon Chronicle*, Everyman.

Ayer, Fred, Jnr (1971). *Before the Colors Fade: Portrait of a Soldier, George S. Patton, Jr.*, Norman Berg.

Beevor, Antony (1998). *Stalingrad*, Viking.

Bird, Antony, and Bird, Nicholas (ed.) (2006). *Eyewitness to War*, Summersdale.

Blainey, Geoffrey (1973). *The Causes of War*, Macmillan.

Bullock, Alan (1952). *Hitler: A Study in Tyranny*, Odhams.

Caulfield, Michael (2007). *The Vietnam Years*, Hachette.

Collins, Owen (1998). *Speeches That Changed the World*, HarperCollins.

Gilbert, Martin (1992). *Churchill: A Life*, Henry Holt and Company.

Goldwag, Arthur (2007). *Isms & Ologies*, Quercus.

Green, J. (1886). *The Conquest of England*, Macmillan.

Grey, Viscount E. (1925). *Twenty-five Years, 1892–1916*, Hodder & Stoughton, quoted in:

Ross, Stewart (1988). *The Origins of the First World War*, Wayland.

Jones, B. and Dixon, M. (1986). *The Macmillan Dictionary of Biography*, Macmillan.

Lacey, R. (2003). *Great Tales From English History: Cheddar Man to the Peasant's Revolt*, Little Brown.

Lee, F. N. (2000). *King Alfred the Great and Our Common Law*, Department of Church History, Queensland Presbyterian Theological Seminary.

Lewis, J. (2001). *The Mammoth Book of How It Happened in Britain*, Robinson.

Klemperer, Victor (2000). *The Language of the Third Reich*, Athlone Press.

Manser, Martin H. (2007). *Buttering Parsnips Twocking Chavs*, Weidenfeld & Nicolson.

Mayr-Hartling, H. (1972). *The Coming of Christianity to Anglo-Saxon England*, Batsford.

Montefiore, Simon Sebag (2005). *Speeches That Changed the World*, Murdoch Books.

Pollard, J. (2005). *Alfred the Great: The Man Who Made England*, John Murray.

Poole, Steven (2006). *Unspeak™: Words are Weapons*, Little, Brown.

Pratt, D. (2007). *The Political Thought of King Alfred the Great*, Cambridge University Press.

Safire, William (1997). *Lend Me Your Ears*, Norton.

Schama, S. (2000). *A History of Britain 1: At The Edge of the World? 3000BC–1603AD*, BBC Worldwide.

Trevor-Roper, H. R. (ed.) (1953). *Hitler's Table Talk 1941–1944: Secret Conversations*, Weidenfeld & Nicolson.

Various (translated by Keynes, S. and Lapidge, M.) (1983). *Alfred the Great: Asser's Life of King Alfred and Other Contemporary Sources*, Penguin.

Warhaft, Sally (ed.) (2004). *Well May We Say...The Speeches That Made Australia*, Black Inc.

INDEX

Page numbers in *italic* refer to photographs and illustrations

ACKNOWLEDGMENT

The author wishes to thank Sean Maher and Sarah Baker for their invaluable help.

PHOTOGRAPHY CREDITS

AAP: page 356
Corbis: front cover and pages 8, 13, 25, 30, 32, 34, 36, 43, 50, 55, 59, 62, 65, 68, 76, 82, 89, 91, 93, 98, 103, 118, 120, 121, 124, 130, 133, 137, 141, 142, 157, 162, 174, 177, 178, 185, 187, 193, 195, 196, 200, 203, 207, 208, 210, 213, 217, 220, 223, 226, 235, 241, 244, 249, 252, 256, 258, 261, 275, 277, 278, 292, 295, 300, 305, 316, 318, 325, 328, 340, 344, 348, and 360.
Getty Images: pages 4, 6, 23, 33, 38, 41, 46, 60, 66, 73, 79, 94, 115, 116, 123, 134, 146, 161, 166, 168, 170, 176, 183, 189, 192, 229, 236, 247, 268, 272, 283, 285, 286, 289, 283, 285, 286, 289, 299, 302, 308, 311, 315, 331, 332, 335, 338, 343, 351, 355, 359, and back cover.
Library of Congress: pages 80, 108, 127, 151, and 154.
Newspix: pages 320 and 322.
Photolibrary: pages 15, 18, 29, 40, 45, 53, 56, 61, 64, 86, and 112.

TEXT CREDITS

Every effort has been made to contact the copyright holders of the material. Please contact the publisher for any disputed copyright.

Extract from John F. Kennedy's speech on Cuban missile crisis, page 282. © Gerhard Peters. Reprinted with permission from The American Presidency Project website: http://www.presidency.ucsb.edu

John F. Kennedy quotes, page 285. © Gerhard Peters. Reprinted with permission from The American Presidency Project website: http://www.presidency.ucsb.edu

Martin Luther King's speech, "I have a dream," page 288. Reprinted with arrangement with The Heirs to the Estate of Martin Luther King Jr., c/o Writers House as agent for the proprietor New York, NY. Copyright 1963 Dr. Martin Luther King Jr; copyright renewed 1991 Coretta Scott King.

Nelson Mandela's speech, "I am prepared to die," page 294. © http://www.nelsonmandela.org

Extract from Margaret Thatcher's speech on Falkands War, page 309. © Lady Thatcher. Reproduced with her permission from www.margaretthatcher.org, the official website of the Margaret Thatcher Foundation.

Speech by George Bush Snr on attack on Iraq, page 313. © Gerhard Peters. Reprinted with permission from The American Presidency Project website: http://www.presidency.ucsb.edu

Speech by Mikhail Gorbachev, accepting the Nobel Peace Prize, page 316. © Nobel Foundation. Reproduced with permission from http://www.nobelprize.org, the offical website of the Nobel Foundation.

Speech written by Don Watson for Paul Keating, page 321. Reprinted with permission from the Australian War Memorial website: www.awm.gov.au/